ASIAN AMERICAN VOICES

ENGAGING, EMPOWERING, ENABLING

Lin Zhan, PhD, RN, FAAN
Editor

National League
for **Nursing**

National League for Nursing
61 Broadway
New York, NY 10006
212-363-5555 or 800-669-1656
www.nln.org

ISBN 1-934758-00-0

Cover design by Brian Vigorita
Art Director, Laerdal Medical Corporation

Printed in the United States of America

ASIAN AMERICAN VOICES

ENGAGING, EMPOWERING, ENABLING

TABLE OF CONTENTS

List of Tables.. VII

Foreword... IX

Preface.. XI

Acknowledgments.. XVIII

Dedication XIX

Chapter 1   Culture, Health, and Nursing Education 1
             Lin Zhan, PhD, RN, FAAN

Chapter 2   A Thematic Analysis of Persistence and Long-Term Educational Engagement
             with Southeast Asian American College Students 21
             Peter Nien-chu Kiang, EdD

Chapter 3   A Critical Analysis of the Exclusion of Asian Americans from Higher Education
             Research and Discourse 59
             Samuel D. Museus, PhD

Chapter 4   Mentoring Asian Students toward Entering the Health Professions 77
             Ivy K. Ho, PhD & Khanh T. Dinh, PhD

Chapter 5   Diversity Research Initiatives: Reflection and Thoughts 91
             Lin Zhan, PhD, RN, FAAN

Chapter 6   Chinese American Children, Families, and Special Education 107
             Lusa Lo, EdD

Chapter 7   Bridging the Broken Narrative: How Student-Centered Teaching Contributes
             to Healing the Wounds of Trauma 123
             Nancy J. Lin, MA & Karen L. Suyemoto, PhD

Chapter 8   Community Cultural Development and Education with Cambodian American Youth 147
             Shirley Suet-ling Tang, PhD

Chapter 9   Cá Trí Nho: Roles of Vietnamese American Studies and Education Post-Katrina 171
             James Đien Bùi, MSW & Peter Nien-chu Kiang, EdD & Shirley Suet-ling Tang, PhD
             & Janet Hong Võ, BA

Chapter 10 Asian American Models of Leadership and Leadership Development in U.S. Higher
             Education 191
             Patricia Akemi Neilson, EdD, MPH

Chapter 11 Integrating Disciplines for Transformative Education in Health Services: Strategies
             and Effects..209
             Karen L. Suyemoto, PhD & John Tawa, MA & Grace S. Kim, PhD & Stephanie C. Day, MA
             & Susan A. Lambe, EdM & Phuong T. Nguyen, MA & Julie M. AhnAllen, PhD

Appendix A Author Profiles 229

LIST OF TABLES

LIST OF TABLES

Table 2-1   Massachusetts Southeast Asian American Applicants to NSRCF, 2000 49

Table 2-2   Reported Family Income of Massachusetts Southeast Asian American Applicants to NSRCF, 2000 50

Table 6-1   Number of Students Served Under IDEA, Part B, Ages 3-21, by Race and Ethnicity..........108

Table 6-2   Demographics of the Families 109

Table 10-1 Ethnic Representation in LDPHE 1997-2007 204

FOREWORD

Asia is our largest continent, in both physical and population terms. Culturally, it is the most complex continent, as well. Over past 25 years, Asia has been undergoing some of the most profound socioeconomic changes the world has ever witnessed, perhaps on its way to becoming the site of the world's largest economy. Within the United States, where Asians have lived for over 200 years, Asian Americans have become one of the fastest growing minority groups, and now constitute a population of over 11 million. They are to be found in many areas of the United States' social and cultural life and will be central to any definition of its future.

Asian Americans, although frequently described as the "model minority," are not well known and are still largely invisible in most areas of public discourse, as well as policy-making forums. Were one to examine the discussions in the current national political campaigns, for example — campaigns within which we have had considerable demographic emphasis, including immense focus on minority groups — rarely has there been any reference to Asian Americans. It is as if they were not a part of the political terrain.

Asian American Voices: Engaging, Empowering, Enabling commendably seeks to give greater visibility to the lives, experiences, and articulations of Asian Americans from a variety of backgrounds. Written by a group of distinguished authors, the book's chapters embody an admirable number of contexts within which unfolds a rich tapestry of human journeys, of ways of being, and of modes of becoming.

Asian Americans do not live in isolation; and the social, cultural, moral, and spiritual features that define their lives and living do not inhabit sites exclusive to them. They and those features interact and are interconnected with (and are somewhat the product of) the socio-cultural web we call the United States, as well as the transnational networks of which that country is a part. In reading the book, therefore, one is also learning about a United States of which one may be largely unaware.

The volume, edited by Dr. Lin Zhan, Dean and Professor, Massachusetts College of Pharmacy and Health Sciences, constitutes an important contribution to our understanding of Asian Americans, and educators at all levels — health care providers, researchers, policy makers, and practitioners from a variety of fields (psychology, psychiatry, nursing, and education, for example) — will benefit from reading it.

Winston E. Langley, PhD, JD
Provost and Vice Chancellor for Academic Affairs
University of Massachusetts Boston

One troubling fact in our nation is the existence of disparities in health, education, and social opportunities among ethnic minority populations, who have experienced higher rates of morbidity and mortality in health, limited access to health care and higher education, higher attrition rates in higher education, and tremendous obstacles in social mobility. The nation has called for eliminating disparities by bringing ethno-culturally accessible, appropriate, and adequate education and services to the underserved and underrepresented, including Asians in America. To this end, critical reflection and intellectual dialogue are needed to answer the questions: "Why do disparities stubbornly continue to exist?" "How does this disparity affect Asian Americans?" "What are the struggles and strengths of Asian Americans?" "How do multifaceted and complex pathways (race, gender, class, culture, health, and society) intersect, interact, and interplay in the educational process?" "What are the ethno-culturally responsive, informative, and innovative educational processes that help fulfill our mission of education?" and "How can we translate a body of knowledge and knowing about inter- and intra-ethnic and racial variations into classrooms, service sectors, and other areas to, ultimately, eliminate disparities in health and education in this nation?"

Asian American Voices: Engaging, Empowering, Enabling (hereafter, *Asian American Voices*) assembles reflections and intellectual dialogues for educators across disciplines and settings. Each chapter is written by an Asian American scholar(s) who share(s) his/her or their experiences, assertions, analyses, thoughts, and intellectual inquiries. Single voices, collected voices, all call for reform and leadership in higher education. Traditional pedagogical approaches — excessively content and teacher-centered pedagogy — have limited flexibility, critical connection, and multicontextual environments to *engage, empower,* and *enable* diverse student populations across the campuses in the nation. *Asian American Voices* focuses on critical issues, needs, and challenges faced by Asian Americans, and particularly Asian students in higher education. *Asian American Voices*, based on the authors' experiences in education, research, and public and community service, examine existing barriers that lead to many Asian Americans experiencing unequal treatment and missing opportunities for education, service, and health care. Authors of this book critically analyze the intersection and interplay of race, class, culture, immigration, and social and political contexts in relation to the vulnerability of Asian Americans, notably, Southeast Asian Americans, and demystify the pervasive and perpetual "model minority" stereotype. Educational reform is needed to create ethno-culturally appropriate curricular and learning environments and to develop leadership of Asian Americans in higher education. *Asian American Voices* presents compelling model interventions within a holistic framework and reflective of culturally responsive practices in higher education. Emerging agendas in this book provide clear directions for future research, advocacy, collaboration, and interventions.

Asian American Voices is organized into 11 chapters. **Chapter 1, Culture, Health, and Nursing Education** offers an overview of Asian cultures and Asian Americans' experiences in health care. Higher education is at the heart of the crossing of cultures as students and educators bring different ideas with them to classroom, clinical, and community learning experiences, and create anthropological perspectives essential to the theory and practice of education. Understanding social and cultural contexts and recognizing intra-ethnic variability are keys to successful educational practice. The application of multiculturalism to education must not be considered as optional or peripheral since the science and art of health and education are the science and art of human relationships and existential experiences. In this chapter, Dr. Zhan reflects on her own research and teaching, and presents voices from Asian American students. A single voice, shared voices, all boil down to simple, yet poorly understood, questions: Who are Asian Americans? And what barriers have they experienced when seeking education? Asian Americans, particularly immigrant elders and women, the poor, and refugees, encounter tremendous demographic, cultural, and structural/system barriers. This chapter offers descriptive and explanatory analyses of how these barriers impact the health and well-being of Asian Americans, and what changes need to be made to improve cultural competence in education and service. The author calls for concerted efforts from all levels — individual, group, community, institution, and society — to address these critical issues and to improve health and education for all.

What are the voices, needs, and strengths of Southeast Asian American college students? In **Chapter 2, A Thematic Analysis of Persistence and Long-Term Educational Engagement with Southeast Asian American College Students,** Dr. Peter Kiang, a prominent scholar in the field of higher education and Asian American studies, presents an in-depth analysis of educational experiences of Vietnamese and Cambodian immigrant/refugee students, whose strengths and survival strategies often are ignored in the mainstream analyses of college student achievement and persistence. Inspired by those same students, Dr. Kiang has explored how specific curricular and pedagogical commitments in Asian American studies can serve as models of transformative practice for U.S. higher education. In this chapter, Dr. Kiang describes various phases of applied research and reflection over the past two decades, focusing on questions of pedagogy, student learning, and persistence for Southeast Asian American students within the structure and culture of Asian American studies classrooms at one urban public university. Dr. Kiang suggests that an active engagement of educational researchers in ethnic studies classrooms produces rich opportunities for advancing theory/ practice, particularly with underresearched and traditionally marginalized populations. Still, some critical questions remain to be answered, which calls for continued research and policy development in higher education.

"Why have Southeast Asian Americans been excluded from higher education research and discourse?" Dr. Museus explores the question, in **Chapter 3, A Critical Analysis of the Exclusion of Asian Americans from Higher Education Research and Discourse,** as an important, yet poorly researched, issue is raised. The author identifies three sources of perpetual exclusion of Asian Americans from literature and discourse in higher education: a) the model minority myth, which reinforces the common assumption that Asian Americans need no attention or resources in higher education, which in turn leads to their being excluded from discussions of race on campus; b) the nonexistence of disaggregated data that fails to sufficiently examine the disparities within the entire Asian American group; and c) overemphasis of degree attainment while ignoring other important student outcomes in higher education discourse. The author calls for inclusion, not exclusion, to gain a full understanding of the needs and strengths of Asian Americans in higher education. Particular attention needs to be paid to Southeast Asian college students, who share many of the same disadvantages as their Black and Latina/o peers. In addition, the author notes that, "... the absence of informative research and knowledgeable practitioners who understand the cultural nuances may prevent Asian Americans from seeking needed mental health services on the campus." The author discusses ramifications of the model minority myth, prejudice and discrimination, cultural adjustment and cultural conflicts, and psychological distress and coping as they are relevant to Southeast Asian Americans on many college campuses across the nation. A call for ethno-culturally sensitive and scientifically rigorous research to recognize diversity in Asian Americans and to generate much needed knowledge that will inform the discourse in higher education is issued.

An increasing need for diversifying the nation's health professionals prompts educators to consider learning about Asian college students and mentoring them to become health professionals. **Chapter 4, Mentoring Asian Students toward Entering the Health Professions,** written by Drs. Ho and Dinh, discusses the struggles Asian college students face. Cultural collision occurs when Asian cultures, which tend to favor silent reflection and attentive listening, encounter Western culture, which openly encourages verbalization and extraversion. Stereotyping as a cognitive strategy is used to reduce the complexity of Asian American groups into a simple generalization. Racism creates a hostile educational environment, and evidence of prejudice and discrimination against Asian American students exists in university settings. Asian college students may also have to contend with their family's attitude toward career choices. A lack of parallel words for psychology and nursing in some Asian languages, for example, forces Asian college students to explain to their parents what these fields are about. Intergenerational conflicts result as families may prefer their children to pursue fields with security and lucrative salary, which may cause emotional and physical distress among Asian students. Drs. Ho and Dinh present an intervention model that uses practical and successful strategies to help Asian college students enrolled in a public university succeed in becoming health professionals.

As America becomes ever more diverse, the nursing profession calls for increasing the diversity of its workforce. Currently the majority of nurse educators are from the dominant Euro-American culture while an increasing proportion of nursing students are from cultures with different beliefs, values, traditions, learning styles, and languages. Quite often, students of diversity struggle to understand and to be understood in nursing education. **Chapter 5, Diversity Research Initiatives: Reflections and Thoughts,** presents a qualitative study[1] that explored learning experiences of Asian American nursing students in one urban public university. Unlike teaching a research course in a classroom, Dr. Zhan, the author of this chapter, collaborated with undergraduate and graduate nursing students to conduct a study that aimed to understand Asian American students' learning needs and experiences. Using a content-sensitive, student-centered learning approach, students were able to synthesize their previous knowledge while learning about the concept of diversity, research design and methods, and the site of inquiry — the college and the campus. Most significantly, both the researched and the researchers had meaningful reflections and made meaningful connections as a result of the research process. The data collected from focus group and individual interviews revealed that Asian American students regularly experienced prejudice and thought their learning needs were ignored. Some were told "nursing is not for you" while others were evaluated as having "poor communication skills" due to their accented English. Asian American students called for increasing cultural sensitivity in nursing education, improving teaching pedagogy, and creating a humane, caring, and conducive learning environment. The author calls on nurse educators to respond to the academic needs of diverse students and include diversity as a vital component of academic excellence.

A paucity of research exists to describe the lived experience of Asian families with disability in the United States. Dr. Lo, in **Chapter 6, Chinese American Children, Families, and Special Education,** describes how three Chinese immigrant families of children with disabilities struggled and navigated in an unfamiliar school system. Their struggles were further compounded by language difficulties and a lack of linguistic and cultural support services in special education. The author recommends a) parent education training that helps families with diverse backgrounds become familiar with the special education system for their disabled children; b) bilingual and bicultural professionals in special education who are able to respond to families' needs in a culturally and linguistically appropriate way; c) parent support groups that help parents cope with their children's disabilities; d) increased funding that supports training, culturally appropriate services, and increased preparation of bilingual practitioners in this field; and e) development of culturally appropriate assessment methods, procedures and action plans that inform Asian communities about services for disabilities.

"What is the best way for educators to reach students who have personal and familial experiences with sociocultural trauma? How can health service educators convey information in a personally and socially sensitive manner that helps students negotiate their own experiences?" Drs. Lin and Suyemoto, in **Chapter 7, Bridging the Broken Narrative: How Student-Centered Teaching Contributes to Healing the Wounds of Trauma,** present effective pedagogies for promoting the optimal outcome of education. Their pedagogical approaches are based on four major principles: learning is connected to students' contexts, learning is relational and interactive and requires taking relational risks, learning involves trust and respect, and learning is personal, changing students and the way they see others. Drs. Lin and Suyemoto question traditional learning and teaching methods in which "facts" and "content" are presented without a relevant context. The authors contend that to promote learning and personal growth for students of refugee backgrounds, it is essential to make conceptual and emotional linkages between the content and the context, between facts and meanings, between self and others, between learning and healing, and between classroom and communities. There is no single best way to reach students who have personal and familial experiences with sociocultural trauma. Yet, Drs. Lin and Suyemoto's research-based analysis sheds light on how to promote a sense of agency, a sense of responsibility, and a sense of belonging for the vulnerable — students of refugees or families that have experienced sociocultural trauma.

Chapter 8, Community Cultural Development and Education with Cambodian American Youth, written by Dr. Tang, presents her work in engaging urban Khmer American youth to achieve authentic learning. Interaction, shared experiences, and active learning are some strategies that can enable young Khmer American students to identify and analyze issues, engage others in public dialogue and action, and make sense of their own community. Dr. Tang connects higher education to the Youth Art in Action (YAIA) program in a community of Southeast Asian Americans, as she notes, "...Youth artists in YAIA have modeled powerful practices of learning, teaching, and preserving cultural traditions through cultural immersion and historical research...." The connection enhances not only generating knowledge and expressing creativity, but also creating new spaces and new worlds for student learning and faculty teaching. Dr. Tang's work deconstructs the conventional deficit-based paradigm of youth development, which focuses on "fixing problems," and showcases a positive model of youth development that draws on strength, resiliency, creativity, and power in disenfranchised and vulnerable youth.

Service learning is an educational approach that aims to meet both learning and community needs. Students are active partners in service learning by identifying community needs and planning and evaluating service activities related to these needs. Service learning also empowers students to take control of their learning, develop leadership skills, and take their places as valuable, decision-making members of their communities. A group of educators from the Asian American Studies Program at University of Massachusetts Boston, James Điền Bùi, Peter Kiang, Shirley Tang, and Janet Hong Võ, in **Chapter 9, Cá Trí Nho: Roles of Vietnamese American Studies and Education Post-Katrina,** present a case study that exemplifies an empowering and enabling model that aims to achieve educational goals and rebuild a Gulf Coast Vietnamese community following Hurricanes

Katrina and Rita in fall 2005 in the Gulf Coast region of the United States. Using an integrative methodological approach, students became involved in community organizing, asset rebuilding, and community cultural development. Students' learning experiences transformed schools and empowered the community. Culturally responsive service learning grounds students in the real world where they make sense of, attach meaning to, and pursue knowledge in the context of rebuilding and empowering the community.

Despite an increased number of Asian American faculty in higher education, the troubling reality is that less than 2% of these academics hold senior leadership positions in colleges and universities. Dr. Neilson, in **Chapter 10, Asian American Models of Leadership and Leadership Development in U.S. Higher Education,** explores ten Asian Americans' career pathways to senior leadership positions in higher education. Stereotypical assumptions and structural barriers, characterized as a "glass ceiling," have limited the entry of Asian Americans into senior level leadership positions. As qualified Asian Americans try to climb the career leadership ladder, they sometimes are considered as "finalists," but often only because they are people of color, and with that they create the "diverse" pool of candidates required by affirmative action guidelines. Qualified Asian Americans may be perceived as "not assertive enough" for leadership positions, as Asian cultures value modesty and social consideration. Dr. Neilson documents the remarkable success of ten individuals who were able to "break the glass ceiling" by being persistent, resilient risk takers who work hard, hold high standards for themselves, and collaborate effectively with others, enabling them to achieve beyond the "norm" and join the 2% of Asian Americans who are in senior leadership roles in higher education nationally. Dr. Neilson identified three themes that emerged from this qualitative study, including a) hard work as honor, legacy, and moral obligation; b) collaboration as interconnection in the present, and c) risk taking. Dr. Neilson calls for leadership development that values specific cultural norms that lie at the heart of both Asian American leaders' philosophical commitments and their daily leadership practices.

How do educators effectively teach increasingly diverse students and prepare them for providing health services to increasingly diverse health care consumers? Are traditional approaches to nursing education that emphasizes "objective" knowledge effective? Dr. Suyemoto and associates, in **Chapter 11, Integrating Disciplines for Transformative Education in Health Services: Strategies and Effects,** describe curricular strategies of transformative education that engages, empowers, and enables students to become active participants and contributors to social justice in their education, health professions, and social milieus. Transformative education emphasizes pedagogies that examine complex social variables and power relations, include marginalized voices, value personal knowledge, and explore epistemological validity. Multiple levels of power in the individual, interpersonal, and systemic levels exist. Transformative education encourages students to question how problems might lie within systems and reflect on inequities in power and privilege. A system-focused conceptualization enables students to move beyond an individual analysis to examine the complexities of privilege and lack of privilege posed by the intersection of race, ethnicity, gender, language, and socioeconomic class. Personalizing knowledge helps students connect principles and facts, and the experiences of other individuals and their own experience. As the authors note, how we teach can model critical examination of knowledge production and maintenance, or it can encourage students to passively accept what is taught as the single truth. To engage, empower, and enable students to think critically, educators need to embrace transformative education as a philosophical approach to education.

Asian American Voices is a collection of scholarly work by Asian American educators. Each chapter — understanding Asian Americans, mentoring Asian students to become health professionals, teaching Asian students with psychosocial trauma, understanding Asian students' learning needs, engaging, empowering, and enabling students in service learning and cultural development, or developing higher education leaders among Asian Americans — reflects an unyielding commitment by Asian American educators and scholars to connect what has been disconnected in higher education: experience, meaning, and students' realities, and to develop students for what has been ignored: a sense of agency, and a sense of responsibility, and accountability. No doubt, the experimental and experiential teaching practices negate traditional approaches to education, where individuals disconnect with their realities, struggle with abstractions, and probe "false" separation and differences from real connections. Does education contribute to a progressive form of social change? If so, the relationships of power, domination, and submission must be disrupted so that intellectual liberty is equally celebrated and pursued, multiculturalism is integrated throughout curricula, and places and spaces are created where students and educators together examine the past, study the present, and explore future possibilities.

Asian American Voices: Engaging, Empowering, Enabling is written by educators and researchers who continue to care deeply about the betterment of higher education. If our vision is to achieve diversity in higher education, and our vision is to be realized, we must ask where students and educators can find their own "voices," and how faculty and administrators can create environments where diverse student populations are educated, empowered, and enabled; where intellect can safely range and speculate; and where diverse voices can be heard and respected.

Lin Zhan, PhD, RN, FAAN
Dean and Professor, School of Nursing
Massachusetts College of Pharmacy and Health Sciences

---

1   *This diversity research project was part of the university-wide Diversity Research Initiative, funded by the Ford Foundation, and took place at University of Massachusetts Boston.*

ACKNOWLEDGMENTS

I would like to acknowledge all contributing authors who worked collaboratively on the production of *Asian American Voices*. Their willingness to share their knowledge and expertise humbled me immediately. I thank them for their spirit of scholarly inquiry and enthusiasm.

Deep appreciation goes to Dr. Terry Valiga and Ms. Justine Fitzgerald for their skillful edits of this book, and for their dedication to the betterment of education.

Gratitude goes to the faculty, students, families, men and women who never fail to teach me to be a better educator and a better person.

Lin Zhan, PhD, RN, FAAN, Editor
Asian American Voices
Summer 2008

DEDICATION

Voices

Begging to be heard

Burst into telling

New and different stories

Echoing somewhere

Perhaps

Perhaps someday

We will hear all voices

By Lin Zhan

CHAPTER 1
CULTURE, HEALTH, AND NURSING EDUCATION[1]

Lin Zhan, PhD, RN, FAAN

Nursing, the largest health care workforce in the United States, is experiencing unprecedented challenges in caring for increasingly diverse clients. Racial and ethnic minorities represent a third of the U.S. population. Yet, the profession of nursing itself severely lacks diversity, with only 11.6% of registered nurses in the United States representing racial or ethnic groups other than white (U.S. Department of Health and Human Services, 2004). To achieve diversity within the nursing profession, concerted effort must be made to critically examine the curriculum and ways we teach future nurses, the environment in which students learn best, and the connections we make to the reality of existing health disparities among racial and ethnic minorities in the nation. The Institute of Medicine (2004) reports that the lack of diversity affects the quality of health care delivery, since minority professionals' presence, practice, and commitment to underserved communities and populations improve access to and quality of health care.

To prepare a diverse nursing workforce, nurse educators need to ask critical questions, such as: "To what extent are nurse educators informed about culture and health outside their own?" and "How do nurse educators integrate knowledge of multiculturalism into teaching and learning?" Integration is not adding one cultural dimension to existing content; rather, it takes knowledge, deep understanding, appreciation, and a thoughtful design to create integrative curricula and appropriate pedagogies. The dynamics of interaction and interplay between nurse educators and an increasingly diverse student body require nurse educators and academic leaders to rethink what we teach, how we teach, what kind of educational environment we create for learning, how we evaluate what we teach, and how we integrate cultural knowledge to be part of the essential competencies we use to prepare new members of our profession.

Nursing education prepares graduates to provide nursing service for patients and families from diverse ethnocultural backgrounds. Understanding cultural influences on human health beliefs and behaviors is essential for culturally competent care. This chapter will present some results of the author's research focusing on culture and health among Asian Americans.

SCHOLARLY INQUIRY

Over the years, much of the author's funded research and scholarly work has focused on cross cultural studies: health promotion and practices in ethnic elderly women; substance abuse among Chinese women of childbearing age: exploring resilience factors; self-care and self-consistency among African American elders[2]; medication practices in community-dwelling elderly Chinese Americans; experiences of Chinese family caregivers with persons with Alzheimer's disease; best practice in caring for Asian American elders; senior health care service in Boston's Chinatown[3]; and Asian American students' learning needs, to name a few. While the author was investigating health issues among ethno-cultural groups, particularly

Asian Americans, some academicians and even some academic officers viewed this kind of work as being "out of focus," and not mainstream research. But existing health disparities in the nation are the correct focus for ethno-cultural studies and intellectual inquiries that help us elucidate the complex pathways of human health and behavior and identify useful interventions for eliminating health disparities and promoting health for all.

In addition, the author has worked with community leaders and other advocates for providing accessible and culturally appropriate health care for underserved and vulnerable populations; has designed and taught the course, "Asian American Cultures and Health Practices" in an urban public university; and engaged in dialogue with scholars, educators, service providers, community leaders, and policy makers across the United States. From caring for an Asian elder in the community to giving speeches in conferences to teaching students to studying health issues in ethno-cultural groups, I hear voices speaking of barriers and difficulties that ethno-cultural group members experience as they encounter the educational and health care systems, of the impact of cultural misunderstandings and unequal treatment on their health and well-being, and of the less than adequate quality of care they receive. It is clear that many voices are begging to be heard, and new voices want to tell their stories. Consider the following real life stories:

I am having bleeding, but I am afraid of calling my doctor, I can't speak English (Vietnamese American elder);

I had eye surgery. I did not understand what they said to me nor did I ask them. I waited for a while and then walked home. I felt so dizzy and passed out on the street near Chinatown. What would happen if my friend did not pass by and take me home? (Chinese American elder);

Why did my doctor keep telling me to forget about the past? I am the only one who survived the Pol-Pot killing in my family. The past is the connecting tissue to my home, my family, my soul, and my current life (Cambodian American man);

We took my mother to a long-term care facility due to her dementia condition. We were rejected because we were told that my mom did not speak English. My mom lost her access to needed health service (Chinese family caregiver);

Why did the professor tell me, "Nursing is not for you"? "Whose nursing is it"? (Vietnamese male nursing student).

A single voice, shared voices, all boil down to one simple yet poorly understood question: Who are Asian Americans? What barriers have they encountered in trying to receive health care? How can their culture, health needs, and health care experiences be made more visible in nursing education? Whose right is it to tell a student that "nursing is not for you"? Such questions are important for both nurse educators and health providers to ask, since we have a professional and social responsibility to understand the populations we serve and the colleagues with whom we work.

ASIAN AMERICANS

Our nation continues to become increasingly diverse. By 2050, forty-eight percent of the population will be non-white. Latino Americans will outnumber the population of African Americans, and Asian Americans will continue to be the fastest growing ethnic group, expanding from the current 3% (approximately 11 million) to 10% (41 million). Such diversity in our nation speaks to a new concept, the "browning of America." Many cultures and many ethnicities intersect, interact with, and challenge the existing dominant Western culture. Among Asian Americans, more than 70% are immigrants who came to the United States in different waves of immigration — from building railways or searching for gold mountains in the 19th century, immigrating to achieve family reunion or escaping political persecution to filling a demand for highly skilled technology jobs or pursuing higher education and professional advancement. The population of Asian Americans is extremely diverse in culture, language, custom, religion, political and immigration experience, and socio-economic status. Of Asian Americans, there are more than 50 sub-ethnic groups, speaking more than 30 different languages and many more dialects.

It is noteworthy that distinct differences exist between Asian immigrants and refugees. People immigrated to the United States in search of opportunities — educational, economic, or for purposes of family reunion. Refugees, however, were driven by the circumstances or powerful forces of war, violence, or political persecution; thus, they are persons outside the borders of their home country who are fearful of returning because they fear persecution at the hands of their government, persecution based on their race, religion, political opinions, nationality, or membership in a particular social group (Winter, 1997). Indeed, the refugee situation is political — from why they became refugees and how they escaped their devastating situation to where they settled and the new lives they have established.

Most Asian refugees are from Southeast Asia. They fled from the horrors of war and escaped from abusive governments. The refugee experience is traumatic — physically, psychologically, and politically — and many refugees suffer from post-traumatic stress disorder (PTSD), a serious health outcome of refugee flight. PTSD symptoms range from nightmares, sleep disorders, and somatic complaints to psychological complaints such as depression, loneliness, apathy, withdrawal, avoidance, and persecution reactions.

Refugee women are particularly vulnerable in flight, at the point of entry into another country, and at the military base of the host country where they are targets of sexual abuse, exploitation, and discrimination. Many were raped, forced to work, and tied up in flight (Mayotte, 1997). Reexperiencing the traumatic events of discrimination, abuse, sexual violence, and prejudice once refugees resettle can have a profound impact on the quality of their lives. Some never fully recover, spiritually or physically, as they continue to reexperience traumatic events. Therefore, when people flee as refugees, they need, and indeed deserve, to be rescued, protected, and cared for.

SOCIOECONOMIC STATUS

Socioeconomic status (SES) refers to a person's position in a social system that differentially allocates the major resources enabling them to achieve health or other desired goals. The major resources are income, education, occupation, and assets (House & Williams, 2002). Contrary to the pervasive myth of Asian Americans as a "model minority," socioeconomic status among Asian Americans tends to be a bipolar distribution. Some groups enjoy good economic status while others endure poverty. Asian Americans have not achieved parity with respect to personal income (Takaki, 1987), and recent refugees from Southeast Asia and immigrant elders are among the poorest in our nation. The National Center for Health Statistics (1998) reported that, in 1995, the poverty rate for Asians was almost twice that of whites. Education disparities also exist among Asian Americans. While there is a high rate of college completion, there also is a high percentage of functional illiteracy. Lack of educational preparation limits one's opportunity for better paying jobs and social mobility, which often leads to poverty, and poverty itself is a major barrier to health care access. People who are poor have higher mortality and morbidity rates than those who are not. Poverty, a determining factor for poor health, must be taken into account in our efforts to improve health for all.

There is a strong association between race/ethnicity and SES in the United States. Historically, Asian Americans have been discriminated against. Between 1882 and 1892, the Chinese Exclusion Act prohibited Chinese from coming to the United States. The 1924 National Origin Act prohibited all Asians from entering the United States. Finally, in 1942, Executive Order 9066 forced 120,000 Japanese to relocate. Such discriminatory legislation has limited the opportunities and social mobility of many Asians and generated prejudice and sentiments against Asian Americans that remain in the 21st century. Quite often, Asian Americans are frustrated and saddened by constant reminders that they "do not belong," and many suffer equally because of outright hostility and bias toward them on a daily basis. Unfortunately, Asian Americans have experienced discrimination based on not only their race, but also on their national origins. Racial discrimination and prejudice in health care can lead to diagnostic errors, unequal treatment, and psychological damage to clients. In the example noted earlier, a Chinese family caregiver describes[4], "I took my mom to a nursing home. We were rejected because I was told that my mom did not speak English." Another Asian family caregiver said, "My doctor told me that if I did not speak English, he would not refer me to the leading hospital for my mom's Alzheimer's disease evaluation." In these cases, the patients and families lost access to needed service; they found themselves being rejected or relegated to a lesser level of service. Indeed, much of the tension in these clinical encounters is a reproduction of larger class, racial, and gender conflicts in the broader society (Singer, 1995).

Many factors precipitate a lack of access to health care. Chief among them are difficulties with English among many immigrant elders. Linguistic isolation blocks one's communication with others, prevents one from learning new information and gaining new knowledge, and keeps one from discussing his/her health problems with providers. In 2001, the U.S. Department of Health and Human Services Office of Minority Health established national standards for culturally and linguistically appropriate services in health care, calling on health care organizations to provide care to patients/consumers in their preferred language, to make available easily understood patient-related materials, and to post signage in the languages of the commonly encountered group or groups represented in the service area. However, most of health education information is still disseminated in English. One Chinese elder, a college professor in his original country and an author of several books, described, "It is very hard for me here. I do not understand English. I can't even discuss my headache with my doctor, and I am like a disabled person here." A Japanese student recommended: "Even if patients do not speak English fluently, nurses and doctors need to find a way to communicate with them. They need to have a cultural broker or a language translator. They need to understand their feelings. Asians and Asian Americans are really afraid of being rejected in conversations; so health care workers need to understand that."

CULTURAL CONFLICT

Many Asian immigrants and refugees experience tremendous cultural conflicts when they interact with the American health care system. "If anything was made to be taken for granted, it is culture" (Gallagher & Subedi, 1995, p. 4). A culture refers to shared and learned knowledge that people in a society hold (Loustaunau & Sobo, 1997). It guides people's health beliefs and practices and the way they interpret and conceptualize health and illness. When people encounter different cultures, they are searching for a cultural fit, a phenomenon known as acculturation. However, no one totally gives up his/her culture to become acculturated; rather, one moves along the continuum of acculturation. Some Asian American groups may become acculturated to a greater degree in some areas than in others. Some may keep their traditions while others become bicultural or multicultural. Health providers, therefore, need to have an appreciation of the various cultures and cultural practices of the diverse people they serve.

The American health care system is based on a biomedical model that determines what typology is legitimate, which practice is appropriate, how treatment is implemented, which language is considered proper, and who has the authority to make decisions. Based on this paradigm, folk medicine is not valued. Ethnocentrism in health care can create barriers for those who seek health care yet believe and practice in different cultural modes. Traditional medicine, for example, has been practiced in Asia for several thousand years. The introduction of Western medicine to Asia has resulted in integrated medicine, in which both medicines are practiced and encouraged in the health care system. Under this kind of system, patients may be diagnosed by Western medical technology, but prescribed traditional medicine for treatment. When Asian American immigrants interact with the U.S health care system, Western practices are contrary to their familiar, integrated medical system, different cultures collide and cross-cultural misunderstandings take place. Some may not want to take prescriptions and do end up doing so. Some may visit doctors for diagnosis, but not for treatment. Indeed, cultural health practice is partly responsible for what clinicians call "noncompliance." Without a cross-cultural understanding, the effectiveness of any intervention can be compromised.

Here are voices from Asian American patients:

When I had my annual physical, my doctor asked me "have you been physically abused?" How could he ask me that kind of question? And 'black and blue' on my skin was caused by my using of a coin to rub my neck when I feel under the weather (Vietnamese American student);

It still upsets me when my doctor kept telling me that I needed not to worry about it when I felt a lump in my breast. They told me that, "Chinese women rarely get breast cancer." But I was soon to learn that I had a breast cancer (Chinese woman);

Sometimes, Western doctors think that it is absurd to use folk medicine. Folk medicine has the ability to make me get well, and sometimes it works. I wish they could learn about folk medicine (Cambodian American student).

People's health-seeking behaviors are influenced by whether health services are culturally responsive and linguistically appropriate. The majority of health care providers are from the dominant Euro-American culture, while an increasing proportion of clients are from cultures with different beliefs, traditions, values, and practices. When health care providers interact with the clients from a different culture, the more vulnerable group is often subjugated to the authority of the more powerful group. This presents an array of problems having to do with professional ethics, quality of care, well-being of the client, and the general health of society (American Academy of Nursing, 1995).

CULTURE AND HEALTH PRACTICE

Decision-Making. Decision-making in health care may depend upon the degree of agreement between the client and the health professional (Kleinman, 1980). Family, for example, in many Asian cultures, means an extended group, including one's immediate family, parents, grandparents, and/or other relatives. Based on an extended family structure, when a patient comes to health care, his/her decision is not merely personal; rather, it is made through a collective process in which an extended family may be involved and affected. How a person defines illness, interprets the onset of symptoms, and evaluates the effects of the treatment regimen determines his/her health care decision-making process. If the person's health belief and practice differ greatly from that of the health provider, he/she is less likely to seek health care or adhere to the treatment regimen. Decision-making also is structurally determined. In some Asian cultures, for example, men may make a family planning decision, or a patient's family member may make a decision for the patient, as one Filipino American stated,

> American health care puts a great deal of emphasis on patient autonomy and patient's right to know, which may not be shared by all cultures, and is contrary to the dominant beliefs of many societies. The custom in many cultures, such as Filipino, Chinese, and Iranian, is for a patient's family to be the first to hear about a poor prognosis, after which the family decides whether and how much to tell the patient. Members of such cultural groups may believe that it would be insensitive for a patient to be told bad news and that this would only cause the patient great stress and even hasten death by destroying hope.

Food. Food, in Asian cultures, is considered to be a source for restoring health and preventing illness, but it also carries significant symbolic meanings and religious significance. A Chinese American elder was told he could have nothing by mouth the day before his gastric surgery. He was nodding his head while his doctor was giving him instruction through the translator. Immediately as his doctor stepped out of the room, he began to peel an orange. In his view, an orange is not food, but a symbol of healing. Another Chinese American man was hospitalized for cancer treatment. On his arrival, he requested a cup of tea. A staff gave him a glass of iced tea. The patient was very upset because he believed that cold-water could shock a sick person's body system. A hospitalized Indian American patient was in tears and refused to eat lunch. She was given green beans, rice, and beef. Eating beef is against her religious belief and she felt she was being insulted. Incidences like these could be avoided if health providers were aware of the meaning food held for their patients.

Yin and Yang. In traditional Chinese medicine, two Chinese philosophical doctrines define the theory and causation of diseases: yin and yang. Yin and yang refer to two great opposing material forces that coexist, even within each other, and regulate the ceaseless emergence, variation, and change in all things (Wang & Wu, 1936). The concept of yin and yang applies to everything, including nature, human body systems, food, health and illness, and the relationship between humans and their environment. Yin and yang influence people's health beliefs and practices and must be balanced in order to be healthy and prosper. With respect to illness, yin refers to "cold" illnesses such as depression and hypothyroidism, whereas yang refers to "hot" illnesses such as hypertension, fever, or seizure. If one has fever, he/she is considered to have too much yang; therefore, food and medicine in the yin category need to be considered. The key practice for maintaining the balance of yin and yang involves prevention. Yin and yang is used as a framework in the *Yellow Emperor's Classic of Internal Medicine,* or the *Nei Jing.* Balancing yin and yang is a way of disease prevention and health promotion (Veith, 1970, p. 12).

Medication Practice. Some Asian Americans define health as "free from symptoms." Managing the onset of symptoms involves changing one's diet (if the onset is perceived as a small problem), taking herbal remedies, and/or using over-the-counter drugs (if the onset is getting worse). In traditional Chinese medicine, diet and herbal remedies are always practiced together. Some may visit a healer instead of a Western doctor, as seeing a Western practitioner is the last step that one takes for diagnosis and/or prescription.

The author conducted a funded study to understand medication practices in community-dwelling elderly Chinese Americans[5]. Using both interviews and a structured survey, more than 200 elderly Chinese Americans participated in the study. Findings showed that a majority of the participants took medications based on symptoms. Either relieving or worsening of symptoms caused their discontinuation of taking prescribed medications. Comments made by the study subjects included the following: "If the prescription does not make me feel better, why bother? I stop taking it." "If I feel better, I do not need to take a pill." Some indicated self-medication without consulting a physician or nurse practitioner. Some combined herbs with prescriptions. Some went to see a Western doctor for diagnosis and then self-medicated with traditional Chinese medicine and were not aware of the possible adverse effects of some herbal medicines (e.g., Ma Huang, Tian Ma, and Jingshen root) that could be contraindicated in combination with anti-hypertension drugs (Zhan & Chen, 2004). This study provided new knowledge that helps both educators and clinicians identify potential risk factors of drug-drug interactions and adverse drug reactions and be mindful about their clients' medication practices and their ways of managing symptoms. In education, cultural context and content need to be an integral component of pharmacology as educators teach this topic to nursing, medicine, and allied health students.

Cultural Perceptions. Culturally, some Asian Americans may view hospitalization as a sign of impending death. With this view, when a patient is hospitalized, an extended family may be involved, and a spiritual or religious ceremony may be performed. Some may refuse to have their blood drawn because they consider blood as the vital component of the body. Some may consider a physician's delayed diagnosis as a sign of incompetence due to their experience with traditional medicine doctors who usually diagnose the problem at the initial visit.

Culture and Communication. Maintenance of social harmony is highly valued in some Asian cultures, which stand in stark contrast to the North American value of individualism and individual rights and choices, as well as to Western medical ethics that emphasize personal autonomy and view individuals as self-determining moral agents. To maintain social harmony, one may not complain about his/her pain. Family members may hide bad news (such as being diagnosed with cancer) from their loved one (the patient) because they believe such an act will prevent the patient from being emotionally distressed and preserve the patient's internal harmony.

Contrary to what health providers advocate regarding "advance directives," in some Asian cultures, it is not advisable to discuss death when a person is alive. In addition, "informed consent" may be a totally foreign concept for recent Asian immigrants, because it is not practiced in their original country. The Western notion of informed consent changes the historically uneven relationship where the authority figure is in charge; this concept is very difficult for Asian immigrants to understand or accept. Without such understanding, Asian immigrants may sign a consent form merely to *conform*, rather than to consent. Moreover, complications and risks noted in the informed consent may be perceived as an impending danger, as one elderly immigrant described, "Why before the surgery, did the doctor tell me so many risks and complications. After all, why do I need surgery if so many problems are involved?" Health care providers, therefore, need to collaborate with the patient's family about the consent to ensure their full understanding of the purpose, content, and implications of the consent.

To respect health providers, Asian Americans may be reluctant to question or say "no," even though they disagree. A nodding head may show respect, politeness, and attentiveness. However, it does not necessarily mean, "I agree with you"; rather, it means, "I hear you." Health providers need to be aware of such culturally bound behaviors. A simple statement like "You heard me. Do you also agree?" can clear misunderstandings. Cultural beliefs influence health practices, and such cultural knowledge needs to be integrated into the nursing curriculum.

STIGMATIZATION

Mental Illness. Asian Americans suffer a disproportionate burden of mental illnesses. Elderly Asian American women, for example, have higher rates of suicide than whites. For women aged 75 and older, the suicide rate for Asian American was 7.95 per 100,000, compared with the rate for whites of 4.18 (Centers for Disease Control and Prevention, 2007), yet, a paucity of research exists to help provide better understanding this phenomenon. Some explanations for the higher suicide rate can be that older Asian American women a) have difficulties adapting to U.S. culture; b) are not treated with the level of respect they receive in their native cultures; c) experience a lack of social support and connectedness; and d) feel strong stigma attached to mental illness such as depression, thus leading to suicide (Kim & Taylor, 2006; Sue & Sue, 2003).

Asian Americans do not access mental health treatment as much as other racial groups do, perhaps due to the strong stigma attached to mental illness. Stigma — viewing a person with a set of powerful negative images — is often rooted in cultural beliefs and shaped by norms of social interaction (Guo, 2001). One study (Zhang, Snowden, & Sue, 1998) found that Asian Americans are significantly less likely than whites to mention their mental health concerns to a friend or relative (12% vs. 25%), to a mental health professional (4%

vs. 26%), or to a physician (2% vs. 13%). Influenced by cultural traditions, the process of stigmatization of mental illness places more of its significance on the family than on the individual who is labeled as mentally ill (Kleinman, 1986; Phillips, 1993). Asian families may view mental illness as "shameful," "evil spirit," "soul loss," "wrongdoing," or "punishment." In some cases, families shelter the patients for months or years before getting treatment. Stigmatization of mental illness hinders Asian patients from obtaining early diagnosis and receiving timely intervention (Zhan, 2004b). Because of the social stigma attached to mental illness, some Asian American patients may not want others to know about their mental illness. As a result, they may fail to show up for a scheduled appointment. Blocking in an extra 15 or 20 minutes between appointments may help reduce the chance that people might run into someone they know. This workable strategy may help increase the access of Asian American patients to mental health services.

Mental illness may be manifested by culture-bound syndromes in Asian Americans. Culture-bound syndromes are culturally influenced expressions of mental distress and reflect underlying values, morals, and traditions embedded in the social and cultural context within which they exist (Kirmayer & Young, 1999; Lin & Cheung, 1999). For example, Koro (genital retraction syndrome) occurs in China and Southeast Asia. Koro is associated with a sudden, intense anxiety that the penis will recede into the body and possibly cause death. This phenomenon is explained as a sign of fatal exhaustion of the yang element within the framework of the yin-yang balance, and is attributed to guilt and anxiety over real or imagined sexual excess, especially autoerotic (Hall, 1998). Asian Americans also may express mental distress through physical symptoms (somatization), such as complaining about somatic or physical pain, sleeping problems, chronic pain, dizziness, or fatigue. Somatization describes symptoms caused by stress but experienced as bodily sensations that cannot be defined biomedically, as the following case illustrates:

Mrs. Wong came to a senior center with her husband. They both were in their later 60s. While Mr. Wong was asking questions about social and health service in the community senior center, Mrs. Wong appeared to be apathetic and lacked any interest in conversation. When Mrs. Wong was asked (in Chinese), "How are you doing?" she began to complain about sleeping problem: "I could not sleep well for a long time. I am fine, except feeling fatigue, experiencing pain. I even do not know where the pain came from. This is a small problem, do not worry." After three weeks, Mr. and Mrs. Wong came [again] to the senior center. Mrs. Wong seemed to have lost a good deal of weight. She complained, "I can't eat well. No appetite." The community health nurse conducted a depression assessment and referred Mrs. Wong to a Chinese psychiatrist. Mrs. Wong was diagnosed with depression and went on receiving treatment, after which her depressive condition improved and more significantly, she participates in community activities and smiles.

Of special emphasis is the importance of engaging in compassionate dialogue with Asian American patients, who would feel more comfortable discussing their mental health problems with someone they trust and with someone who understands their culture and how things are expressed in their culture. Particularly among refugees whose trust was violated, rebuilding that trust takes time, patience, compassion, sensitivity, and caring.

Sexually Transmitted Disease (STD). There is also strong social stigma toward Asian women who suffer from STD, and who are victims of domestic violence. In these situations, women often are blamed. Domestic violence has emerged as a critical issue in Asian communities. In Massachusetts, for example, although Asian Americans comprise 2.4% of the population, they account for 13% of the women and children killed as a result of domestic violence. Studies among several Asian sub-ethnic groups in Massachusetts found that while most of the respondents did not approve of domestic violence, men tended to hold strong patriarchal attitudes and women tended to be blamed for being battered (Yoshioka & Dang, 2000). It is important to educate women about STDs, and it is even more important to empower Asian women to say "no" to unsafe sex. Of special concern is the need to listen to the voices of battered women, which is the first and most critical step in making their lives safer.

Dementia. The author conducted a qualitative study that interviewed Chinese family caregivers for persons with dementia. The study found that dementia was intensely stigmatized by the Chinese community. Dementia was viewed as "contagious," "worrying too much," "evil spirit," and being caused by "bad Feng Shui." Traditional Chinese culture considers Feng (the force of wind) and Shui (the flow of water) as living energies that form around one's home and workplace. Feng Shui must be properly aligned to bring peace, happiness, and fortune to the family. Sample comments from Chinese family caregivers were: "My dad's friends told us to move to another place. They thought that bad Feng Shui caused my mom's Alzheimer's"; "Some people in Chinatown were scared when they found out that my mom had Alzheimer's disease. They would walk away from us because they thought they would get Alzheimer's disease as well if they get close to us. It is just so hard"; and "People talked about Alzheimer's disease as if it happened to your family because you did something terribly wrong. They made you feel too ashamed to tell others" (Zhan, 2004a).

Social and family support is needed for Asian family members who care for loved ones with devastating illness. Understanding the intense degree of stigma associated with mental illness, sexually transmitted disease, and Alzheimer's disease in Asian Americans may help explain their health seeking behavior and low level of utilization of related health services. Demystifying social stigma takes collaborative and concerted effort made by Asian communities and health care providers. It also takes education of the public about cultural perspectives, yet, how to integrate cultural perspectives into the educational curriculum remains a challenge.

CULTURAL COMPETENCY

Health care deals with diverse people and their responses to health and illness. Human responses are complex, dynamic, and powerful. They are influenced by factors that are biological, psychological, sociopolitical, economic, and cultural. We have known for some time that culture and ethnicity have profound influences on health and illness, health-seeking behaviors, and access to health care. Therefore, health care providers have a moral obligation to understand the cultural perspectives of their clients and the meanings of health and illness held by various ethnic groups. In health care, cultural competence should not be something added to the health care agenda; instead, it should be an integral component of quality care (American Academy of Nursing, 1995).

Cultural competence involves formulation of a complete picture of ethno-cultural group members' responses to health and illness that helps health care providers develop the ability to distinguish between social status and cultural factors and identify the interaction among these factors. As described earlier, Asian Americans are extremely diverse. Not all Asian American group members are poor, nor do they like to eat the same food. Not all speak the same language, nor do they have the same historical past. Considerable harm can be done to the intercultural engagement process if ethnic groups are viewed simply as low-income individuals, if the ethno-cultural dimensions of their lives are ignored, if they are relegated to the category of being victims of discrimination, or if they are treated as functional illiterates (Valle, 1998). In the academic arena, knowledge about various cultures and human diversity must gain widespread legitimacy in education. Cultural competence requires health care providers to use culturally sensitive and appropriate approaches. Diagnostic procedures and treatment regimens need to be explained in appropriate language. Technical terms must be balanced with colloquial language. Health care providers themselves, as products of their own cultures, may exhibit ethnocentric attitudes when interacting with diverse clients. To prepare health care providers to better respond to the social and demographic changes occurring in our nation, educational institutions need to have policies and practices in place that integrate cross-cultural knowledge as part of their mission and curriculum.

However, much of health care profession education is based on Eurocentric models that offer health providers limited knowledge about traditions of healing and the meaning of illness for the diverse patients for whom they will care. Most professional education does not help students learn how to communicate with a family who defines seizure as "soul loss"; instead, we learn about bacteria and germs and how they cause diseases. Students rarely learn the meanings of illness in the world of their patients; instead, they learn neurological diseases and functions of neurotransmitters. They rarely learn about emotional pain, social pain, political pain, or how social structure and context cause these pains; instead, they learn the physiology of pain and how to manage it with medication. To be culturally competent in health care, the education of health professionals must be reformed to include cross-cultural knowledge and experience in other definitions of health and illness as part of the core curriculum. Of equal importance is that education must be responsible for recruiting, facilitating the education of, and graduating students of diversity.

Anne Fadiman, the author of the book *The Spirit Catches You and You Fall Down: A Hmong Child, Her American Doctors, and the Collision of Two Cultures* (1997) vividly describes a tragic story, in which a Hmong child suffered from seizures and eventually slipped into a coma. The story reflects the collision of and painful struggle between two cultures: Hmong culture and biomedical culture. The Hmong family, in the process of seeking and receiving health care from American doctors, encountered intense conflict between the dominant culture and their own. The Hmong family and the American doctors were all caught in the interplay of a complex, dynamic situation, in which each culture stubbornly claimed its place. As powerful an influence as the Hmong culture was in this case, so too was the culture of biomedicine. This tragic story is about excessive cross-cultural misunderstandings and the amazing power of biomedicine. A lesson we all can learn from this tragic story is that health care providers and educators need to examine their own culture, interests and biases, for without cultural understanding, health care providers can be perfect clinicians, but far from perfect healers.

One dangerous approach in clinical practice or education is to take a single piece of cultural observation and generalize to all. Under the label of "multiculturalism" in some nursing textbooks, a single observation is generalized. For example, "Asians do not like eye contact" or "Asians are quiet in social settings." In this case, a stereotype is further perpetuated toward Asians, and it derails ongoing intellectual inquiry to learn about diverse cultures, health practices, and the context and content or fabric of human lives.

Equally dangerous is perpetual ignorance and prejudice toward minority students in higher education. For example, one doctoral student was told "you have to quit your job in order to study well in the doctoral program." This doctoral student, a nurse practitioner and a refugee, serves Cambodian refugees in the community who are otherwise underserved or not served at all. "Working" not only provides income for this student to support his doctoral study and his family of four, but also enables him to identify major health issues among this underserved population as his research interest for his dissertation work. Without knowing the context and experience of students like this, faculty blind themselves to the realities of these students' lives. They may even further traumatize students who already feel unwelcome and misunderstood (in this case, the student was in tears when he was told to quit his work). Without first knowing about students from different racial and ethnic backgrounds, how can we integrate cultural knowledge in nursing, and how can we help students *know how* to care for and to meet health care needs of diverse clients?

In closing, here are student voices[6]:

As increasing numbers of new immigrants and persons of color have sought health care, it has become evident that the health care system must adapt in order to meet their needs. Culturally appropriate health care requires openness to the expectations, perceptions and realities of various communities (Burmese American student);

Many health professionals think that, treating each patient with respect will avert most cultural problems. But more than often, that is not the case. Understandably enough, some cultural knowledge can help avoid misunderstandings and enable practitioners to provide better care for diverse patients (Hispanic American student);

We must not let our ethnocentrism blind us to the merits in the beliefs of other cultures. If health care professionals are serious about their desire to provide the best care for all patients, regardless of their race, gender, ethnic origin, and religion, it is so essential that they are culturally competent. Obviously, it is not possible to know everything about every culture, but the first important step is an awareness of one's own ethnocentrism. That said, we can confidently work towards achieving a culturally competent health care system, successfully serving patients of all cultures and races (African American student).

The aforementioned often reminds us what responsibility we have. If we truly embrace diversity in higher education, we must deconstruct a dualistic, "either/or" approach. Until we do that, we will not begin to hear voices, all voices…

REFERENCES

American Academy of Nursing. (1995). *Promoting cultural competence in and through nursing education.* [Position Paper]. Washington, DC: Author.

Centers for Disease Control and Prevention: National Center for Injury Prevention and Control. Web-Based Injury Statistics Query and Reporting System. (2007). [Online]. Available: http://www.cdc.gov/ncipc/wisqars.

Fadiman, A. (1997). *The spirit catches you and you fall down: A Hmong child, her American doctors, and the collision of two cultures.* New York: Farrar, Straus and Giroux.

Gallagher, E., & Subedi, J. (1995). *Global perspectives on health care.* Englewood Cliffs, NJ: Prentice-Hall.

Guo, Z. B. (2001). *Ginseng and aspirin: Health care alternatives for aging Chinese in New York.* Cornell University Press.

Hall, T. M. (1998). Glossary of culture-bound syndromes. http://homepage.mac.com/mccajor/cbs_frame.html

House J. S., & Williams, D. R. (2002). Understanding and reducing socioeconomic and racial/ethnic disparities in health. In B.D. Smedley & S.L. Syme (Eds.), *Promoting health: Intervention strategies from social and behavioral research* (pp. 81-124). Washington, DC: Institute of Medicine, National Academies Press.

Kim, S., & Taylor, K. (2006). Pursuit of comfort and pursuit of harmony: Culture, relationships, and social support seeking. *Personality and Social Psychology Bulletin, 32* (12), 1595-1607.

Kirmayer, L. J., & Young, A. (1999). Culture and context in the evolutionary concept of mental disorders. *Abnormal Psychology, 108, 446-452.*

Kleinman, A. (1980). *Patients and healers in the context of culture.* Berkeley: University of California Press.

Kleinman, A. (1986). *Social origin of distress and disease: Depression, neurasthenia, and pain in modern China.* New Haven: Yale University Press.

Institute of Medicine. (2004). *In the nation's compelling interest: Ensuring diversity in the health care workforce.* Washington, DC: National Academies Press.

Lin, K. M., & Cheung, F. (1999). Mental health issues for Asian Americans. _Psychiatric Services_, 50, 774-780.

Loustaunau, M. O., & Sobo, E. J. (1997). _The cultural context of health, illness, and medicine._ Westport, CT: Bergin & Garvey.

Mayotte, J. A. (1997). Protection and health needs of refugee women and girl children. In American Academy of Nursing (Ed.), _Global migration: The healthcare implications of immigration and population movements_ (pp. 15-46). Washington, DC: AAN.

National Center for Health Statistics. (1998). _Health, United States, 1998, with Socioeconomic Status and Health Chartbook._ Hyattsville, MD: U.S. Department of Health and Human Services. [Online]. Available: http://www.cdc.gov/nchs/data/hus/hus98.pdf.

Phillips, M. R. (1993). Strategies used by Chinese families coping with schizophrenia. In D. Davis & S. Harrell (Eds.), _Chinese families in the post-Mao era_ (pp. 277-306). Berkeley: University of California Press.

Singer M. (1995). Beyond the ivory tower: Critical praxis in medical anthropology. _Medical Anthropology Quarterly,_ 9(1), 80-106.

Sue, D. W., & Sue, D. (2003). _Counseling the culturally different: Theory and practice,_ 4th ed. New York: John Wiley & Sons.

Takaki, R. (1987). _Strangers from a different shore: A history of Asian Americans._ New York: Penguin Books.

U.S. Department of Health and Human Services. (2004). _The national sample survey of registered nurses._ Washington, DC: Author.

Valle, R., & Gait, H. C. (1998). _Caregiving across cultures: Working with dementing illness and ethnically diverse populations._ London: Taylor and Francis.

Veith, I. (Trans.). (1970). _The yellow emperor's classic of internal medicine._ Berkeley: University of California Press.

Wang, C. M., & Wu, L. T. (1936). _History of Chinese medicine._ Shanghai: National Quarantine Service.

Winter, R. (1997). Keynote Address. In American Academy of Nursing (Ed): _Global migration: The healthcare implications of immigration and population movements_ (pp. 7-14). Washington, DC: AAN.

Yoshioka, M., & Dang, Q. (2000). *Asian family violence report: A study of Cambodian, Chinese, Korean, South Asian and Vietnamese communities in Massachusetts.* Boston: Asian Task Force Against Domestic Violence.

Zhang, A. Y., Snowden, L. R., & Sue, S. (1998). Differences between Asian and White Americans' help-seeking and utilization patterns in the Los Angeles area. *Journal of Community Psychology, 26*, 317-326.

Zhan, L. (2004a). Caring for family members with Alzheimer's disease: Perspectives from Chinese family caregivers. *Journal of Gerontological Nursing, 30(8),* 19-29.

Zhan, L. (2004b). Improving mental health for ethnic older adults. *Journal of Gerontological Nursing, 30(8),* 3.

Zhan, L., & Chen, J. (2004). Medication practices among Chinese American older adults: A study of cultural influences. *Journal of Gerontological Nursing, 30(4),* 24-33.

FOOTNOTES

1   Permission to use the part of the content of this chapter that is adapted from the book, <u>Asian Americans: Vulnerable populations, model interventions, and clarifying agendas,</u> L. Zhan, ed. (2003),was granted by Jones and Bartlett, Sudbury, MA, publisher and copyright owner.

2   Co-investigator with Dr. Jane Cloutterbuck, associate professor at the College of Nursing and Health Sciences, University of Massachusetts Boston.

3   Co-researcher with Dr. Connie Chan, professor in the Public Policy Program, University of Massachusetts Boston

4   The narrative is based on a qualitative study on Chinese family caregivers' experience for persons with Alzheimer's disease.

5   The study was funded by the Boston Medical Foundation.

6   These narratives are from students' work for the course AsAmSt 345 "Asian American Cultures and Health Practices" offered at University of Massachusetts Boston.

CHAPTER 2

A Thematic Analysis of Persistence and Long-Term Educational Engagement with Southeast Asian American College Students

Peter Nien-chu Kiang, EdD

Introduction

In November 2007, the University of California (UC) system boldly announced that its next undergraduate application form includes, for the first time, 23 ethnic categories for Asian American and Pacific Islander populations, rather than the eight categories recorded previously. UC Vice President for Student Affairs Judy Sakaki stated at the public announcement of the policy change: "My goal is for improved data reporting to spur greater accountability regarding overlooked populations in our student body" (UC Newsroom, 2007).

By instituting this reform, data collection and analysis become possible for disaggregated Asian American populations, including Chinese (except Taiwanese), Taiwanese, Asian Indian, Pakistani, Japanese, Korean, Filipino, Vietnamese, Hmong, Thai, Cambodian, Laotian, Bangladeshi, Indonesian, Malaysian, Sri Lankan and other Asians. Expanded Pacific Islander categories include Native Hawaiian, Guamanian/Chamorro, Samoan, Tongan, Fijian and Other Pacific Islander. As Sakaki noted, "Our student data represent a chorus with many voices, and everyone wins when more voices, such as a Hmong student from Fresno and a Cambodian student from Long Beach, can be heard," — a pedagogical and policy perspective shared by the authors included in this volume of *Asian Voices*.

The UC system's decision to recognize disaggregated Asian American and Pacific Islander data follows the conclusions and recommendations made by the U.S. federal government's watchdog agency, the General Accounting Office (GAO), which released its own remarkable report in July 2007 about challenges that face specific Asian American and Pacific Islander subgroups, particularly among Cambodians, Lao, Hmong, and Native Hawaiians (GAO, 2007a). Based on its independent analysis of U.S. Census and U.S. Department of Education data, the GAO found that, "Asian American and Pacific Islander subgroups differ in their levels of academic preparedness, ability to pay for college, and their need to balance academic, employment, and family obligations" (GAO, 2007b, p. 2).

This breakthrough in perspective, policy, and practice represented by the 2007 GAO report and UC system's change in categories finally responds to critiques that have appeared in every major synthesis of Asian American educational research produced during the past two decades, which has clearly shown how aggregate "Asian American" data distort the diverse realities of Asian American and Pacific Islander students, families, and communities (Chang, 2008; Chun, 1980; Gándara, 1999; Lee, 1996; Nakanishi & Nishida, 1995; National Commission on Asian American & Pacific Islander Research in Education, 2008; Olsen, 1997; Pang & Cheng, 1998; Park & Chi, 1999; Suzuki, 1977; Suzuki, 1989; Trueba, Cheng, & Ima, 1993; Trueba, Jacobs, & Kirton, 1990; Weinberg, 1997).

Much of my own agenda as a biracial, Chinese American teacher/researcher and organizer/advocate working at the intersections between the fields of education and Asian American Studies has focused on documenting and analyzing the voices, strengths, and needs of Vietnamese and Cambodian immigrant/refugee students, precisely because mainstream analyses of college student achievement and persistence have typically ignored the strengths and survival strategies employed by Southeast Asian refugee students that I witness empirically at my working-class university. Inspired by those same students, I have also explored how specific curricular and pedagogical commitments in Asian American Studies can serve as models of transformative practice for U.S. higher education.

This chapter documents various phases of applied research and reflection over the past two decades focusing on questions of pedagogy, student learning, and persistence for Southeast Asian American students within the structure and culture of Asian American Studies classrooms at one urban public university. Moreover, it suggests that the active engagement of educational researchers in ethnic studies classrooms can produce rich opportunities for advancing theory/practice, particularly with underresearched and traditionally marginalized populations. Finally, it presents recent local data collected through a national scholarship fund that supports Southeast Asian American high school students to attend college. From this analysis of recent data, questions for continued research as well as policy development then follow.

Phase I: Intuitive Analysis and Early Grounded Theory

I have written at length about the challenge facing the Asian American Studies field to reconceptualize its curricular content and pedagogy in order to be meaningful to working class, immigrant/refugee students (Kiang, 1989; 1997; 1998). Such a vision of curriculum and program development, however, is only viable if grounded in the experiences and perspectives of those students. For faculty like myself who are typically not Southeast Asian Americans, this necessitates a learning process much like the practices of ethnographic participant observation and teacher research (Cochran-Smith & Lytle, 1993).

My entry to Southeast Asian American educational research began when many second wave Cambodian, Vietnamese, and Chinese Vietnamese refugee students enrolled in my initial Asian American Studies classes at UMass Boston in 1987. Their interests and needs led me to develop a new course focusing specifically on the migration, resettlement, and adjustment experiences of refugees from Vietnam, Laos, and Cambodia in the United States. At that time in 1989, "Southeast Asians in the U.S." was one of only four such courses in the country and the only one offered at a university outside California. In reviewing potential readings for the course, I found most of the available literature to be rooted in dominant, uncritical paradigms of cultural assimilation and client/provider social services. My critique of the dominant literature was twofold. First, it was breathtakingly blind to or silent about the asymmetrical power dynamics inherent in its assumptions. Secondly, it ignored the realities of racism that were deeply implicated in both the involvement of the United States in Southeast Asia (del Rosario, 1999; Kiang, 1991) and in the subsequent dispersal of Southeast Asian refugees enacted through federal resettlement policy (Kiang, 1997). I refused to center my course around those distorted perspectives in the literature, and began searching for alternative frameworks.

Thankfully, my instincts as a student-centered teacher and curriculum designer led me to listen, observe, and engage with students in my own classrooms as a way of generating new theory. A crucial breakthrough occurred one day in 1989 when a student mentioned to me after class:

Mai's not acting like herself lately.[1]

I had noticed it, too. Mai had been quiet and unengaged in class all week long. She was usually one of the most dynamic students in the room — voicing ideas and experiences more readily than others who shared her background as a second-wave Vietnamese refugee. Later, when I asked Mai privately how she was doing, she revealed with a mixture of sadness, frustration, and anger:

My family's car was burned, right on the street in front of our house! I don't know why. But I couldn't study. Just keep thinking about it. So depressed...I didn't tell anybody.

As she disclosed her story in fuller detail, I realized that she had felt helpless as a new immigrant after the incident because she did not know how to handle it — how to call or communicate with the police or fire department at the time. She had internalized the problem as a Vietnamese — not telling people outside the family about what had happened. Furthermore, the actual arson of the car had triggered memories of the war in Vietnam, which depressed her even more — reflecting her experience as a refugee. Yet, whether or not she realized it, the source of the problem was racial conflict in the neighborhood — reflecting her reality as a racial minority.

Recognizing each of these distinct dimensions of Mai's identity enabled me to understand more clearly why her participation had changed in class, and, more importantly, how I could better respond to her situation. Viewing her as "not acting like herself" was incorrect. In fact, Mai was being herself — a fully bicultural individual within a complex, multifaceted social context. We needed to see who she really was.

My understanding of Mai's story led me to conceptualize a multidimensional, theoretical framework that integrated various aspects of the Southeast Asian refugee experience and that suggested coherent ways to recognize their strengths and struggles in school. I defined these background characteristics along four distinct dimensions (Kiang, 1991; 1995):

- as Southeast Asians with distinct linguistic, cultural, and historical characteristics determined by growing up in their home countries and, to some extent, maintained by their continuing integration in their basic family and community structure in the United States;

- as refugees with survival skills and psychologies adapted to war, famine, flight and forced migration, loss of family members, secondary trauma from refugee camp, and resettlement;

- as immigrants in America adjusting to drastic changes in status, opportunity, living conditions, climate, and other aspects of daily life, especially in relation to culture and language;

- as racial minorities facing discrimination, disenfranchisement, racism, and violence as social, economic, and political realities in the United States.

As Southeast Asians, students' expectations, learning styles, and performance in school reflected traditional values and educational practices of their homelands. Differences, as well as similarities, between each country and between regions within a single country in culture, language, history, religion, and geopolitical development were important to consider. For example, pursuit of higher education was especially important for Vietnamese and ethnic Chinese influenced by the standards of Confucian society. Along this dimension, Southeast Asian students experienced problems with cultural dislocation, but also were able to draw from traditions and cultural values to achieve in school.

Having fled their home countries as refugees, Southeast Asian students revealed through life history narratives and their own writings common stories of war, rape, escape, and victimization together with themes of guilt, survival, loneliness, family loyalty, and hope for the future. While facing experiences of loss — loss of family, friends, and social networks; loss of homeland, property, and culture; loss of identity, security, and self-esteem, they also demonstrated strengths — strengths of survival and sacrifice; strengths of shared support and loyalty; and strength of values, especially with regard to education. The tragedy of the refugee experience may have limited some in their pursuit of higher education, and motivated others to do so with even greater determination. Southeast Asian refugee students faced a variety of mental health issues arising from their past experience of trauma and loss, but their strengths, if recognized and engaged, could also enable refugees to overcome their difficulties.

Over time, Southeast Asian refugees were reconstructing new lives as immigrants — maintaining aspects of traditional identity while integrating into U.S. society. Themes for students also especially concerned intergenerational conflict with parents and the importance of education to the family. Though immigrant motivations to achieve may have paralleled those of other immigrant groups, immigrant family responsibilities and expectations also intensified the problems and pressures faced by many Southeast Asian students.

Southeast Asians were also facing a racial dynamic in U.S. society not experienced by European ethnic immigrant groups. As racial minorities, Southeast Asian students confronted social conditions and institutional categories that situated them in a racialized category as Asian American minorities. Social-psychological problems of Southeast Asian students were exacerbated by growing anti-Asian sentiment and racial violence on campuses and in neighborhoods throughout the country. At the same time, minority student support services and pan-Asian student advocacy enhanced the persistence of Southeast Asian refugee students in school. Group mobilization and coalition-building provided vehicles with which to gain greater access to resources and demand political power.

Individually, each of these dimensions brought into focus a distinct set of issues facing Southeast Asian American students and pointed to specific directions for intervention and further research. When integrated together, as shown by Mai's story, they illustrated multi-dimensional obstacles and possibilities for strength that Southeast Asian students were bringing to the university. Developing this framework created an alternative to the dominant, assimilationist paradigms that defined majority writings about Southeast Asian Americans during that period. Furthermore, it offered a model for analyzing parallel, multidimensional backgrounds of other non-white refugee/immigrant populations, such as Salvadorans and Haitians, who were also entering schools in growing numbers at that time (Suarez-Orozco, 1989), followed more recently by Somali, Sudanese, Iraqis, and others. Most importantly, though, it enabled me to move beyond simply understanding the backgrounds of Southeast Asian refugee/immigrant students to consider their actual status and needs within the university.

Phase II: Mapping Stories of Persistence

At this point, I moved to explore the mainstream literature on college student attrition and persistence — hoping to find some theories or models to help me make sense of how Southeast Asian American students were struggling and surviving in school. Once again, however, the dominant analyses seemed to discount the realities with which I was most familiar. Mainstream studies concluded, for example, that student degree completion was more likely at private versus public institutions and at residential versus commuter campuses, but said nothing about how students actually did persist at public, commuter institutions.

> The most influential work at that time was sociologist Vince Tinto's *Leaving College* (1987). According to Tinto, college student persistence entails the incorporation, that is, integration, of the individual as a competent member in the social and intellectual communities of the college.... Student institutional departure is as much a reflection of the attributes of those communities, and therefore of the institution, as it is of the students who enter that institution.... Thus the term membership may be taken as connoting the perception on the part of the individual of having become a competent member of an academic or social community within the college (pp. 126-127).

Tinto found that faculty contact was the most important predictor of student persistence, and that its impact was heightened for minority and working-class students and for older students who have families or other external demands — the typical profile of my students at that time. Tinto also emphasized that possibilities for persistence were substantially enhanced if student integration were taking place both academically and socially within the institution. These ideas seemed compelling and theoretically compatible with the community development strategies and sensibilities that I had brought to my own teaching, but I questioned whether Southeast Asian American students' persistence stories matched Tinto's model. This led me to look and listen even more carefully for my own students' perspectives about surviving in school.

Through two years of in-depth research based on student life history narratives, structured student interviews, participant observation as a teacher/adviser, and formal/ informal student writings, my grounded theory of Southeast Asian American student persistence emerged with three major findings (Kiang, 1991; 1996):

- Southeast Asian American students, including those who persisted, were not integrated either academically or socially within the university;

- Southeast Asian American students' motivation to persist in college was based on reference points outside the university;

- Asian American Studies classrooms provided Southeast Asian American students with a university context in which to experience academic and social integration.

The following subsections illustrate each of these points in greater depth.

Stories of Academic and Social Isolation

"On My Own" Stories

In their school experiences, Southeast Asian American students described receiving little direct assistance from family members, friends, or school personnel. Students typically defined their approach to dealing with difficulties in terms of being "on my own" or "by myself." Sokal, a Cambodian male, lamented, "You have no guideline, you know. Your parents don't know really what they want you to be. And you lost, you know, searching for it by yourself." At the same time, he felt, "there was nobody in school to talk to, you know... seem not to find anybody."

Students also made decisions not to ask for help. Khamkeaw, a Chinese Cambodian, who first escaped to Laos with his family before coming to the United States at age seventeen, admitted, "since I came to this school, I never tried to look for any help. Everything I do is on my own." Sounthara, a young Lao woman agreed, "it's like you're kind of on your own. Yeah, professors seem like they don't care... you on your own." Sokal added:

Always on my own...I rarely go see professors or TAs.... Most of the time I can figure it out. If I can't, just do the best I can and pass it in. And sometimes when the grade comes back, there's writing on the bottom — "why didn't you come for help?", you know. I've seen many of those.... I don't think I have any teacher ever follow up.

None of the students gave examples of seeking help from or being assisted by university personnel in any consistent manner. For example, Sok, who came to the United States from Cambodia with her family at age 13, reported, "Since I have been in college, I had never used the support from school service. When I have problem with school, I would talk to my friends or solve it myself." The isolation perceived and experienced by Southeast Asian American students within the university's academic domain, particularly in terms of student-faculty relations and utilization of academic support services, was striking. "On My Own" stories and strategies — defined in relation to classroom dynamics as well as issues such as course selection, academic advising, career preparation, and major choices — expressed not only how students viewed their reality within the university, but also how they attempted to survive academically within it.

Students' feelings of social isolation, both in school and the larger society, were equally striking. Danielle, a Chinese Vietnamese woman, noted about school:

In the classes, like most of the American students, they don't like to be your friend...even when you walk in the hall, you see them, they don't even say hi. Or probably they don't recognize me.

Similarly, but with reference to the larger social environment, Chanda wrote poignantly:

The more I absorb the environment I live in, the more I have a better sense of real life. I continue to see things that divide me from American society. But I could not recognize what it is and why? Everyday living just puts a lot of pressure on me, the anger and struggle I am facing are never overcome. It is crying inside me. No one wants to hear or even cares and I have no one to turn to.

These students were clearly not integrated academically or socially within the university. Though some relied on other Asian students for friendship and support, such informal friendship networks provided only limited assistance in terms of dealing with difficulties in school. "On my own" stories dominated their discourse and their reality in concrete ways at particular times, such as when choosing majors.

"Major" Stories and "Dropping Out" Stories

Related to feeling "on my own," especially academically, many Southeast Asian American students described themselves as "lost" — not knowing how to take care of problems or where to get good advice and not feeling able to "speak up" or ask questions. Furthermore, feeling "lost" had real meaning for them, given their refugee experiences. Recalling his family's escape across the Mekong River, for example, Khamkeaw vividly remembered feeling "like you don't know where you going." Similarly, Seng recalled, after finally reaching the refugee camp in Thailand, the anxiety of having, "no idea where we going, what we are going to do."

Pathways through the university curriculum, though far safer than the jungle, were also difficult to find and negotiate. Sokal recalled:

> I take different courses and I was lost. I do not know what I want to study. I keep looking for it, and searching for it. And I missed one whole year just looking for what I want to do.

In the face of these difficulties, Phat, a Chinese Vietnamese refugee man, concluded, "We can't rely on whatever the major we're interested in, but we have to go from the major whichever is easiest for us to accomplish." Chanda initially followed advice from an admissions counselor who told her that Asian students are good in math. When she failed her first math class, Chanda recalled feeling, "depressed, cry many times that I could not make it. And never think I would graduate." Sokal's major story was also revealing:

> I was watching the film on [public television]. They do it on Southeast Asians, on rice...all this genetics, I mean biologists and biochemistry, they always studying how to find a better way to grow rice, you know. Cambodia, once, was exporting rice. Now they couldn't find enough rice to feed the people. There's something wrong, you know. And I say, well, I want to go in that field and study...I did not consult anybody at all. Just based on my decision. I didn't even talk to my mother or anybody....

A television program, rather than the university curriculum or advising system, directed him to choose chemistry as his major. But frustration, stress, and resignation, rather than satisfaction, then followed as consequences of his choice:

> Once I made the decision, it's too late to turn back because it's my second or third year.... I have to go back to review all the science courses that I haven't had for a long time.... I forgot everything.... I fail every test I took in Physics.... I got a D+, which is the worst grade I ever get in my school career.... I'm not that happy with my major, but I have to find something, you know... so there's no turning back. If I can't make it, I drop out of school.

Not surprisingly, given their "on my own" stories of isolation and confusion, many students like Sokal considered dropping out as an alternative:

I thought about it many times, and say, why I am doing this, you know. Go to school and working. And my family is having a tough time financially. Should I drop out a couple of years, and work outside and then help support the family and then come back? I think about it and say, well, you heard your parents' conversation. They say over and over again, "go to school," you know.... I see my friends, a couple of friends gone. Disappear. You see your friends working, buying brand new car, sports car. It's tempting, you know. But then I say, no it's not worth it. That's not my goal.

He went on to describe the situations of friends:

Nothing you can do about it.... Two or three of them dropped out. And I thought they'd take a semester or two off, but they never come back.... Financially they couldn't do it and they dropped out, get married.... And then having children, you know, couldn't come back. Another friend of mine dropped out a year ago. He says he'll come back when he gets older. I say, yeah, right.

Like Sokal, Phat also referred to friends who left, "A lot of students dropped out because they don't know where to go...there was nobody to help them." Chanda, who during her first year, thought she would never graduate, agreed:

The Southeast Asian students, particularly the Cambodian students, it's just hard, it's very tough for them. The first year I came here, we have four or five Cambodian students, but I'm the only one who stick with school...they all drop out from university because they could not handle it, and no one really guide them or help them throughout the difficult time.

"Dropping-out" stories documented both the substantial obstacles facing Southeast Asian American students and the failure of college personnel to guide those students appropriately. Given students' pervasive lack of integration academically as well as socially, the odds of Southeast Asian American student persistence — especially at an urban, public, commuter institution — seemed terribly slim.

Nevertheless, Chanda, Mai, Khamkeaw, Danielle, Phat, Sokal and others successfully graduated — making their stories all the more significant to learn from. Clearly, their college experiences, like much of the rest of their lives, were characterized by struggle and survival. Rooted in their family contexts and background dimensions as refugees, immigrants, and racial minorities, Southeast Asian American students turned to reference points outside the university for powerful sources of motivation and direction. These reference points, described in stories of refugee flight, family life, and race/gender discrimination, enabled them to persist in college, despite their marginal relationships to the academic and social domains of the university.

Recognizing Reference Points of Persistence Outside the University

Refugee Stories as Reference Points

Students' experiences and status as refugees — reflected in both chilling and inspiring stories of survival — shaped their views of getting through college. Khamkeaw was separated from his family by the Khmer Rouge when he was nine years old and evacuated to a labor camp where he was forced to work 18-20 hours each day. He whispered in an interview, "You never stop...365 days a year...I almost died a couple of times over there." Sokal added, "You never had a childhood life, so you never dreamed what you want to be when you grow up, you know...more important things to think about: survival."

Mental health issues resulting from trauma and family separation confounded the difficulties confronted by many students in school. Post-Traumatic Stress Disorder (PTSD) and related symptoms of depression, guilt, anxiety, and anger marked the continuing effects of their traumatic experiences (Herman, 1992; Nidorf, 1985; Welaratna, 1993). Yet, students' refugee stories also provided powerful reference points of resilience and determination that supported persistence in school. Recognizing his own PTSD, Hai, a Vietnamese man, noted, "Sometimes I thought, just a couple of times, I'm crazy. But I'm strong. My spirit is strong enough to fight." Referring to her major story, Minh, a Vietnamese woman, agreed, "I'm a survivor. I mean, I don't have to do things I want to do or are interested to do. But I have to do things I have to do." Seng added:

> I think I am a strong person, you know. I have gone through a lot of things during Khmer Rouge; the day I escaped from Cambodia; I lived in the camp. Over there I faced so many things...the experience I'd gone through before and my family in Cambodia, all those things is just in my mind. It always pushes me to work hard, to get a good education, to get more money and try to survive. Another thing I want to go back to see my people, to see my homeland, to see my friends in Cambodia. All of those things push me.

Students' refugee stories resonated deeply as motivating forces for persistence within the university. Seng's memories of and commitments to his family in Cambodia also served as significant reference points for his continued survival as a college student.

Family Stories as Reference Points

The context of family had significant meaning for Southeast Asian American students in relation to their responsibilities, expectations, and roles as the first generation in their families to go to college in the United States. Sok, for example, described her family's expectations as follows:

> *I do a little housework, I cook when no one is home. I help my sisters with math, English. Sometimes I have to take care of the bills for my family contribution. In addition, well, my parents expect something from me which they never told me what. However, I knew what they are expecting. They expect me to finish school.*

Students shouldered major responsibilities to provide financial support for their families. Sokal, for example, worked 20-25 hours each week during the school year and three jobs during the summer in order to "help with everything that I can...every dime I make, I give to my mother." This led to a confrontation with the university's financial aid office over his earnings from three jobs:

> *They say, what you do with this money, you know? And I say, I help my family. And he said, what?! You know, they don't understand that. Usually they hear the parents helping the students. Instead, it's the reverse. And it's tough.*

Students also served as the interpreters and intermediaries between their families and U.S. society. Khamkeaw described his duties as: "translate problems and reading English writing, go to hospital, pay the bill, writing letter, making phone calls, communicating with outside." Students played essential roles in enabling their families to survive in this country. But their studies suffered as a result. Exhausted from her daily schedule, Sok sighed, "I return home around nine o'clock, take a shower and do my homework until four o'clock in the morning. I never have enough time for sleep, I go to bed at three or four in the morning and get up a few hours after at seven or seven-thirty." Sokal also complained:

> *I can't study at home. I have room to study but when I get home, your sister tell you about this happened, your mother says, well, you have to do this, all the oil is gone, you know, the boiler is not working. There's so many things going wrong, and you say, well, I got to do this, I got to do that, and I can't study.*

Although students identified strong family expectations that motivated them to persevere in college, those expectations were not accompanied in any tangible way by direct family involvement. This further contributed to the isolation experienced by students, and contradicted studies of first-wave refugees and other Asian immigrant groups who have class and educational advantages that support strong family involvement in students' schooling and educational achievement (Caplan, Whitmore, & Choy, 1989). Sokal argued convincingly, for example, that he would do better in school if he did not live with his family:

I can handle myself [in school] if I live alone. I can take care of it. I can do pretty well, but I got to help my family. That affects a lot, take a lot out of you. Mentally you're not concentrating. Something always happen. If I'm alone, I'll probably do better.

Furthermore, many students did not have intact families in this country. Though separated by distance, if not death, family expectations still motivated student achievement by exerting powerful influences through guilt, grief, and pride. Recalling his escape story, Seng sighed, "When I left my family, I feel really bad, I don't know what to do. But try to survive, you know. Just keep thinking that someday, someday I will see them if they still alive." Sokal agreed, reflecting on his family's survival story and his deceased father's continuing influence:

I look through my past, you know. I say, well, I've been through this and I've seen many things. I've been through a lot of stuff that, you know, I thought I never come out of it alive. And then, you know, here's my father who brought me here...he want you to get through education and he struggle to get here, and, you know, you don't want to disappoint your parents. It really motivates you, you know. Psychologically, that's what I live by.

Although she nearly lost her entire family and lived by herself, Chanda concluded, "I am on my own, but I live to the expectation of the culture. I just try to do well and prove to them that I can do it.... The only thing is I have to struggle."

Race/Gender Discrimination Stories as Reference Points

As with their refugee stories, many students shared discrimination stories that illustrated their own and their families' experiences as urban, racial minorities and low-wage, immigrant/refugee workers. Racism, especially in the workplace, acted as a powerful motivating force for students to complete their higher education. Lien recounted the sentiments of her parents' generation that served as reference points for her own educational persistence:

They all complain that they were treated like a stupid person. And they said if they were in Vietnam, probably not the same here. Because some of them, they were teachers or dentists or somebody in Vietnam. But they went here. They was nothing. Just do something, wash dishes, something like that. Because they didn't pass the test for the dentist or something like that. And they feel terrible.

Chanda bitterly recalled from her own life:

When I first came to America, I work in a cleaning company in a nursing home. They treated me very badly, the boss. They pay me less than other people and some people that were hired at that time, in a later period, they got higher wage than I did. The way they treated me like in a very cruel behavior... sometimes I want to kill them.... I cannot live in a society that put you down because you are an ethnic group. And without education, you are nothing. So that's why, you know, I think no matter how hard it is, I have to struggle in school. I have to have education so people would not treat me that bad.

Chanda also linked her motivation to persist in school with gender discrimination and feudal attitudes in her own community. She explained, "Since I am a woman, you know, my people tend to think that women cannot do anything as good as men. So, by having a degree to prove it, that I have achieved, then probably they take me a little bit seriously." The shifts in expectations and gender roles resulting from women gaining higher education, however, made this a complex and difficult process. Chanda continued:

> From school I learn a lot. And I want to share those things with my people, with the community. But the question is how? They would not allow me. It so hard just to be part of the community. If you are there, you do what they tell you to do. You act very submissive, always take the orders, then it's fine. But if you gain your voice, you try to suggest things — what should be done, what should not be done — then, forget it. They don't like you.

Mai's description of gender dynamics in the Vietnamese community was strikingly similar:

> It's very hard for us [women pursuing higher education], you know, some of us have this idea we can do something – men can do something, so women can do something...women are the ones who recognize all this stuff, all these issues that we have to deal with. But men, they kind of, they just want to keep, you know, controlling power. They always look back to go back there [to Vietnam]. But, you know, now we live here. We have to deal with things here.

Though entering school and the workforce out of socioeconomic necessity, Southeast Asian immigrant/refugee women, nevertheless, experienced a resulting expansion of opportunities that sharply contrasted with the concomitant decline in status and options for men who lost their traditional social roles. Seng, a Cambodian man, also noted the strains of changing gender roles within the community, albeit with ambivalence:

> Women change faster than men...like men, because they don't want to change anything. They like the way it is. But women, they want to change because they want the equality, they want the freedom, they want to be independent. They want to show men how strong they are. They want to be aggressive. Right now in the Cambodian community, girls seem to be more succeed than men. A lot of girls stay in college....Men care too much about money, they care too much about what's going on in family economics, what's going on in the family. They decide to give up school to go to work because they want to support the family economics. And girls, they just want to be in school, to get ahead. I see a lot of girls, a lot of women work in the offices, stay in school while men are out working in the factories somewhere else.

While becoming increasingly acculturated to notions of women's equality and economic independence, Chanda's experiences of social alienation and racial discrimination also intensified, and her critique of U.S. society deepened: "I'm happier here in a way because I can look for a better future. But in spirit, no. In Cambodia, I would feel shoulder to shoulder with the people. Even if I were a farmer, I would be proud; I would be qualified. Here, I feel so bad spiritually." Reflecting on these seemingly contradictory tendencies, she explained:

When I first came, I just want everything just imitate American way. Everything Western way is just great, civilized! But when I grow older, I think how important my culture, the heritage. I realize how much I miss, I lose, and feel so sad, feel like why all this time I deny it? I deny it, I just think even being a Cambodian or anything part of Cambodian is just come from a Third World country, is just so bad! Now I feel like nothing should be ashamed of it. I should keep it and maintain it because it's something I can identify with...not just for myself, but for my children, for the Cambodian population here. It's so important since the refugees, especially the Cambodians, are not treated as equals, are not treated as part of the mainstream. Why deny our own and want something that never never accept me? Before I never think that Cambodian is good, the language. But now I suddenly just think it is so important and I try to learn more. Even write in Cambodian. I never wore a traditional Cambodian dress, I just hate it! It's too feminine to me. But now, you know, I love it. I even imagine to see if I have a wedding I would wear it. It's just beautiful! [laughs]

Interestingly, while developing her sense of gender consciousness as an outspoken, college-educated, Cambodian American woman, Chanda's awareness of racism and inequality reawakened her love of her heritage and returned her to her community. In identifying more closely with her traditional culture, however, Chanda continued to advocate critically for women to look and move beyond the community in order to gain higher education, "My dream is like to play a role model, to tell them how much education is important. Without it, they cannot move up. To tell many young women there that life is not only married and have children...life has to have some education."

Mai attributed similar meaning to the effects of her college education on her racial, ethnic, and gender identity, noting on one hand that, "dealing with my father, I used to be quiet, not saying things back to him...so now I change, well, now I argue with him, but before I just listen." On the other hand — and also paralleling Chanda's expression of love for her traditional cultural aesthetics and values — Mai explained:

I cannot say I'm Vietnamese, but I'm saying I'm Vietnamese American because I keep some and I, because I'm exposed to this society, to this custom, so I'm not being completely Vietnamese. I'm not being completely American....But I still leave my hair long [laughs].

By articulating fully with their own reference points of persistence outside the university — as expressed through stories of refugee survival, family commitments, racism in the workplace, and gender inequality in the community — Chanda and Mai transformed themselves from lost first-year students who were failing math and nursing to graduating seniors who completed majors in women's studies and sociology. With an emerging sense of herself as a role model, Chanda realized that she could construct and represent new reference points of persistence for others. Like Chanda, Mai also recognized that her own process of transformation provided her with experience and a vision to construct new reference points of educational persistence and community empowerment that could benefit others:

> My dream is just to help the new people aware of what is going on here in this society. They need to get involved in fighting for their beliefs, I mean what they think is right for justice and equality. You know, set up the program or help the younger generation to go on, like get higher education and help their people. That's all I can do.

Beyond their inspiring stories of struggle and persistence, Mai, Chanda, and others also highlighted the important role of Asian American Studies classrooms in which they were able to experience academic and social integration at the university, and where they not only survived, but thrived. This emerged as a third key finding from this phase of research.

Asian American Studies as a Context for Persistence

Recalling the frustration of her earlier years in not having clear direction, Chanda emphasized the impact of Asian American Studies courses in guiding her to change her major from math and science to sociology and women's studies:

> Even when I was here two years, I still did not know what I really want, did not know what I'm good in.... But when I took the Asian American Studies courses, then it's like a light come in to define what really I am and what I want...for so long I did not know that I would fight for justice....But when I learn, when I see those things that say that's it! That I want to help society to change.... After that, it [my education] improved. You know, I took something that I enjoy and that I learn... if I do not take [the Asian American Studies] course, probably I will never never understand or know who I really am or what I want to do in the future.

Mai described the effect of taking her first Asian American Studies course in much the same way: "That [first] class show me the experience of Asian Americans, that changed me since that time...after that, I have a clear direction. I can do things. I can graduate."

While course content was important, students also emphasized the classroom environment — expressing motivation and appreciation because their voices were encouraged and their experiences were shared by both the teacher and their peers. A Vietnamese student noted, "half of the class are already Asian whose background are similar to mine, including the professor. This way we can be more open to share our problems and experiences because no one would laugh." Sokal, one of the most active participants in an Asian American Studies course, reported being unable to speak up in other classes:

> There's a lot of Asians in there, and they probably have the same basic experience. We're together...similar problems, accents, pronunciation....I always have an opinion, something to say. But somehow, the class also help the fear inside, don't be afraid, you know. Have question, ask. But somehow, after that class, I go into the same pattern again, you know. Not asking questions....

He then described his view of Asian American Studies classes compared to other courses in terms of death and life — concepts with which he was intimately familiar:

In science course, you go there, listen, sit back and write down all the notes or record it, come back and write it down.... I come from there, I saw it change so quick, you know. Get out of [the Asian American Studies] class, you go to another course, sit back and, you know, just write down notes. And then when you get out of from that class, go to another one, same thing. Next day, before you come to [the Asian American Studies] class, you go another class, like you're dead. And then, all of a sudden, you come alive, you know. Full of life!

Lien similarly described the significance of her Asian American Studies class in relation to her memories of Vietnam:

When I talk, I felt like somebody listen to me....I feel like the old times in Vietnam – have a teacher who is concerned about, have friends to share with...you feel like at home...look like everybody is happy. So I thought I wish I had more classes like that.

In effect, students in Asian American Studies courses functioned as competent members of classroom communities supported by both the course content and learning environment. The combination of a critical mass of Asian students with an engaged Asian American teacher and a relevant curriculum enabled students to "come alive" with their questions and share experiences with their peers, thus breaking down both the academic and social isolation that they typically faced on their own in other settings at the university.

By mapping their persistence stories, this phase of research showed, contrary to dominant models of college student persistence: a) that Southeast Asian American students were not integrated in either the academic or social domains of college, and b) that reference points motivating them to persist in college against formidable odds were family- and community-centered rather than college-related. Asian American Studies courses, however, served to establish viable reference points within the university's curriculum, in student-faculty relations, and in student peer relations that explicitly recognized and directly reinforced those external reference points of refugee stories, family stories, and race/gender discrimination stories that were motivating Southeast Asian American students' educational persistence.

As a curricular and pedagogical intervention, then, the praxis of Asian American Studies itself deserved further research and grounded theoretical development. This became a major commitment in my evolving research agenda as I moved to consider more systematically the institutional structures that hindered or supported Southeast Asian American students' persistence.

Phase III: Toward Systemic, Comparative, Long-Term Perspectives

I want to go on.

Her words broke a long silence from the front of the room. A few moments earlier, Trang had faltered in her project presentation about the experiences of Vietnamese Amerasians, and begun to cry quietly. Usually, she sat in the back with one or two other Vietnamese friends, trying to remain safe and unobtrusive. Had the pressure of speaking her second language in front of everyone in class overwhelmed her? Perhaps she was re-living the memories of her own life in Vietnam. Maybe she recalled how hard it was to arrive here five years ago in the land of her father, still not knowing who or where he was.

Are you sure?

Yes, I want to go on.

Trang completed her presentation, filled with emotion in accented English, teaching the class about struggle and survival. On the last day of the semester, I reminded the class of the context and meaning of those words, *"I want to go on."* There were strengths to be shared and lessons to be learned from Southeast Asian refugees, especially in facing and overcoming obstacles. From the back of the room, Trang looked up for a moment and smiled. Everyone nodded in recognition.

The following semester in another Asian American Studies course, Trang's friend Hong began her final project presentation with a poem written by a Cambodian classmate who was too shy to recite it himself:

I have seen starvation at sea,

I have seen a man put his life at the bow, so

His children could know what Freedom means.

I have seen pirates rape a young girl, then throw her overboard;

The sea turned red and my anger raged...

The room was still as she started to weep, unable to read any further. The poet hadn't known that his words revealed the story of Hong's own sister. Others in class didn't realize it either, but could see her sorrow as the sea turned red. We sat quietly, feeling the moment — another living lesson in struggle and survival. Like Trang the semester before, Hong went on, completing the poem and continuing her presentation. After the class, the Cambodian writer apologized to her, saying he didn't know that his poem would affect her so much. She responded:

That's okay. It was important to say. I'm glad you wrote it.

Southeast Asian American students' commitments to persist and share — wanting to go on — have continued to be articulated and sustained in Asian American Studies classes year after year. Not only have their stories been important to say and to write, they have also inspired deeper and wider commitments to curriculum/program development and applied research. In the following section, I offer brief examples of how the research agenda of Phase III evolved during the 1990s, moving beyond thick description and grounded theory to address critical issues of impact in three important ways — institutionally, comparatively, and longitudinally.

Challenging Institutionalized Anguish as a Second Language

During Phase II, Southeast Asian American students engaged in research around issues of their own and their peers' persistence in college. This process not only generated important stories, themes, and challenges to dominant paradigms, it also influenced students' own views and subsequent actions. The research interviews served not only as sources for data collection, but also as interventions in students' lives. Hung, for example, a Vietnamese student who was on academic probation after failing a course, but had not told any of his family members about his difficulties, stated at the conclusion of his interview:

This is the first time I sharing my experience. I never talk to anybody [laughs]. Before, my English teacher told me to see the psychiatrist, you know, talk about it, try to open more. I said, well, I don't think so....You want to know more about the difficulties of Asian people who are trying in university, who have problems with it, so I think that's good for me. So I said okay, I'll share my experience.

Mai similarly noted at the end of her interview:

Yeah, I never thought of these questions...we never have a chance to talk like people asking questions to feed back and forth, but it's in your mind. I see myself different than before. But when you don't talk about it, you don't have the language to describe.

Mai also highlighted the peer support and development engendered through the research process (student focus groups, students interviewing students, etc.), "I feel that I'm not the only one who face those problems...then you feel more comfortable with working in school, like explaining your points because you have, you get support from other people."

Beyond these types of individual effects and interventions within informal networks, however, students also identified larger institutional barriers that needed change in the university. Among the obstacles forcing some students to stop/drop out, for example, was an English writing proficiency graduation requirement that became the target of student advocacy and a new focus of applied research described briefly here and documented in detail elsewhere (Kiang, 1993). Minh, for example, an early participant and peer facilitator in a Southeast Asian student oral history project during Phase I, emerged as one of the campus student leaders who filed a formal Title VI complaint with the U.S. Department of Education Office for Civil Rights (OCR), alleging that the university's graduation requirement of a writing proficiency exam (WPE) had disparate negative impact against minority students. Indeed, anecdotal evidence had always suggested such a reality, but the university had never released data about who passed and who failed the WPE until the OCR's investigation required it to do so. The results confirmed students' impressions.

The data, based on records for all students taking the WPE from 1981 to 1987, showed that 29% of all Black students, 23% of all Hispanic students, and 24% of all Asian students had not passed the WPE after three or more attempts. In sharp contrast, only 7% of White students similarly failed the exam after three or more tries. When students' grade point averages were controlled, students of color still failed the WPE at disproportionately higher rates. Other data offered disturbingly corroboratory evidence. During the same 1981-1987 period, Asian students had a higher retention rate than all other student racial groups during their first four semesters — the critical period according to mainstream studies of student attrition — followed by a dramatic and continued decline after their sixth semester when taking and passing the WPE became mandatory.

Following release of the institutional data, Minh, Mai, Chanda, Seng, and other Southeast Asian American students involved in Phase I and Phase II organized, wrote, and spoke for institutional policy changes. In an emotional commentary for the campus newspaper, a Vietnamese refugee student asserted:

> [This] is the only four-year college that is accessible and affordable for us. This is the only place we have a chance to get a college education. But if we spend four years here and then you kick us out because our writing is not what the school wants, then the school has wasted our time. You have to realize, we Asian students are starting from scratch, trying to build new lives in this country. We don't have any time to waste....Don't bring us out into the middle of the ocean and leave us there. We have already been there once before. (Nguyen, 1989)

From follow-up student/faculty research projects in Asian American Studies classes, we pieced together a critical analysis of the issue to complement the statistical data (Kiang, 1993). For example, a Chinese Vietnamese refugee student complained bitterly about a WPE essay question focusing on Mozart and the Hollywood film, *Amadeus,* which he had never seen. Along with several other students, Chanda, herself faulted the director of the WPE, "She gives you pressure, and says you have to pass the exam or else you'll be expelled from school. Her attitude is not to help you." Other informants noted that many Vietnamese students were enrolling in the two-year engineering program so that they could transfer to another school before their junior year when they would otherwise have to take the WPE. Extending the "major stories" documented in Phase II, these Phase III findings similarly suggested that students may not have been so committed to engineering as a field, but chose to major in it as a survival strategy to avoid being forced out of school by the WPE.

Stories and critical insights generated from the Phase III research bolstered students' civil rights complaint against the university. By the conclusion of OCR's investigation several years later, a wide range of WPE policy reforms had been implemented, including the crafting of less Eurocentric readings and essay questions, the reassignment of the WPE director, and the development of a viable writing portfolio option as an alternative to the essay examination format. Through this process, Southeast Asian American students directly participated in advocacy research that positively impacted the institution.

Furthermore, their work inspired other students to critically examine parallel struggles of Southeast Asian American students at the K-12 level. Though not described in detail here, other examples of research designed to document and challenge systemic inequity in schools during Phase III included a project to examine Vietnamese American students' views of race relations at a local urban high school immediately following a race riot that closed the school for one week in 1993. This study concretely challenged the black-and-white paradigm of race relations and offered insights about school climate through the views and experiences of students who were usually silent or silenced (Kiang & Kaplan, 1994).

With similar goals in mind, two former undergraduate students and I designed a project to capture how recently arrived Vietnamese elementary students in a fourth-grade bilingual classroom were making sense of the daily racial conflicts they experienced or witnessed at school and in their neighborhoods (Kiang, Nguyen, & Sheehan, 1995). The project grew out of concerns expressed by Nguyen Ngoc-Lan, a first-year Vietnamese American teacher who observed her students being harassed frequently. I still recall the afternoon when she first came to see me in frustration:

Some of my kids just got into a fight with older boys who were harassing a younger Vietnamese student on the way home from school. It happens every day and I get so angry. People need to know about it. Sometimes I just want to shout, "DON'T IGNORE IT!" to the school and the community.

Two years earlier, Ngoc-Lan was struggling with the WPE at UMass Boston herself. Having failed the exam, she agreed to try the alternative portfolio option, and with targeted support from another student majoring in Asian American Studies, she eventually passed — after much anguish. Like many other immigrant/refugee students, Ngoc-Lan experienced failure and discouragement within those educational environments where her linguistic and cultural background was viewed by individuals and institutional policies as a deficit. But within the fourth-grade bilingual classroom where she taught professionally, Ngoc-Lan was successful, motivated, and respected by students, parents, and school colleagues. In turn, she affirmed and reinforced those same strengths for the newcomer children in her care.

Ngoc-Lan had also been successful in her Asian American Studies classes, often sharing her desire to become an elementary school teacher — a dream she had carried from childhood in Vietnam. Asian American Studies not only provided a learning environment in college where Ngoc-Lan's linguistic and cultural backgrounds represented valuable assets, but also served as a structure of support that sustained her visions as a critical, bilingual teacher/researcher following her graduation. Ngoc-Lan's example also raised a larger question: what kinds of impact and meaning did Asian American Studies courses have in the lives of former students and alumni over time?

Comparative Perspectives on Long-Term Curricular Impact

As a second important commitment of the research agenda during Phase III, we launched a two-year Asian American Studies alumni research project in conjunction with a campus diversity research initiative funded by the Ford Foundation. Utilizing both quantitative and qualitative methods to reach alumni who had taken at least one Asian American Studies course prior to graduating between 1987 and 1999, the study found that the greatest effects reported by alumni were increased understanding of the immigrant experience, greater awareness of racial stereotypes, increased clarity about their own identities in U.S. society, and enhanced abilities to interact comfortably with Asian Americans. For example, 91 percent of survey respondents specifically indicated that their Asian American Studies courses had much or very much increased their understanding of the immigrant experience; 86 percent stated that their learning had much or very much raised their awareness of racial stereotypes. Seven out of ten of respondents (70%) noted that the courses had much or very much enabled them to make friends with people different from their own backgrounds. Eight out of ten (83%) indicated that the courses had much or very much helped them to interact more comfortably with Asian Americans. For nonresidential university settings in which the development of student attitudes and competencies related to diversity are largely limited to what happens in the classroom, these were powerful effects (Kiang, 2000).

While these positive impacts cut across all groups, regardless of race, gender, number of courses taken, or year of graduation, Asian American alumni specifically pointed to growth in their identity — becoming more aware of who they were in U.S. society — as being nearly as powerful as their gains in social awareness through learning about the immigrant experience and racial stereotyping. Furthermore, when the responses of Asian American alumni were differentiated by gender, two dramatic results became evident. Asian American men showed far greater course impact in the domain of family than Asian American women. In contrast, Asian American women found much more impact from their learning about jobs and careers than Asian American men. All other domains of impact showed little variation by gender. These striking results suggested that learning from Asian American Studies courses laid an important foundation of understanding and experience for Asian American students and alumni, not only to develop social awareness and clear identities, but also to redefine traditional gender roles and relationships.

The alumni research focus in Phase III also provided a qualitative way to explore comparative perspectives with those former students of non-Asian backgrounds who had taken Asian American Studies courses. Marisol, for example, a Latina who graduated in 1996 and was working as a job developer for low-income communities while raising her one-year-old child at the time of the interview, recalled:

> I learned that I have a lot more in common with the Asian community....I found a lot of pieces of my identity with my friends of countries like China, Korea, Japan, etc....I felt connected and it was very exciting to feel and know that I had friends who are Asian American who really care for me....I can communicate and relate to people when I have knowledge of their history and struggles as well as achievements. This is what I learned and pass on to others.

Tanisha, an African American alumna who graduated in 1990, was teaching social studies in an elementary school at the time of her interview. Like Marisol, Tanisha was one of many interviewees who described the significance of cross-racial learning facilitated by the courses:

> As a Black person, I hate to be stereotyped, and I'm sure that Asians feel the same way....When people of different races have an opportunity to interact and get to know each other, they often like each other. Like, I meet many people I probably would have never had the opportunity to meet and get to know (from the courses). I learned that I liked them and respected them as people.

The important professional teaching roles played by graduates like Tanisha and Tara, a White alumna who graduated in 1989, further illustrated the long-term effects of Asian American Studies in reaching new generations. Tara asserted:

> I finally decided to become a teacher of English as a second language, and I am sure that the Asian American course had some effect on that decision, partly by giving me a stronger sense of empathy for the immigrants' experience and at the same time giving me a greater sense of respect.

In addition to research focusing particularly on cross-racial comparisons, we also developed a specific qualitative research focus on the experiences of alumni with learning disabilities who had taken Asian American Studies courses. Interviews conducted by a graduate student in special education who had majored in Asian American Studies as an undergraduate and who co-led the "Don't Ignore It" study in Nguyen Ngoc-Lan's fourth grade Vietnamese bilingual classroom five years earlier, suggested how course advising could be linked effectively with classroom pedagogy in Asian American Studies courses to address the needs of students with learning disabilities. Crystal, a White alumna who graduated in 1997, for example, recalled, "The adviser would tell LD [learning disabled] students to take these [Asian American Studies] courses because the professors accept these kinds of students. They make them feel at home as they do with immigrants." She then added:

*I was probably one out of six...Caucasian people in the class and there were about 30 of us...
and the other White students in the class were learning disability students and this is because
[the adviser] always suggested that we take that class because there's a good teacher....When she
suggested that to me, I was like, "what are you crazy? I'm not going to take a class like that. You
must be crazy!" I took it and I'm like, oh God, this class is going to be awful but I really enjoyed
it...after the first few classes, it was really interesting....And I loved it through the end.*

Interviewees highlighted important connections between their own struggles with
learning disabilities and those of Asian Americans that they witnessed through their
classroom interactions and course work. Echoing the "on my own" stories of Southeast Asian
American students several years earlier, Crystal explained: "When you're an immigrant or a
person with LD you can find yourself lost, find yourself needing help most of the time."

Educationally and philosophically, Asian American Studies was never intended to
serve only Asian American students. The comparative foci in our Phase III alumni research,
however, empirically showed how a curriculum and learning environment designed
explicitly to support Asian immigrant/refugee students could also be empowering for other
marginalized populations. Findings from this type of comparative diversity research deserve
much more attention.

EMERGING DIRECTIONS AND FRESH QUESTIONS

Much of my research agenda during the past twenty years has taken shape in response to my
frustrations with dominant paradigms. Although presented here as "phases" based loosely
on a chronology of research/advocacy projects, the insights and interventions represented
in the design and development of each of the discrete projects have never been linear in
their trajectories or conceptualizations. Indeed, the student and community populations
served by urban public universities are so diverse and dynamic that — to work effectively
with and for them — teachers, researchers, curriculum developers, service providers,
and organizers must constantly intuit, map, and re-ground theories (Phases I and II) in
order to revitalize commitments, systemically assess impact, and sustain comparative,
longer-term connections (Phase III). Looking toward the future, particularly in relation to
a continuing research agenda focusing on Asian American Studies and Southeast Asian
American student persistence, the following section describes three emerging directions
that represent proactive strategies and fresh questions.

Toward Contemporary Curricular Commitments with Southeast Asian American Students

One critical way through which this research agenda can have continuing impact is by
informing curriculum development and pedagogical innovation. For example, I regularly
teach the course, "Southeast Asians in the U.S.," which examines the processes of

migration, refugee resettlement, and community development for Vietnamese, Cambodians, and Lao nationally and locally, and the interplay of themes of trauma, healing, and resilience with changing contexts of families, communities, schools, public policies, and homeland relations. Each time I teach the course, I center it around an in-depth, semester-long project based on principles of authentic assessment to which I am deeply committed. In recent years, for example, I have asked students to apply and extend what they were learning about Southeast Asian American history, culture, and community life by producing children's books with original Southeast Asian American themes and characters. Students were assigned to:

- recall their own childhood experiences with children's books;

- review and critique what is commercially available in terms of published Vietnamese, Cambodian, Lao, and Hmong children's stories;

- design and produce their own original books based on story lines or themes inspired either by personal experiences or from the course;

- read and discuss their original books with a small group of children at the age/grade level they targeted;

- reflect on the entire learning process through a class presentation and written essay.

To support students' efforts while providing concrete examples that modeled high expectations, two Asian American professionals — a children's book author/illustrator and a children's trade book editor — visited the class and offered practical strategies for writing, illustrating, and publishing Asian American children's books. The two also returned at the end of the semester to review the completed projects and to suggest next steps for those students who were interested in pursuing publishing opportunities for their stories.

This project design was directly inspired both by the persistence stories of Southeast Asian American students mapped during Phase II, which represented core content for children's book story lines, and by the alumni research project in Phase III, which convincingly showed that our Asian American Studies courses could have significant long-term effects. Though I did not expect most students in the course to shift their career plans to become children's book writers/editors, I was hoping that the project would enable them ultimately to become more critical, engaged, and effective as parents and advocates for their children now or in the future. In order to extend the impact of students' projects beyond the classroom and university, I have also shown some of the completed children's books in my presentations at national meetings for audiences such as the Children's Defense Fund. Furthermore, the *Boston Globe* highlighted one student's story, illustrations, and reflections in conjunction with a feature story about new directions in the local Vietnamese American community that appeared in a special section commemorating the 25th anniversary of the fall of Saigon (Zuckoff, 2000). Other Asian American Studies Program faculty at UMass Boston have also adapted this project focus on Southeast Asian American children's books as a way to support their own course goals of documenting community stories and producing relevant, fresh resources (Bui, Tang, & Kiang, 2004).

Toward Longitudinal Research, Portraiture, and Southeast Asian American Life Stories

When interviewed for the alumni research project in Phase III, many former students like Marisol and Tanisha also spoke about applying their learning from Asian American Studies courses in their roles as parents. For example, Kunthea, a Cambodian interviewee who took one Asian American Studies course in 1989 and was raising two children at the time of her interview, stated:

> *[The course] will have an effect on my way of raising my children. I will raise my children to be aware of their parents' root and to respect others, regardless of race, class, and gender....I gain a lot of knowledge from Asian American Studies courses and it will always stay with me.*

At a more recent Asian American Studies alumni gathering, Lien and Mai each came with two children. When asked about her seven-year-old daughter's experiences in elementary school, Lien replied, "I know it's tough for her sometimes, being a minority. I always tell her to hang in there and tell me whenever she has problems." Listening to her closely, I remembered that Lien had used the exact same phrase, "hang in there" to describe the essence of her own approach to persist in college ten years earlier. Since then, I have often wondered how the survival strategies and motivating reference points of persistence utilized by Southeast Asian American students in college continue to be adapted and applied developmentally throughout their lives.

Seng also attended the alumni gathering. Working as a classroom ESL teacher at an urban middle school, Seng sounded a familiar theme — being "on his own" as the only Cambodian and only refugee among the school's adult staff. While connecting intimately with the strengths and struggles of students from Haiti, Bosnia, Korea, Vietnam and elsewhere around the world in his own classroom, he found his White colleagues to be profoundly disconnected and ineffectual. Recalling their reactions to the Columbine High School shootings in Littleton, Colorado, Seng recounted:

> *They just sat in the teachers' room talking about it, like what if it happened at our school and they got trapped inside. They were so scared, they had no idea what to do. I just said, "Look, just open that window and jump down to the roof and climb down from there. Don't you see that!?"*

From these recent perspectives offered by former students like Lien and Seng, it is clear that Southeast Asian American stories of survival, struggle, and persistence continue to be real and relevant. For example, Lien is both a mother of two children and also an accountant for a nonprofit education center that provides support services and resources for students who have disabilities. After teaching in an urban middle school, Seng directed a local refugee mutual assistance association and is now focusing on Southeast Asian American community capacity-building related to public health issues. Chanda is a mother of two and a successful small business owner and leader within the local Cambodian community. Mai serves as a Vietnamese outreach worker for a state mental health agency and is a community/parent organizer for her local church and its affiliated school, which her two children attend. Finally, Sokal is also a successful small business owner who has been able to support many members of his own family as well as projects in his home village in Cambodia. Like Sokal, Seng and Chanda are also involved with education projects in their home villages in Cambodia — reflecting the diasporic commitments and contributions of their generation. Every individual is involved in multiple ways with issues of education at home, at work, in their communities, and in their home countries. By following their evolving life stories over time — in the spirit of Cliff Adelman's counsel to "follow the student" rather than the institution (Adelman, 1999) — I expect their voices, perspectives, and experiences to continue to inform (and challenge) practices of persistence and development as well as broader conceptualizations of "cultural capital" and "civic engagement" in the literature of educational research and policy.

Profiling New Generations

While needing to invest more fully in this kind of sustained, long-term research over the lifespan of Southeast Asian Americans, I also recognize the critical importance of documentation and analysis with the new generation of Southeast Asian American students entering secondary and post-secondary education currently. One significant opportunity to analyze new data has been facilitated by the Nisei Student Relocation Commemorative Fund (NSRCF), a voluntary group of Nisei (second generation) and some Sansei (third generation) Japanese Americans who have provided annual scholarships to support college-going Southeast Asian American youth from various cities throughout the United States since the early 1980s.

The little-known story of the NSRCF is, itself, remarkable, with origins beginning during World War II, when the efforts of predominantly White educators, church groups, and service organizations established the National Japanese American Student Relocation Council and enabled roughly 4,000 college-age Nisei interned in U.S. concentration camps to leave camp and continue their education at colleges and universities, primarily in the Midwest and eastern United States. The impact of this effort on the Nisei was both immediate in transforming their life opportunities and life-long in transforming their values concerning social justice and civic responsibility. Forty years later, some of those impacted

Nisei identified with and responded to the urgent needs of Southeast Asian refugee youth by establishing the Nisei Student Relocation Commemorative Fund (NSRCF). According to Yutaka Kobayashi, a former president of the NSRCF:

This group was started back around the summer of 1979 in New England by a group of Nisei at a picnic. In swapping stories and recalling experiences of the war years, it became apparent that many of them were among those who had left their relocation camps for college. The picnickers came up with the idea of starting a commemorative fund to honor the memory of the grassroot movement in the United States which resulted in the relocation of Nisei students from camp to college. The plight of the "boat people" from Southeast Asia was in the news at that time and the problems faced by the college-age students of that group were reminiscent of the problems faced by the Nisei college-age students in the Relocation Camps. It seemed appropriate to help needy Southeast Asian college-bound students in the same spirit as the Nisei were helped during World War II under similar circumstances. Since the first scholarships were awarded in 1981, this volunteer group has doggedly managed to plod along running annual fund-raising campaigns and arranging awards in various cities in the continental United States where needy Southeast Asian students were concentrated. Awards have been given in Philadelphia, New York City, Houston, Los Angeles, Seattle, Boston, Minneapolis-St. Paul, Fresno and Stockton. Local award committees were organized at each city to select recipients and award the scholarships.

In 2000, the NSRCF scholarship award process rotated to Massachusetts. A total of 132 applications were received that year, each with background/demographic information about the applicant, a narrative essay, and other relevant documentation, such as high school transcripts and letters of recommendation. Recognizing the research value of the information, I asked for and received formal permission from the NSRCF board to have access to the 132 applications for educational research purposes after the awards process was completed. The pool of applications represented a unique cross-sectional profile of the new generation of Southeast Asian American college-going youth in Massachusetts. Some of the findings from my analysis are summarized here.

**Table 2-1: Massachusetts Southeast Asian American Applicants
to NSRCF, 2000 (n=132)**

	# female	% female	# male	% male	# total	% of total sample
Cambodian	22	73%	8	27%	30	23%
Hmong	4	57%	3	43%	7	5%
Lao	2	50%	2	50%	4	3%
Vietnamese	60	70%	26	30%	86	65%
Viet Chinese	4	100%	0	0%	4	3%
Thai	0	0%	1	100%	1	1%
TOTAL	92	70%	40	30%	132	100%

Of the total applicant pool (see Table 2-1), Vietnamese Americans comprised 65% and Cambodian Americans comprised an additional 23%. The third largest subgroup was Hmong, representing only 5% of the sample. All other groups were 3% or less. Particularly striking is the gender distribution. Female applicants represented 70% of the total applicant pool. This pattern is also true for the large subgroups of Vietnamese and Cambodian American applicants, among whom males comprised less than 30% of their respective totals. In addition, all the Vietnamese Chinese applicants were female, although their sample size was small. In none of the groups represented did male applicants comprise a majority. Clearly, this raises questions about possible gender differences in college-going behavior or in access to scholarship information within Southeast Asian communities in Massachusetts. This gender imbalance may also parallel similar patterns among other minority and immigrant populations.

Over 70% of the applicant pool resided in the six urban centers in the state where Southeast Asian American communities are physically concentrated (Cambodians in Lynn/ Revere and Lowell; Hmong in Fitchburg/Leominster; Vietnamese in Dorchester/Boston, Worcester/Auburn, and Springfield). For those applicants who reported family incomes (n=123; see Table 2-2), nearly 60% claimed less than $20,000 in earnings from the previous year. Only 15% of this sample reported family income of more than $40,000 during the previous year. Though self-reported, the data show a distressingly low family income level overall for this college-going population.

Table 2-2: Reported Family Income of Massachusetts Southeast Asian American
Applicants to NSRCF, 2000 (n=132)

	less than $20,000	$20,000 to $30,000	$30,000 to $30,000 to	more than $40,000
Cambodian	61% (17)	21% (6)	4% (1)	14% (4)
Hmong	50% (3)	0%	17% (1)	33% (2)
Lao	50% (2)	0%	25% (1)	25% (1)
Vietnamese	61% (49)	9% (7)	19% (15)	11% (9)
Viet Chinese	0%	25% (1)	25% (1)	50% (2)
Thai	100% (1)	0%	0%	0%
TOTAL	59% (72)	11% (14)	15% (19)	15% (18)

Beyond reaffirming the continuing geographic concentration and low socioeconomic status of Southeast Asian American youth/families in Massachusetts, though, the NSRCF data revealed other insights that suggest fresh or emerging themes to explore further. For example, in response to a question about intended majors in college, nearly 60% listed the predictable areas of health sciences/pharmacy, business/management, and engineering/ computer science/information science, while another 15% were undecided. However, other areas such as social science/psychology/communications, design/architecture/graphic arts, and education/teaching /Asian American Studies accounted for 25% (8.3% each). These are important fields with few pathways or precedents from previous generations of Southeast Asian Americans in higher education. These fields deserve focused attention from teachers, advisers, and mentors as well as supportive family and community constituencies.

In addition, themes articulated in the applicants' essays also confirm the continuing impact of family expectations and struggles with poverty and racism, while introducing fresh ideas that need further study. For example, many essays reveal specific issues faced by the applicants at home, such as the absence of fathers and sacrifices of mothers or caretaking challenges with family members who have health problems and disabilities. These subjects have yet to be explored by teachers, researchers, or policy makers.

Within the domain of school and future careers, some essays refer to the importance of community service/activism and leadership programs[2] — most of which were not available for an earlier generation of Southeast Asian refugee students in urban schools twenty years ago. This generational difference is notable, particularly in the sense of creativity that many applicants express about their futures. Even for those who state intentions to major in traditional fields like the sciences or health professions, many describe visions of integrating various academic, career, and sociocultural interests such as computer science with fashion design or biotechnology with traditional Chinese medicine. Despite dealing with substantial obstacles, their resilience directed toward the future is inspiring. A Cambodian American female NSRCF applicant wrote:

> My mother and three younger sisters offer little guidance for my aspirations. My parents did not complete junior high. In Cambodia and Vietnam, sheer survival mattered more than equations and poetry. I was raised to follow these views....It took me a long time to break free from my parents' views because I felt alone in my struggle. I will insure that others will not feel alone, and that they will realize their options. There are no limits.

Refusing to be constrained by stereotypic assumptions or static categories of culture, many also write about their own hybrid identities, which include, for some, complex, multi-ethnic, multicultural backgrounds, as noted by another female applicant:

> I come from a family that is striving to succeed in America, the land that is so different from our own. My sisters and I are Cambodian, Chinese, and Vietnamese. I am proud that we are. Being part of three different cultures, I can help create a new generation of cultural appreciation.

The NSRCF 2000 data illustrate both the continuing struggles and emerging themes for this new generation of Southeast Asian American students. Their continuing stories — across multiple pathways — are valuable to gather, share, and study.

Conclusions

The various phases of research described in this chapter have, over time, documented Southeast Asian American student stories, generated alternative theories of college persistence at urban commuter universities, and influenced the reform of specific campus-based policies and the design of curriculum and pedagogy for one particular Asian American Studies program. This body of work has demonstrated not only the importance of gathering disaggregated data and following life stories of Southeast Asian American students with their holistic, multidimensional identities over time, but has also modeled how Asian American Studies curricular/pedagogical interventions and investments can have long-term impact on individuals and their families and communities (Kiang, 2003a; 2003b; 2004a).

Furthermore, by indexing my own university — a severely underresourced, urban, public school — as the site for these sustained commitments of research, teaching, mentoring, and advocacy, I am also implicating a larger structural reality in which the institutions that hold substantial resources, status, and influence in U.S. society are typically NOT sites where Southeast Asian American students and communities tend to be concentrated. The unfortunate irony of such asymmetric arrangements contradicts the Cambodian American young woman's bold but subjective optimism that, "there are no limits." Thus, the equity-centered commitments and sustained, voluntary intervention of the NSRCF for more than two decades deserve recognition as well (Kiang, 2004a).

Indeed, with demographic and other changes in U.S. society, the NSRCF has recently questioned whether its commitments, after twenty plus years, should shift away from Southeast Asian American youth to support other struggling populations. Given evidence of continuing realities of inequality facing Southeast Asian American communities, however, the NSRCF decided in 2003 to continue its dedicated support, while also noting that other populations, including those who may not be Asian American, are becoming important to consider. Communicating this perspective in the wake of 9/11, then-President Yutaka Kobayashi reflected in a 2002 memo to the NSRCF board:

> As WWII becomes a more distant memory with each passing year, it is clear to me that we need to look at the Nisei experience of that time, not so much as a Japanese American experience, but as a lesson in American history. It is a lesson of how democracy can fail in a time of crisis. Persons of the Islamic faith in America, both immigrants and their American children, have experienced what happened to the Nisei in 1942, in part, since September 11, 2001. We must take a firm stand to defend the civil liberties guaranteed by our Constitution to all of its citizens. The Nisei experience during WWII must not be allowed to happen ever again to any other ethnic group in America. Our democracy, which is the envy of the world, is our birthright. To have any real meaning, democracy must work equally during war as it does so well during peace. It is this aspect, an important lesson of democracy failed, which is timeless. Although our mission is focused on the children of SE Asian immigrants from the Vietnam War period today, the time will come when our Fund's help will not be critical for their success. We, as a Fund, need to look ahead to that time and think about how best to fulfill our mission.

As time passes, will the nearly one thousand Southeast Asian American awardees of NSRCF scholarship funds across the United States internalize the Nisei example, and feel compelled in future years to mobilize collective support for other vulnerable populations beyond themselves? Clearly, their struggles to persist in higher education are far from resolved, as this chapter has documented. But by considering the cumulative impact of their own long-term educational engagement, together with transformative interventions by relevant school- or community-based Asian American Studies programs and groups such as the NSRCF, however, we can at least envision possibilities for the continuing life stories and contributions of Southeast Asian Americans to become limitless.

REFERENCES

Adelman, C. (1999). *Answers in the tool box: Academic intensity, attendance patterns, and bachelor's degree attainment.* (Document No. PLLI 1999-8021.) Washington, DC: U.S. Department of Education, Office of Educational Research and Improvement.

Bui, J. D., Tang, S. S., & Kiang, P. N. (2004). The local/global politics of Boston's Viet-vote. *AAPI Nexus: Policy, Practice & Community,* 2(2) 10-18.

Caplan, N., Whitmore, J. K., & Choy, M. H. (1989). *The boat people and achievement in America.* Ann Arbor: University of Michigan Press.

Chang, M.J. (2008). *Beyond myths: The growth and diversity of Asian American college freshmen: 1971-2005.* Higher Education Research Institute Research Brief, University of California, Los Angeles.

Chun, K. (1980). The myth of Asian American success and its educational ramifications. *IRCD Bulletin, Teachers College,* 15(1,2) 1-12.

Cochran-Smith, M., & Lytle, S. L. (1993). *Inside outside: Teacher research and knowledge.* New York: Teachers College Press.

del Rosario, C. A. (1999). *A different battle: Stories of Asian Pacific American veterans.* Seattle, WA: Wing Luke Museum.

Gándara, P. (1999). *Priming the pump: Strategies for increasing the achievement of underrepresented minority undergraduates.* Washington, DC: The College Board.

GAO (General Accounting Office). (2007a, July). *Asian Americans and Pacific Islanders' educational attainment. A report to congressional requesters.* (Document No. GAO-07-925). Washington, DC: Author.   [Online]. Available: http://www.gao.gov/cgi-bin/getrpt?GAO-07-925.

GAO (General Accounting Office). (2007b, July). Information sharing could help institutions identify and address challenges that some Asian American and Pacific Islander students face. *Highlights of GAO-07-925.* Washington, DC: Author.

Herman, J. L. (1992). *Trauma and recovery.* New York: Basic Books.

Kiang, P. N. (1989). Bringing it all back home: New views of Asian American studies and the community. In G.M. Nomura, R. Endo, S.H. Sumida, & R.C. Leong (Eds.), *Frontiers of Asian American studies* (pp.305-314). Pullman: Washington State University Press.

Kiang, P. N. (1991). About face: Recognizing Asian & Pacific American Vietnam veterans in Asian American studies. Amerasia Journal, 17(3), 22-40.

Kiang, P. N. (1993). Stratification of public higher education. In L. A. Revilla, G. M. Nomura, S. Wong, & S. Hune (Eds.), Bearing dreams, shaping visions (pp. 233-245). Pullman: Washington State University Press.

Kiang, P. N. (1995). Bicultural strengths and struggles of Southeast Asian American students. In A. Darder (Ed.), Culture and difference: Critical perspectives on the bicultural experience in the United States (pp. 201-225). New York: Bergin & Garvey.

Kiang, P. N. (1996). Persistence stories and survival strategies of Cambodian Americans in college. Journal of Narrative and Life History, 6(1) 39-64.

Kiang, P. N. (1997). Pedagogies of life and death: Transforming immigrant/refugee students and Asian American studies. Positions, 5(2), 529-555.

Kiang, P. N. (1998, Fall). Writing from the past, writing for the future: Healing effects of Asian American studies in the curriculum. Transformations: A Resource for Curriculum Transformation and Scholarship, 9(2), 132-149.

Kiang, P. N. (2000). Analyzing the impact of Asian American studies in the lives of alumni from an urban, commuter university, University of Massachusetts Boston. [Online]. NASPA Programs & Initiatives: Diversity on Campus: Reports from the Field. Available: www.naspa.org/programs/reports.cfm.

Kiang, P. N. (2003a). Voicing names and naming voices: Pedagogy and persistence in an Asian American studies classroom. In V. Zamel & R. Speck (Eds.), Crossing the curriculum: Multilingual learners in college classrooms (pp. 207-220). Mahwah, NJ: Lawrence Erlbaum.

Kiang, P. N. (2003b). Pedagogies of PTSD: Circles of healing with refugees and veterans in Asian American studies. In L. Zhan (Ed.), Asian Americans: Vulnerable populations, model interventions, clarifying agendas (pp. 197-222). Sudbury, MA: Jones & Bartlett.

Kiang, P. N. (2004a) Checking Southeast Asian American realities in Pan-Asian American agendas. AAPI Nexus: Policy, Practice & Community, 2(1), 48-76.

Kiang, P. N. (2004b). Linking strategies and interventions in Asian American studies to K-12 classrooms and teacher preparation. International Journal of Qualitative Studies in Education, 17(2), 199-225.

Kiang, P. N., & Kaplan, J. (1994). Where do we stand: Views of racial conflict by Vietnamese American high school students in a Black-and-White context. *The Urban Review,* 26(2) 95-119.

Kiang, P. N., Nguyen, N. L., & Sheehan, R. L. (1995). Don't ignore it!: Documenting racial harassment in a fourth-grade Vietnamese bilingual classroom. *Equity and Excellence in Education,* 28(1) 31-35.

Lee, S. J. (1996). *Unraveling the "model minority" stereotype.* New York: Teachers College Press.

Nakanishi, D. T., & Nishida, T. Y. (1995). *The Asian American educational experience.* New York: Routledge.

National Commission on Asian American and Pacific Islander Research in Education. (2008). *Asian Americans and Pacific Islanders - Facts, not fiction: Setting the record straight.* Research report. New York: New York University and the College Board. Available at: www.nyu.edu/projects/care.

Nidorf, J. F. (1985). Mental health and refugee youths: A model for diagnostic training. In T. C. Owan (Ed.), *Southeast Asian mental health: Treatment, prevention, services, training and research,* (pp.391-429). Rockville, MD: National Institute of Mental Health. (ERIC Document Reproduction Service No. ED266199)

Olsen, L. (1997). *An invisible crisis: The educational needs of Asian Pacific American youth.* New York: Asian Americans/Pacific Islanders in Philanthropy.

Pang, V. & Cheng, L. R. V. (Eds.). (1998). *Struggling to be heard: The unmet needs of Asian Pacific American children.* Albany: SUNY Press.

Park, C., & Chi, M. M. Y. (1999). *Asian-American education: Prospects and challenges.* Westport, CT: Bergin & Garvey.

Suarez-Orozco, M. M. (1989). *Central American refugees and U.S. high schools.* Stanford, CA: Stanford University Press.

Suzuki, B.H. (1977). Education and socialization of Asian Americans: A revisionist analysis of the "Model Minority" thesis. *Amerasia Journal,* 4(2) 23-51.

Tinto, V. (1987). *Leaving college: Rethinking the causes and cures of student attrition.* Chicago: University of Chicago Press.

Trueba, H. T., Cheng, L. R. L., & Ima, K. (1993). _Myth or reality? Adaptive strategies of Asian Americans in California._ London: Falmer Press.

Trueba, H. T., Jacobs, L., & Kirton, E. (1990). _Cultural conflict and adaptation: The case of Hmong children in American society._ Philadelphia: Falmer Press.

UC Newsroom. (2007, November 16). _Asian American, Pacific Islander data collection launches.[Online]._ Available: http://www.universityofcalifornia.edu/news/article/16826.

Weinberg, M. (1997). _Asian-American education: Historical background and current realities._ Mahwah, NJ: Lawrence Erlbaum.

Welaratna, U. (1993). _Beyond the killing fields: Voices of nine Cambodian survivors in America._ Stanford, CA: Stanford University Press.

Zuckoff, M. (2000, April 30). Vietnamese American stories. _The Boston Globe,_ pp. F13-14.

Footnotes

1   *Unless otherwise specified or cited, italicized "voices" from informants are based on personal interviews, classroom conversations, and student writings collected and maintained by the author.*

2   *Several applicants, for example, refer to the importance of the Coalition for Asian Pacific American Youth (CAPAY), a regional leadership network in Massachusetts. For further information, go to www.capayus.org.*

Acknowledgments

Some data in this chapter are provided with permission by the Nisei Student Relocation Commemorative Fund. Funding support was provided by the SAVE Project of the Southeast Asia Resource Action Center and Harvard Civil Rights Project. Significant sections of the chapter are adapted from Kiang (2002).

CHAPTER 3

A CRITICAL ANALYSIS OF THE EXCLUSION OF ASIAN AMERICANS FROM HIGHER EDUCATION RESEARCH AND DISCOURSE

Samuel D. Museus, PhD

In 2007, the Association for the Study of Higher Education (ASHE) announced the formation of the ASHE Institute on Equity Research Methods and Critical Policy Analysis. The equity institute was created to respond to the need to think more critically about race and ethnicity in the field of higher education. The institute was created with the intentions of (1) supporting the development and greater inclusion of minority scholars in the field, (2) promoting increased attention to the needs of minority communities, and (3) fostering an enhanced network of minority scholars in higher education who might be called upon to help shape future policy agendas. Finally, the announcement indicated that the institute would focus specifically on addressing inequalities that exist for African American, Latina/o, Native American, and Native Hawaiian populations.

The ASHE Institute is an initiative that offers hope for several racial and ethnic minority populations that are at risk or underrepresented in postsecondary education, while simultaneously contributing to the continued exclusion of other important groups in higher education. That is, the institute constitutes a major step forward in enhancing the voices of African American, Latina/o, Native American, and Native Hawaiian people, but also represents[1] another missed opportunity to include Southeast Asian American[1] and other Asian American populations in discussions that will play a major role in shaping those groups' future experiences and opportunities in higher education and society. This omission of and lack of voice among Asian Americans in higher education research and discourse is not uncommon. In fact, a recent review of five of the most widely read peer-reviewed academic journals in higher education reveals that only approximately one percent of the articles published in those journals during the last decade have given specific attention to Asian American populations[2].

Asian Americans constitute a population of significant size in American society and postsecondary education. They comprise one of the fastest growing populations in the nation (Hune, 2002). Moreover, it is projected that, by 2050, one of every ten United States residents will be of Asian descent, suggesting that the number and proportion of students on college campuses who are of Asian descent will most likely continue to increase rapidly as well (National Education Association, 2005; U.S. Census Bureau, 2000). The fact that this growing segment of the American population lacks adequate voice in higher education, therefore, is inequitable and unacceptable.

This chapter begins with an overview of some factors that contribute to the omission of Asian American populations from higher education research and discourse. Understanding how these phenomena collectively help perpetuate the aforementioned exclusion is important in efforts to address that omission and enhance voice among Asian Americans in higher education. Second, the chapter offers a discussion of why this exclusion is injurious for Asian American populations, and especially Southeast Asian Americans. Giving specific attention to Southeast Asians is important because excluding Asian Americans from higher education research and discourse can exacerbate the disadvantages already faced by this underserved and at-risk population. Finally, the chapter highlights some important implications for responsible and responsive researchers, policymakers, and practitioners who believe that they should and hope to include these populations in future discussions about race, ethnicity, equity, and opportunity in higher education.

THREE SOURCES OF PERPETUAL EXCLUSION

This section focuses on highlighting factors contributing to the exclusion of Asian Americans from research and discourse in higher education. The omission of Asian American voices from the field of higher education is perpetuated, at least in part, by three phenomena. First, the model minority myth, or the belief that Asian Americans achieve universal and unparalleled academic and occupational success, has historically shaped and continues to drive common assumptions that Asian Americans do not need the attention of educators because they will automatically succeed on their own (Suzuki, 1989, 2002). The second phenomenon that contributes to this exclusion is the continued absence of sufficient empirical data on the Asian American population, which inhibits researchers, policymakers, and practitioners from gaining a critical understanding of the diversity within and needs of the Asian American population (Nakanishi, 1995a; Teranishi, 2005). Finally, educational researchers and policymakers, while overemphasizing the importance of degree attainment in higher education discourse, too often ignore other important educational outcomes. As I argue below, these three factors perpetuate one another and have resulted in the continued failure of researchers and policymakers to acknowledge, understand, and address the problematic exclusion of this group from higher education research and discourse.

Source of Exclusion #1: Model Minority Myth

Scholars have previously noted that the model minority myth helps perpetuate the exclusion of Asian Americans from policy considerations in higher education (Teranishi, 2007; Zia, 2006). The negative consequences of this stereotype, however, permeate research and discourse more broadly in postsecondary education as well. This section provides a brief overview of the model minority myth.

The model minority stereotype emerged in the mid-twentieth century and has dominated common assumptions about Asian Americans since that time. Researchers have examined the rise of this stereotype in the 1960s (Suzuki, 1977, 2002; Uyematsu, 1971). Prior to that time, Asian Americans were most often portrayed in Western media with almost uniformly negative connotations as the *yellow peril*, or uncivilized heathens who threatened the American way of life (Miller, 1969; Ogawa, 1971). When explicit racial conflict peaked during the mid-1960s, however, images of Asian Americans as academic superstars began to emerge in the media (Peterson, 1966). After studying the concurrence of the fight for civil rights and the rise of the model minority myth, scholars and activists have posited that Asian Americans were promoted as the model minority at this time to discredit demands for racial equality in the Civil Rights Movement (Suzuki, 2002; Uyematsu, 1971). In other words, civil rights opponents created the model minority myth to argue that equal rights were not necessary for minorities to succeed in American society.

Although the model minority myth is not the only stereotype that shapes contemporary thought about Asian Americans in the United States, evidence from both academic arenas and mainstream society suggests that it continues to be one of the most pervasive stereotypes about this group (Museus, 2007, 2008; Suzuki, 1977, 2002; Wong, Lai, Nagasawa, & Lin, 1998). Stereotypes of Asian Americans as socially awkward, unable to speak proper English, cheap, sly, and untrustworthy foreigners also have been perpetuated in American culture (Kim & Yeh, 2002; Miller, 1969; Ogawa, 1971). Nevertheless, the model minority myth does provide the foundation for prevalent assumptions about Asian Americans, and one does not have to look very far to see its manifestation in popular culture and media. Indeed, popular cartoons, television sitcoms, and Hollywood movies all tend to limit the appearances of Asian Americans to a few stereotypical roles, one of which is the model minority stereotype. This stereotype has helped generate and sustain the common assumption that Asian Americans do not need the attention and resources of higher education researchers, policymakers, and practitioners; the few critical analyses of data on Asian Americans that *do* exist, however, suggest that this is a faulty assumption.

While aggregated data indicate that Asian Americans, in general, exhibit high rates of educational and occupational success, a different picture emerges when critical analyses of the Asian American population are invoked (Hune, 2002; National Education Association, 2005; Suzuki, 1977; Teranishi, 2007). Suzuki (1977), for example, demonstrated that the average Asian American family income was higher than the average income of White American families only because they had more individual income earners per household and were concentrated in high cost-of-living geographic regions. Moreover, his analyses indicated that, when these factors were taken into account, Asian Americans actually had lower levels of family income than their White counterparts, earned considerably less than Whites with equal levels of education, and were more likely to live in poverty than Whites. Despite evidence contradicting the model minority myth, the stereotype has persisted.

Moreover, related to the model minority myth is the fact that analyses of Asian Americans in higher education are often based on the collection and use of insufficient data. Specifically, when data are collected on Asian Americans, they are usually collected in such small numbers that disaggregation of those data result in sample sizes that are inadequate for statistical analyses. The failure to collect sufficient data on this population is the focus of the next section.

Source of Exclusion #2: Insufficient Data

The persisting model minority myth and the failure of higher education researchers and policymakers to collect data on Asian Americans that can be disaggregated and analyzed have created a vicious cycle, in which the myth and the absence of data on this population function to consistently perpetuate one another. Indeed, the model minority stereotype has contributed to the prevalent notion that Asian Americans do not require attention because they do well enough on their own (Suzuki, 2002; Yeh, 2002); the common assumption is that energy and resources should, therefore, not be invested in serving this population. In turn, the absence of data that permit disaggregation and critical analyses of specific subgroups contributes, in part, to the fact that higher education researchers often analyze Asian Americans as one massive group, thereby masking the differences and inequities that exist within the population and inaccurately confirming the model minority stereotype (see, for example, Berkner, He, & Cataldi, 2002).

The assumption that Asian Americans achieve universal educational and occupational success has, in part, resulted in the continued use of insufficient data to examine this population. In turn, this insufficient data analyzed, and knowledge produced from those analyses, often reinforce the model minority myth. Berkner and colleagues (2002), for example, analyzed nationally representative data collected by the National Center for Education Statistics (NCES) and reported that Asian and Asian American college students exhibited the highest levels of six-year degree completion rates among all racial groups. When Asian American students in the NCES sample are extracted and disaggregated, however, some Southeast Asian subgroups consist of as few as 14 students. Thus, the NCES data are adequate for producing aggregated statistics that confirm the model minority myth, but are insufficient for examining the disparities from which some Asian American subpopulations suffer and generating information that challenges that prevailing stereotype. Unfortunately, as scholars such as Teranishi (2005, 2007) have noted, the collection of such inadequate data is a pervasive problem and most federal education databases do not include sufficient data on Asian American subpopulations to permit the disaggregation and critical examination of specific Asian American ethnic subpopulations.

The nonexistence of data that permit the disaggregation and analysis of particular Asian American subpopulations forces researchers to choose between either excluding them from analyses altogether or examining them in the aggregate by default. In other words, researchers are forced to choose between treating Asian Americans as invisible and perpetuating the model minority myth. Unfortunately, the invisibility of Asian Americans from most higher education research and the production of these few aggregated analyses in the absence of more critical inquiry and examination has proven to be misleading at best and harmful at worst. Often intertwined with the model minority myth and examinations of aggregated data on Asian Americans is an overemphasis on degree attainment as the primary or only measure of success, which is the focus of the next section.

Source of Exclusion #3: Overemphasis on Degree Attainment

The third phenomenon highlighted herein for its contribution to the exclusion of Asian Americans from higher education research and discourse is the emphasis, or overemphasis, that higher education scholars and policymakers often place on educational attainment (see, for example, Burd, 2003; Zumeta, 2001). Indeed, when Asian Americans are depicted as the model minority, such portrayals are often a function of assertions exclusively focused on their exhibiting high levels of degree attainment. By contrast, scholars have acknowledged many alternative measures of success that are frequently overlooked, including cognitive, civic, and moral growth, as well as post-college occupational attainment and quality of life (Pascarella & Terenzini, 1991, 2005). These alternative outcomes, however, are too often only peripheral concerns.

Furthermore, postsecondary degree attainment is not necessarily linearly related to other indicators of success. For example, evidence from the 1990s suggests that, even in fields in which Asian Americans have the highest levels of educational attainment among various racial/ethnic groups, they face a "glass ceiling" that prevents them from advancing in the workforce after college (Woo, 1994). Such evidence also indicates that, as a result, even in fields where they are the most qualified, Asian Americans are less likely to occupy managerial positions than other racial/ethnic groups, including their Black and Latina/o peers. With regard to per capita income, on average, in 1993, Asian Americans ($18,907) earned less than their White counterparts ($22,952). Moreover, some Southeast Asian American groups earned only one-tenth that of Whites. Hmong Americans, for example, had a per capita income of $2,692 (Hune, 2002; U.S. Census Bureau, 1999). Even when earnings among college graduates are examined, disparities manifest, with the median annual earnings of full-time Asian American college graduates ($36,844) remaining below that of their White college degree holding counterparts ($40,240).

While the glass ceiling for Asian Americans could primarily be a function of many factors, such as racial discrimination, it may also be a result of the fact that Asian American college graduates do not possess the traits that Western cultures deem desirable for leadership (Cheng, 1996). Moreover, existing research suggests that, regardless of their academic performance, Asian American college students might not be making the same developmental gains as their non-Asian American peers with regard to overall competence (Ying, Lee, Tsai, Hung, Lin, & Wan, 2001). Thus, because the few discussions in which Asian Americans are included usually focus on their overrepresentation in college and disproportionately high levels of educational attainment, questions remain about whether colleges are equipping these students with the skills they need to succeed in a predominantly White workforce. If higher education researchers and policymakers fail to generate and analyze data to question assumptions that they are adequately serving Asian American college students, they may be severely neglecting the real needs of this population.

In sum, the model minority myth, the insufficient collection and use of data, and the overemphasis on degree attainment all function, in part, to perpetuate the exclusion of Asian Americans from research and discourse in higher education. It is important to note that the omission of the voices of Asian Americans from the field of higher education, while unfair for the entire population, may be most detrimental for Southeast Asian American populations. This is because Southeast Asian Americans, on average, suffer from many similar inequities faced by their Black, Latina/o, and Native American counterparts. Accordingly, the following section highlights some of these critical disparities from which Southeast Asian Americans continue to suffer.

UNDERREPRESENTED SOUTHEAST ASIAN AMERICAN COLLEGE STUDENTS

As mentioned, while the lack of consideration of Asian Americans in higher education research and discourse disadvantages all Asian Americans, the exclusion of voice among these groups may be particularly harmful for Southeast Asian American populations. Indeed, stereotypes of all Asian Americans as the model minority, data that mask the real disparities and diversity within the Asian American population, and discussions that ignore the diverse needs of this population are especially damaging for Southeast Asian American students because they, compared to other Asian Americans and the national population, originate from the most poorly resourced communities (Chang & Kiang, 2002; Kiang, 2004; U.S. Census Bureau, 2004). Moreover, some Southeast Asian groups, such as Cambodian and Hmong American populations, are severely underrepresented in college student and college educated populations (Suzuki, 2002; U.S. Census Bureau, 2004).

Researchers have begun to underscore the diversity that exists among Asian Americans (Hune, 2002; Suzuki, 1977; Teranishi, 2007; U.S. Census Bureau, 2004). In doing so, they have highlighted some of the disparities from which Southeast Asian American populations suffer. These Southeast Asian American groups differ dramatically from their East and South Asian American counterparts in characteristics such as average levels of poverty, income, and educational attainment (Hune, 2002; U.S. Census Bureau, 2004). Data from the U.S. Census Bureau (2004) suggest that less than ten percent of Asian Indian, Filipino, and Japanese Americans were living under the federally defined poverty level in 2000, while that figure was 38% for Hmong Americans. Furthermore, Cambodian, Chinese, Hmong, Korean, Laotian, Pakistani, Thai, and Vietnamese Americans all exhibited higher poverty rates than the national population during that year.

The U.S. Census Bureau (2004) has also highlighted the large disparities that exist, with regard to educational attainment, in the Asian American population. For example, the proportion of the adult Asian Indian population (64%) holding a bachelor's degree was approximately seven times that of their Cambodian (9%) and eight times that of their

Laotian (8%) and Hmong (8%) counterparts. Moreover, the latter Southeast Asian American populations exhibited degree attainment rates far below the national population (24%). These differences in educational attainment are so salient that scholars have asserted that the Asian American population appears to be most accurately represented by a bimodal distribution (Kim, Rendón, & Valadez, 1998). One of those distributions is comprised of many East and South Asian American groups exhibiting high rates of success, and the other consisting of Southeast Asian American populations who disproportionately originate from more disadvantaged backgrounds and display lower levels of educational and occupational attainment. In sum, much like their Black and Latina/o peers, Southeast Asian Americans originate from disadvantaged backgrounds, are underrepresented in higher education, and suffer from great disparities in degree attainment.

The omission of this population from higher education research and discourse has rendered Asian Americans one of the most misunderstood groups on college campuses. Moreover, given the fact that Southeast Asian Americans suffer from disparities in educational and occupational attainment, it is only fair that higher education researchers, policymakers, and educators give adequate attention to the needs of this population. The next section outlines critical areas in which these groups should be included in future research and discourse in postsecondary education.

INCLUDING ASIAN AMERICANS IN HIGHER EDUCATION RESEARCH AND DISCOURSE

This section includes a discussion of five areas in which Asian Americans have been excluded from higher education research and discourse. They are areas in which little understanding of the experiences of and challenges faced by Asian Americans exists, in part, because they are often ignored by researchers and policymakers in discussions about racial and ethnic minorities in higher education. In highlighting these five areas, I underscore critical knowledge gaps in which the generation of scholarly research on and discourse about these populations must be increased to inform postsecondary policymakers and educators about how they can adequately serve Asian American, and especially Southeast Asian American, populations in higher education.

While issues of exclusion pose negative consequences for all Asian Americans, paying particular attention to Southeast Asian Americans is emphasized herein because, as previously mentioned, Southeast Asian Americans are underrepresented in higher education and experience many struggles, such as high poverty rates and low rates of educational attainment, similar to those of other underserved racial/ethnic minority groups. Moreover, this section focuses on Asian American college students, as opposed to faculty, administrators, and staff. It is not focused on students with the intention of diminishing the importance of considering the needs of these other groups; on the contrary, Asian Americans are underrepresented in these roles as well, and that underrepresentation deserves the attention of higher education policymakers and researchers. Nevertheless, because it is the primary responsibility of college faculty, administrators, and staff to serve undergraduates, I focus on Asian American college students for the purposes of this discussion. Although the list of areas discussed is not exhaustive, this section delineates some of the most critical areas in which postsecondary education policymakers and practitioners should be aware of the challenges faced by Asian American college students.

Ramifications of the Model Minority Myth

Higher education researchers have written about the model minority stereotype and the pressure that this stereotype creates for Asian American students (Museus, 2007, 2008; Suzuki, 1977, 2002; Uyematsu, 1971; Wong et al., 1998). Museus (2008), for example, has demonstrated that pressure to conform to the model minority stereotype may be associated with a tendency for Asian American college students to disengage in and out of classrooms. His research also showed that fear of failing to fulfill expectations of the myth may be associated with an inclination among Asian American students to avoid seeking help from faculty members. Because student involvement is a critical factor in promoting developmental and other positive educational outcomes (see, for example, Astin, 1984, 1993; Pascarella & Terenzini, 1991, 2005), the perpetuation of the model minority myth may pose major barriers to Asian American college students' ability to maximize the benefits of their college experience. This could be particularly detrimental for Southeast Asian American students, who understand that they share many similar disadvantages as their Black and Latina/o peers and, therefore, face major challenges in meeting the excessively high academic expectations perpetuated by the model minority stereotype.

In addition, scholars have noted that the model minority stereotype can engender resentment and hostility toward Asian Americans among other racial/ethnic groups (Nakanishi, 1995b; Suzuki, 1989). Such negative attitudes toward Asian American groups could strain race relations on college campuses and throughout society. Unfortunately, research investigating the harmful consequences of the model minority stereotype is sparse, leaving postsecondary educators ill equipped to understand how to identify and address such ramifications.

Cultural Adjustment and Membership

Because higher education researchers and policymakers often assume that Asian American students adjust to college campuses with few challenges and achieve universal success in higher education, research and literature on Asian American college student adjustment and persistence is almost nonexistent. The few researchers who have studied factors that influence Asian American student adjustment and persistence (e.g., Museus, Nichols,

& Lambert, 2008; Truong & Museus, 2008; Yeh, 2004-05) provide evidence to the contrary, suggesting that Asian American students do, in fact, face difficulties adjusting to, finding membership in, and persisting through predominantly White institutions. Moreover, evidence that Southeast Asian American students can be victimized by within-race discrimination and isolation from other Asian American groups may present added challenges for these groups (Lee, 1994, 1996); at colleges and universities in which Southeast Asian Americans are underrepresented, therefore, postsecondary researchers and educators should be aware that those students may encounter enhanced difficulties adjusting to and finding membership in their campus communities. Until higher education researchers study Southeast Asian American students' experiences and outcomes in-depth, postsecondary educators will know little about the challenges faced by those students and how to sufficiently address them.

Prejudice and Discrimination in the College Experience

Because Asian American students are often ignored in higher education research and discourse, knowledge of the extent to which they face prejudice and discrimination in higher education is sparse. The evidence that does exist suggests that Asian American students continue to be victims of subtle and overt forms of racism, including racially motivated violence on college campuses (Alvarez & Yeh, 1999; Lewis, Chesler, & Forman, 2000; Sue, Bucceri, Lin, Nadal, & Torino, 2007; U.S. Commission on Civil Rights, 1992). In 1999, for instance, a Korean student at Indiana University was gunned down by a White supremacist as he was standing outside a Korean United Methodist Church before Sunday service (Vest, 1999). While this is an extreme example, experiences with prejudice and discrimination are a common aspect of the college experience for many Asian American students. Despite the prevalence of prejudice and discrimination in the experiences of Asian American undergraduates, those students have expressed discontent with the fact that they are often excluded from discussions of race, which are typically focused on Black-White relations, on campus (Lewis et al., 2000).

Equally as important as the fact that Asian American students experience prejudice and discrimination is the fact that existing data may underestimate the salience of these incidents in the experiences of Asian American college students. This is because many Asian American cultures place high value on interdependent harmony (Uba, 1994), which may result in a culturally-based inclination to evade unnecessary conflict and a decreased likelihood that Asian American students will report or complain about being victimized by prejudice and discrimination. Thus, educators should be careful not to assume that failure to report incidents of prejudice and discrimination is the same as not encountering such experiences. Research aimed at developing a better understanding of Asian American and Southeast Asian American students' experiences with racial prejudice and discrimination, as well as their attitudes and dispositions toward reporting and responding to such incidents, would aid postsecondary educators in better understanding how to serve those students.

Also important is the notion that Southeast Asian American students may face both inter-racial and intra-racial prejudice and discrimination. Indeed, there is evidence that more educationally and economically successful Asian American populations may alienate and exclude other historically marginalized Asian American groups (Lee, 1994, 1996). This is an important consideration because many Southeast Asian American groups, as a result of this intra-racial discrimination, may not have access to the same cultural and social networks, resources, and support as their East and South Asian American counterparts in higher education and the post-college workforce.

Psychological Distress and Coping

One consequence that has been associated with Asian American college students' perceptions of racial prejudice and discrimination on campus is their likelihood of experiencing psychological distress and depression (Cress & Ikeda, 2003). This is noteworthy because empirical research suggests that Asian American college students may suffer from disproportionately high rates of depression (Greenberger & Chen, 1996; Kim & Chun, 1993). If researchers and educators, therefore, hope to help their Asian American students cope with the mental health issues that they face, they must better understand the causes and nature of those issues.

Postsecondary educators must possess the knowledge necessary for and be diligent in ensuring that Asian American undergraduates access essential advising and counseling services because those students are less likely than their non-Asian American counterparts to seek and utilize such services on their own (Uba, 1994; Zhang, Snowden, & Sue, 1998). Indeed, research suggests that Asian American students with problems tend to use more avoidant coping strategies than their non-Asian peers (Chang, 1996; Jung, 1995; Sheu & Sedlacek, 2004). Scholars have noted that this avoidance behavior could be due, in part, to a lack of knowledge about resources, reluctance to seek help from strangers, avoidance of seeking assistance from educators who are not culturally sensitive to Asian American cultural issues, and Asian cultural values that emphasize harmonious interdependence and discourage the creation of disharmony by acknowledging and addressing mental health problems (Uba, 1994; Yeh, 2002). Regardless of the source of avoidance, the disproportionately high levels of mental health issues, coupled with choices to avoid seeking help for such issues, requires the attention of postsecondary researchers and educators.

Given the aforementioned pressures emerging from the model minority stereotype, experiences with prejudice and discrimination, and adjustment difficulties among Asian American college students, the fact that Asian American undergraduates may not be seeking the help and services they need should be considered a critical concern by faculty, administrators, and staff in higher education. Again, because of the limited available information regarding Asian American students and culture, administrators and staff often lack the awareness and resources needed to deal with the psychosocial needs of the Asian American students whom they serve.

Suzuki (2002), for example, highlighted how counselors who lack knowledge of Asian American issues can mistakenly and destructively assume that Asian American college students do not seek help because they are well adjusted and experience few personal problems. Due to the fact that Southeast Asian American groups exhibit so many high-risk characteristics and deal with the aforementioned pressure from stereotypes, prejudice, discrimination, and adjustment difficulties, these students may be equally, or more, prone to mental health issues as their East and South Asian peers. The absence of informative research and knowledgeable practitioners who understand the cultural nuances that may prevent Asian Americans from seeking important mental health services can be counterproductive at best or psychologically damaging at worst.

Alternative Measures of Success

As mentioned, the limited research and discourse that includes Asian American college students is disproportionately focused on degree attainment and providing evidence that confirms the model minority myth. This research and discourse often fails to explore questions about whether and why Asian American students are, or are not, succeeding at rates equivalent to their non-Asian peers after they enter the workforce. Given existing evidence that Asian American graduates are not entering leadership positions at rates or earning wages equivalent to their non-Asian counterparts (Woo, 1994), it is critical that higher education researchers and policymakers examine (1) whether Asian American college students are gaining the skills and knowledge that are believed to be critical to success in the workforce and (2) the long-term effects of college on Asian American students.

Indeed, there is a need to better understand how college affects Asian American students' skills and success after graduation, as well as how those effects might differ from the impact that college has on the skills and long-term outcomes of other racial groups. If future research confirms that institutions of higher education are less effective at facilitating the development of critical skills and post-college benefits among Asian Americans than amongst their non-Asian counterparts, higher education policymakers, researchers, and leaders must be held accountable for ignoring the real needs of their Asian American students, as well as retaining and graduating Asian Americans who are not fully equipped to maximize their potential in the post-college workforce.

Conclusion

This chapter discusses how the voices of Asian Americans have historically been omitted from higher education research and discourse. This exclusion poses harmful consequences for Asian American college students in general and Southeast Asian American college students in particular. If postsecondary educators are to adequately serve this growing population, attention to Southeast Asian American and other Asian American college student populations must be included in higher education research and discourse. Although the five areas discussed herein are not the only areas in which researchers, policymakers, and practitioners should include the voices of Asian American college students, they are offered as a starting point to begin discussions about issues relevant to this population that deserve and require adequate attention.

References

Alvarez, A. N., & Yeh, T. L. (1999). Asian Americans in college: A racial identity perspective. In D. Sandhu (Ed.), _Asian and Pacific Islander Americans: Issues and concerns for counseling and psychotherapy._ Huntington, NY: Nova Science Publishers.

Astin, A. W. (1984). Student involvement: A developmental theory for higher education. _Journal of College Student Personnel, 25(4), 297-308._

Astin, A. W. (1993). _What matters in college? Four critical years revisited._ San Francisco: Jossey-Bass.

Berkner, L., He, S., & Cataldi, E. F. (2002). _Descriptive summary of 1995-96 beginning postsecondary students: Six years later._ Washington, DC: National Center for Education Statistics, U. S. Department of Education.

Burd, S. (2003). Education department wants to create grant program linked to graduation rates. _The Chronicle of Higher Education, 49(17),_ A31.

Chang, E. (1996). Cultural differences in optimism, pessimism, and coping: Predictors of subsequent adjustment in Asian American and Caucasian American college students. _Journal of Counseling Psychology, 43(1), 113-123._

Chang, M. J., & Kiang, P. N. (2002). New challenges of representing Asian American students in U.S. higher education. In W. A. Smith, P. G. Altbach, & K. Lomotey (Eds.), _The racial crisis in American higher education: Continuing challenges for the twenty-first century_ (pp. 137-158). Albany: SUNY Press.

Cheng, C. (1996). We choose not to compete: The merit discourse in the selection process, and Asian and Asian American men and their masculinity. In C. Cheng (Ed.), _Masculinities in organizations._ Thousand Oaks, CA: Sage.

Cress, C. M., & Ikeda, E. K. (2003). Distress under duress: The relationship between campus climate and depression in Asian American college students. _NASPA Journal, 40(2), 74-97._

Greenberger, E. & Chen, C. (1996), Perceived family relationships and depressed mood in early and late adolescents: A comparison of Europeans and Asian Americans. _Developmental Psychology, 32(4), 707-716._

Hune, S. (2002). Demographics and diversity of Asian American college students. _Working with Asian American Students: New Directions for Student Services,_ No. 97, 11-20. San Francisco: Jossey-Bass.

Jung, J. (1995). Ethnic group and gender differences in the relationship between personality and coping. *Anxiety, Stress, and Coping, 8*, 113-126.

Kiang, P. N. (2002). Stories and structures of persistence: Ethnographic learning through research and practice in Asian American Studies. In Y. Zou & H. T. Trueba (Eds.), *Advances in ethnographic research: From our theoretical and methodological roots to post-modern critical ethnography.* Lanham, MD: Rowman & Littlefield.

Kiang, P. N. (2004). Checking Southeast Asian American neoconservative renditions of equality: An analysis of the Brian Ho lawsuit. *AAPI Nexus: Policy, Practice, and Community. AAPI Nexus: Civil Rights, 2*(1), 48-76.

Kim, A., & Yeh, C. J. (2002). Stereotypes of Asian American students. *ERIC Digest,* No. 172. New York: ERIC Clearinghouse on Urban Education. (ERIC Document Reproduction Service No. ED462510)

Kim, H., Rendón, L., & Valadez, J. (1998). Student characteristics, school characteristics, and educational aspirations of six Asian American ethnic groups. *Journal of Multicultural Counseling and Development, 26*(3), 166-176.

Kim, L. S., & Chun, C. (1993), Ethic differences in psychiatric diagnosis among Asian American adolescents. *Journal of Nervous and Mental Disease, 181*, 612-617.

Lee, S. J. (1994). Behind the model-minority stereotype: Voices of high- and low-achieving Asian American students. *Anthropology & Education Quarterly, 25*(4), 413-429.

Lee, S. J. (1996). *Unraveling the "model minority" stereotype: Listening to Asian American youth.* New York: Teachers College Press.

Lewis, A. E., Chesler, M., & Forman, T. A. (2000). The impact of "colorblind" ideologies on students of color: Intergroup relations at a predominantly White university. *The Journal of Negro Education, 69*(1/2), 74-91.

Miller, S. C. (1969). *The unwelcome immigrant: The American image of the Chinese, 1785–1882.* Berkeley: University of California Press.

Museus, S. D. (2007). Using qualitative methods to assess diverse institutional cultures. In S. R. Harper & S. D. Museus (Eds.), *Using qualitative methods in institutional assessment: New directions for institutional research,* No. 136, 29-40. San Francisco: Jossey-Bass.

Museus, S. D. (2008). The model minority and the inferior minority myths: Inside stereotypes and their implications for student engagement. About Campus, 13(3), 2-8.

Museus, S. D., Nichols, A. H., & Lambert, A. D. (2008). Racial differences in the effects of campus racial climate on degree completion: A structural model. The Review of Higher Education, 32(1), 107-134.

Nakanishi, D. T. (1995a). Asian/Pacific Americans and selective undergraduate admissions. Journal of College Admissions, 118, 17-26.

Nakanishi, D. T. (1995b). Growth and diversity: The education of Asian-Pacific Americans. In D. T. Nakanishi & T. Y. Nishida (Eds.), The Asian American educational experience: A source book for teachers and students. New York: Routledge.

National Education Association (2005). A report on the status of Asian Americans and Pacific Islanders in education: Beyond the "model minority" stereotype. Washington, DC: Author.

Ogawa, D. (1971). From Japs to Japanese: The evolution of Japanese-American stereotypes. Berkeley, CA: McCutchan.

Pascarella, E. T., & Terenzini, P. T. (1991). How college affects students: Findings and insights from twenty years of research. San Francisco: Jossey-Bass.

Pascarella, E. T., & Terenzini, P. T. (2005). How college affects students: Vol.2. A third decade of research. San Francisco: Jossey-Bass.

Peterson, W. (1966, January 9). Success story: Japanese-American style. New York Times Magazine, p. 21.

Sheu, H., & Sedlacek, W. E. (2004). An exploratory study of help-seeking attitudes and coping strategies among college students by race and gender. Measurement and Evaluation in Counseling and Development, 37, 130-143.

Sue, D. W., Bucceri, J., Lin, A. I., Nadal, K. L., & Torino, G. C. (2007). Racial microaggressions and the Asian American experience. Cultural Diversity and Ethnic Minority Psychology, 13(1), 72-81.

Suzuki, B. H. (1977). Education and the socialization of Asian Americans: A revisionist analysis of the "model minority" thesis. Amerasia Journal, 4(2), 23-51.

Suzuki, B. H. (1989, November/December). Asian Americans as the "model minority": Outdoing Whites? Or media hype? Change, 17(6), pp. 13-19.

Suzuki, B. H. (2002). Revisiting the model minority stereotype: Implications for student affairs practice and higher education. Working with Asian American students: New Directions for Student Services, No. 97, 21-32. San Francisco: Jossey-Bass.

Teranishi, R. T. (2005). Asian American and Pacific Islander participation in U.S. higher education: Status and trends. New York: The College Board.

Teranishi, R. T. (2007). Race, ethnicity, and higher education policy: The use of critical quantitative research. In F. Stage (Ed.), Using quantitative research to answer critical questions: New directions for institutional research, No. 133, 37-49. San Francisco: Jossey-Bass.

Truong, K. A., & Museus, S. D. (2008). Focusing on cultural differences within race: The salience of precollege communities in the experiences of Asian American college students. Paper presented at the 2008 Annual Harvard Alumni of Color Conference. Cambridge, MA.

Uba, L. (1994). Asian Americans: Personality patterns, identity, and mental health. NewYork: Guilford Press.

U.S. Census Bureau. (1999). Money income in the United States, 1998. Washington, DC: U.S. Government Printing Office.

U.S. Census Bureau. (2000). Resident population estimates of the United States by sex, race, and Hispanic origin. Washington, DC: U.S. Government Printing Office.

U.S. Census Bureau. (2004). We the people: Asians in the United States. Washington, DC: U.S. Government Printing Office.

U.S. Commission on Civil Rights. (1992). Civil rights issues facing Asian Americans in the 1990s. Washington DC: Author.

Uyematsu, A. (1971). The emergence of yellow power in America. In A. Tachiki (Ed.), Roots: An Asian American reader. Los Angeles: UCLA Asian American Studies Center.

Vest, J. (1999, July 13). Summer of Smith. The Village Voice. Retrieved January 20, 2008, from http://www.villagevoice.com/news/9927,216729,7022,1.html

Wong, P., Lai, C. F., Nagasawa, R., & Lin, T. (1998). Asian Americans as a model minority: Self-perceptions and perceptions by other racial groups. Sociological Perspectives, 41(1), 95-118.

Woo, D. (1994). _The glass ceiling and Asian Americans._ Washington, DC: U.S. Department of Labor Glass Ceiling Commission.

Yeh, T. L. (2002). Asian American college students who are educationally at risk. _New Directions for Student Services,_ No. 97, 61-71. San Francisco: Jossey-Bass.

Yeh, T. L. (2004-05). Issues of college persistence between Asian and Asian Pacific American students. _Journal of College Student Retention: Research, Theory, and Practice,_ 6(1), 81-96.

Ying, Y., Lee, P. A., Tsai, J. L., Hung, Y., Lin, M., & Wan, C. T. (2001). Asian American college students as model minorities: An examination of their overall competence. _Cultural Diversity Ethnic Minority Psychology,_ 7(1), 59-74.

Zhang, A. Y., Snowden, L. R., & Sue, S. (1998). Differences between Asian and White Americans help seeking and utilization patterns in the Los Angeles area. _Journal of Community Psychology,_ 26, 317-326.

Zia, H. (2006). _Asian/Pacific Americans and higher education: Facts, not fiction – Setting the record straight._ New York: The College Board.

Zumeta, W. (2001). Public policy and accountability in higher education: Lessons from the past and present for the new millennium. In D. E. Heller (Ed.), _The states and public higher education policy: Affordability, access, and accountability_ (pp. 155-197). Baltimore: Johns Hopkins University Press.

FOOTNOTES

1   For the purposes of this chapter, the term "Southeast Asian Americans" is used to refer to American Cambodian, Hmong, Laotian, and Vietnamese populations

2   The journals reviewed included the Journal of Higher Education, Research in Higher Education, The Review of Higher Education, the Journal of College Student Development, and the NASPA Journal.

CHAPTER 4
MENTORING ASIAN STUDENTS TOWARD ENTERING THE HEALTH PROFESSIONS

Ivy K. Ho, PhD
Khanh T. Dinh, PhD

Asians are the fastest growing group of college students in the United States (Higher Education Research Institute [HERI], 2007), with the proportion of Asians in U.S. institutions increasing from 0.8% in 1971 to 8.8% in 2005. Contrary to the "model minority myth" that depicts Asians as being the most successful ethnic minority group, in recent years, Asian students attending college are facing a growing number of obstacles. For example, 30.9% of Asian college students come from low-income households that earn $40,000 or less per year (HERI, 2007). Moreover, given that Asian students are more likely to come from large families that live in metropolitan areas with high costs of living, the burden of paying for a college education may be heavier for these families than their income would imply. Furthermore, although Asian students are increasingly applying to six or more colleges, only 51.8% of them are attending their first choice colleges, compared to 68% in 1974 (HERI, 2007). In contrast, 69.8% of the overall population of new college students in 2005 and 77.2% in 1974 were enrolled in their first choice colleges. Upon enrollment in college, Asian students earn lower grade point averages than do their White counterparts (Tseng, Chao, & Padmawidjaja, 2007), even after accounting for the fact that Asian students tend to major in fields that typically award lower grades, such as science and mathematics.

These trends outline the current profile of the Asian college student in the United States, and alert faculty to the challenges their Asian students may be facing. The present chapter focuses on one sector of Asian college students — those majoring in the health professions — by discussing the struggles they face and providing specific recommendations for faculty who mentor them. Although the issues highlighted in this chapter apply to the health professions in general, we will at times use the field of psychology as an example of a health profession. Even though psychology is a varied field of study, many psychology majors choose careers in the social services, or enroll in graduate programs in clinical and counseling psychology, as well as in social work and other mental-health-related fields. Therefore, within today's increasingly multidisciplinary health care settings, nurses are likely to collaborate with colleagues who have an undergraduate degree in psychology. Finally, college students of Asian descent in the United States include American citizens, permanent residents, and international students. In this chapter, the term "Asian" will be used inclusively to refer to all three groups of students. Readers, however, must be mindful that the term "Asian" is perhaps elusive and too broad to make any generalization, as there are variations among Asian ethnocultural groups, and thus an individual or a case-by-case analysis may be required.

BARRIERS TO BEING SUCCESSFUL STUDENTS IN THE HEALTH PROFESSIONS

Acculturation

Acculturation is a complex and multidimensional phenomenon; however, from a linear or unidimensional perspective, it is defined as "the acquisition of the cultural patterns (e.g., values, norms, language, behaviors) of the core or dominant society" (Atkinson, Morten, & Sue, 1997, p. 11). The majority of Asians in the United States is of immigrant background and many vary in their levels of acculturation and acculturative modes (see Berry, 2003 for more information on acculturation theories and definitions). While some adopt the culture of mainstream American society, others adhere to traditional Asian worldviews and practices; many also manage to integrate aspects of both cultures (Dinh & Nguyen, 2006; Dinh, Weinstein, Kim, & Ho, 2008).

There are several distinct ways in which Asian cultures and the dominant American culture differ and these differences have specific implications for the Asian college student. For example, whereas Western culture values extraversion and encourages young people to openly verbalize their thoughts and opinions, many Asian cultures favor silent reflection and attentive listening. This difference between cultures has direct implications for Asian students majoring in the health professions, especially those of immigrant background. Unlike courses in the physical sciences and engineering (to which the majority of Asian students gravitate), many courses in the health professions rely heavily on class discussion, student participation, and building verbal communication skills. Some Asian cultures' mores of interpersonal interaction place emphasis upon polite restraint and deference to authority (Leong & Serafica, 1995). In contrast, students in these professional courses are expected to share their views in front of the class, be an active contributor to group work and group discussions, and are often even encouraged to disagree with the instructor. Asian students who are relatively less acculturated may find it difficult to act on these expectations. As a result, instructors and peers may perceive these students as being disengaged, unintelligent, and/or "too quiet."

Furthermore, less acculturated Asians may have difficulties with the English language. Yet, as mentioned, many courses in the health professions call for active oral participation and incorporate additional written assignments in the form of essays or lengthier papers. Therefore, in addition to their tendency to be relatively "quiet" in the classroom, Asian students who have difficulty expressing themselves in English are at a further disadvantage. Descriptions of the experience of Asians in the work setting may shed some light onto the plight of the Asian college student. As noted by Leong and Gupta (2007), Asians with limited proficiency in English and who have difficulty communicating their expertise may be deemed by coworkers and supervisors to be relatively inept and unintelligent.

This perception may in turn lead to poorer job evaluations or decreased opportunity for promotion. Similarly, Asian college students may be graded unfavorably by their instructors, and passed up for leadership roles in course-related projects or in the practicum setting.

Attitudes of Asian Families

"What kind of a major is that?" "But you'll never make any money!" Asian students who express a desire to major in the health professions have to contend with their families' reactions. The reactions of family members to a college student's choice of major is an important factor because, among Asians, the family exerts a significant influence over a young person's career choice (Tang, Fouad, & Smith, 1999). First, concern about a young person's ability to obtain financial security may be the primary reason family members are reluctant to endorse a career in the health professions that tend to have lower salaries than, for example, careers in the physical or life sciences and engineering. Traditional Asian families expect grown offspring not only to be able to provide for themselves, but to support their aging parents as well (Leong & Gupta, 2007). One way to ensure that young Asians can do both comfortably is to select careers that offer lucrative salaries (Xie & Goyette, 2003). Second, many Asian immigrant parents have had first-hand experience of racism and discrimination in the workplace. Therefore, they prefer that their children select majors and careers in which other Asians have already enjoyed success (Leong & Gupta, 2007). The Asian value of *filial piety* asserts that offspring should respect and obey their parents' wishes. Therefore, many Asians are likely to heed their parents' preferences regarding their majors and careers (Leong & Gupta, 2007; Liu, 1998).

As stated previously, the careers that meet the above criteria (namely, offer both a generous income and include a high number of successful Asians) tend to be in the physical/life sciences and engineering fields. Asian students who choose to major in the health professions are therefore confronted with the challenge of persuading their parents to give their blessings. Asian students wishing to major in psychology, for example, often find themselves explaining to their parents what this field is all about. As Suinn (1988) noted, some Asian languages do not have a parallel word for *psychology*. He proposed that the presence of an Asian faculty member in that university's psychology department may be one way of "legitimizing" psychology in the eyes of a student's parents (a point we will revisit later in this chapter). This argument may be generalized to other disciplines in the health professions, such as nursing and social work.

Research on the career attitudes of Asian college students is consistent with studies on the attitudes of these students' families. In his comparison of Asian and European American college students, Leong (1991) concluded that Asian college students valued occupations that they perceived to be high in prestige and in earning potential, and that would provide them with a stable financial future. These attitudes, however, may vary among Asian students. For example, whereas Chinese American fifth and sixth graders who are less acculturated tend to place greater emphasis on earning a high salary, their more acculturated counterparts tend to value the opportunity to apply their abilities (Leong & Tata, 1990). This implies that among college-age Asians, those who are more acculturated may select majors that are consistent with their talents, and may place less emphasis on salary and status.

Stereotyping of and Racism toward Asians

Social psychologists regard stereotyping as a cognitive strategy with which people reduce the complex characteristics of a particular group of people into a simple, distilled generalization (Aronson, Wilson, & Akert, 2007). Asians have been the target of numerous stereotypes. In addition to the model minority stereotype, other stereotypic profiles include the "China Doll" Asian female and the shrewd and conniving Asian businessman. One stereotype that pertains to the Asian American college student is that of a small-built, bespectacled, bucktoothed, engineering major with a heavy accent and extraordinary mathematical prowess. It is important to examine stereotypes against Asians because non-Asians who harbor these stereotypes may interpret the behaviors of Asians in a way that serves to confirm those stereotypes. For example, when Asian men were asked to display the characteristics of a good manager in a classroom mini-assessment center, they behaved in ways that they believed a "team player" would — with courtesy, respect and humility, and by not being competitive or "selling themselves" (Cheng, 1996; cited in Leong & Gupta, 2007). Their classmates, however, interpreted those behaviors to reflect gullibility, passivity, and introversion, characteristics that are inconsistent with a good leader (but that are consistent with stereotypes of Asians). Not surprisingly, the Asian men were not selected to be team managers (in the words of one White male, "We don't want nerds. We want real managers." Cheng, 1996, p. 190). Similarly, the behaviors of Asian students in the health professions may be interpreted such that common stereotypes are reinforced. Behaviors that are meant to convey empathy, consideration for others, and mindfulness, for example, may be perceived unfavorably to reflect stereotypes such as being afraid to speak up and being a "pushover."

The consequences of stereotyping for Asian college students can be considered along with the challenges Asians face in the workplace. Leong and Chou (1994) defined occupational segregation as "the distribution of members of an ethnic group across occupations, such that they are overrepresented in some and underrepresented in others" (p. 164). With regard to Asians, occupational segregation is characterized by an overrepresentation in engineering, computer science and the physical sciences, coupled with an underrepresentation in the law, administration, arts and social sciences. A correspondingly uneven distribution can be found in the university setting, where, among the Asian population, there is a disproportionately small number of students who are health professions majors.

Occupational segregation may be attributed to occupational discrimination (Leong & Gupta, 2007). An example of occupational discrimination against Asians is the refusal to hire an Asian job applicant based on the perception that this individual is different from members of the dominant culture (Leong & Chou, 1994). Asians who have been hired may be discriminated against by being awarded lower wages, overlooked for promotions and leadership positions, and given poor performance reviews. Once again, parallels can be drawn in the university environment. Though research on discrimination against Asian students majoring in the health professions is scarce, one can speculate that these students may similarly be viewed with caution because they appear different from the typical student in their chosen major, may be evaluated unfavorably in didactic and practicum settings, and may be deprived of opportunities to develop leadership and administrative skills.

Racism creates a hostile educational environment for Asians of all ages. There is evidence that prejudice and discrimination against Asian students exists in the university setting. In a study on Asian students' perceptions of campus climate, those students who perceived a negative campus climate, characterized by experience and/or perception of racism, sexism and discrimination, were more likely to report higher levels of depression (Cress & Ikeda, 2003). This association has important implications for Asian students' psychological well-being and mental health needs.

Mental Health and Emotional Difficulties

Racism and hostility toward Asian college students are but one source of mental and emotional difficulties that these students face. Mental and emotional difficulties also arise from problematic relationships with one's family. Many Asian college students report some amount of intergenerational family conflicts (Lee, Su, & Yoshida, 2005) that are borne of differing values between immigrant parents and their children who were raised in the United States. Intergenerational conflict is exacerbated with the increasing autonomy among Asian youth as they enter college, coupled with decreasing authority and control that immigrant parents have over their offspring's day-to-day activities and choices. Such family conflict is associated with increased emotional and physical distress among Asian students (Lee et al., 2005). For Asians who defied their families' wishes by choosing to major in the health professions instead of the parent-preferred fields of engineering and the physical/life sciences, the level of intergenerational conflict may be even higher, with implications for the emotional well-being and academic success of these students.

Another potential source of emotional distress is the traditional way in which Asians make attributions regarding their successes and failures (Kawanishi, 1995; Yan & Gaier, 1994). On the one hand, Asians tend to downplay their personal contributions and talents when they are successful, attributing success instead to external factors, such as luck or the kindness of others. On the other hand, they tend to shoulder the blame for their failures, attributing failure to internal factors, such as a lack of ability. This tendency to not give oneself credit for success and to blame oneself for failure may set the stage for low self-efficacy with regard to one's academic abilities. Asians who choose majors in the health professions may be susceptible to emotional distress associated with their attribution styles. As noted earlier, Asians in such majors encounter unique barriers to academic success. These students may likely attribute their initial failure to personal characteristics ("I am not good at speaking in public," "My English skills are poor"), and downplay their own contributions to their success ("I did not really say that much in class").

FACULTY MENTORING OF ASIAN STUDENTS

"Lifting as We Climb"

Asian students majoring in the health professions need the support of their instructors. Faculty members in the health professions can play a crucial role in helping their Asian students overcome the challenges outlined thus far, and guide these students toward embarking upon successful careers in their fields. The motto of the National Association of Colored Women, "Lifting as We Climb," accurately conveys the creed of the authors of this chapter. The authors are Asian faculty members in the Psychology Department at the University of Massachusetts Lowell. The first author is of Chinese descent and was born and raised in Singapore, whereas the second author is of Vietnamese descent and was born in Viet Nam but raised in the United States since age six. Both have had personal experiences of confronting and overcoming the challenges of being Asian undergraduate and graduate students in one particular field where Asian students are scarce, and are now committed to helping minority psychology students attain academic success.

An Example of Faculty-Coordinated Mentoring of Asian College Students: Recruitment and Retention of Cambodian Americans Majoring in Psychology (RRCAMP)

In 2007, the authors, along with a third colleague, Sharon Wasco, received a small grant from the American Psychological Association to coordinate a pilot program to address the gross under-representation of Cambodian Americans in the field of psychology. This program, entitled Recruitment and Retention of Cambodian Americans Majoring in Psychology (RRCAMP), aims to increase the number of Cambodian American undergraduate students majoring in psychology and graduating with psychology degrees at University of Massachusetts Lowell. It also aims to increase the number of Cambodian American psychology undergraduates applying to graduate programs in psychology. Due to limited funding, the program serves only Cambodian American students. However, the coordinators plan to seek out additional funding to establish mentoring programs that also serve other Asian and ethnic minority students. Although RRCAMP involves a mentoring program in psychology, its framework and goals can be applied within nursing and other disciplines.

Background of Cambodian Americans in psychology and in Lowell, MA. The Cambodian American community is extremely underrepresented in the field of psychology. Although there are no published reports of the number of Cambodian American psychologists, based on the American Psychological Association membership directory, we estimate that there are, at most, a handful of psychologists who are of Cambodian descent. It is important to increase the number of Cambodian American psychologists because, given the traumatic history and acculturative stressors that Cambodian refugees have undergone, the Cambodian community faces unique psychosocial issues that need to be addressed presently and in the future.

The Southeast Asian population in Massachusetts grew almost three-fold over the past 10 years (Lotspeich, Fix, Perez-Lopez, & Ost, 2003). In the city of Lowell, population 105,167, Cambodians comprise the largest group of Asians. In fact, Lowell has the second largest Cambodian population in the United States, after Long Beach, California. Although the U. S. Census Bureau (2000) estimated that 10,000 of Lowell residents are of Cambodian descent, Cambodian American leaders in Lowell believe that this is a gross underestimate and that in fact approximately 20,000 or more Cambodian Americans live in this city. Cambodian refugees immigrated to the United States, starting in 1979, to escape the Khmer Rouge regime. Currently, members of the second generation of Cambodian Americans are now at, or approaching, college age. Therefore, this is a timely program that could increase the number of Cambodian American students majoring in psychology.

Components of RRCAMP. RRCAMP employs a three-pronged approach to assisting Cambodian American psychology majors. First, each student is matched with a willing faculty mentor on the basis of the student's interests within psychology. For example, one student expressed interest in working with children who have developmental disabilities; she was therefore assigned to a faculty member who has expertise in this area. The role of the mentor is to provide support and encouragement, involve the student in research, direct the student to professional development opportunities (such as scholarships, conferences and colloquia), and assist in identifying and solving problems that may impede the student's academic success. In order to achieve these goals, RRCAMP students meet monthly with their mentors.

Second, students serve as peer support for one another. They are scheduled to meet at least once per semester to share common experiences, discuss academic-related concerns and issues, trade study tips and strategies, and provide encouragement to one another. Although the first peer meeting is faculty-facilitated in order to get the process started for the peer group, subsequent meetings are student-facilitated and involve only the students.

Third, the program provides a small stipend ($100 per year) that the student can use toward psychology textbooks or psychology-related expenses. Students are also given a copy of the Publication Manual of the American Psychological Association to assist them in scientific writing in psychology. Although this stipend is small, it conveys an acknowledgment of the financial strain college can put on students.

Criteria for joining the RRCAMP program. All students in the program must be psychology majors. Consistent with the goals of this mentoring program, we require students to maintain at least a 3.0 grade point average. Due to the limited number of Cambodian American psychology majors at the time of this writing, students from freshman through junior year status were accepted into the program. There are currently five students enrolled in the program with plans to add 10 more students in the following academic year.

Lessons learned so far. Although the RRCAMP program is currently still in its infancy, we have gleaned a few insights thus far. All five students in the RRCAMP program chose to major in psychology because they enjoy taking psychology classes, and because their career goals are related to this discipline. These students embody many of the challenges outlined in this chapter. Except for one student who came to the United States as a refugee when she was a child, the other students were born here to refugee parents. All are first-generation college students, who, unlike their peers with college-educated parents, often need to grapple with the complexities of college life without the benefit of their parents' experiences. These students live at home with their parents, and divide their attention between school, family, household chores, and a paying job. They also have common and unique mentoring issues that are most pressing to them and their mentors. These mentoring issues span the challenges described in this chapter, from the day-to-day academic workload and performance to acculturation and intergenerational relationships.

Recommendations for Faculty Who Mentor Asian Students

For faculty, mentoring Asian students in the health professions can pose its own set of challenges. To help faculty be more effective mentors to Asian students, we offer the following recommendations:

First, establish a relationship and rapport with the Asian student that acknowledges the student's cultural emphasis on deference and respect for authority, while encouraging the student to feel safe to express issues related to being mentored, as well as cultural issues that the faculty mentor might have overlooked or misunderstood. Some gentle yet direct probing ("Is there any other way in which I can help you that I have missed?") may be needed. If the student does share an area of concern, thank the student for her or his feedback, and then seek clarification to gain complete understanding of the issue. We also recommend that the faculty mentor verbally paraphrase and summarize the student's concern to further ensure accurate understanding and to convey genuine interest.

Second, be mindful of the fact that Asians are a very diverse group who vary in terms of ethnicity, primary language spoken at home, immigration history, level of acculturation, socioeconomic status, culture and so on. There are at least 25 different ethnicities within the Asian population in the United States, with the Chinese, Filipino, Indian, Korean, and Vietnamese being among the largest sectors. Some Asian students come from families who have been living in the United States since the 1800s, while others are recent immigrants. Differing levels of acculturation and acculturative modes mean that while some Asian students adhere to traditional values, others have adopted a predominantly Western worldview. Yet others may integrate elements of both their family's culture and that of the mainstream America. Given these dimensions across which Asians can differ, faculty mentors ought not to assume that the Asian students with whom they have contact are identical in culture.

Third, contrary to the model minority stereotype that paints a picture of middle-class, highly educated Asian families living in beautiful suburban houses, many Asian college students face a myriad of challenges, such as low household income, living in unsafe neighborhoods, immigration status, and others' limited understanding of Asian cultures. Together, these problems can have a cumulative impact on the students' academic performance. When confronted with a host of students' concerns, well-intentioned faculty members can easily begin to feel overwhelmed along with the students they are trying to help. Therefore, we recommend that, if an Asian student chooses to confide her or his problems, the faculty member ought to lend an empathetic ear while adopting a problem-solving approach. How are these problems affecting the student's academic performance, both in the short run and in the long run? Can the student's overall academic objectives be broken down into smaller, more attainable, and more immediate goals? What are some feasible and practical strategies the student can adopt in order to work around personal or familial issues? It is also important to acknowledge and accept that there are limits to what a faculty mentor can do, and that lending an empathetic listening ear can in itself be a significant comfort. Whenever needed, faculty mentors should refer their students to appropriate services or organizations on campus or in the community that are in a better position to provide the necessary information or assistance.

Fourth, encourage Asian students to pursue resources established specifically for Asians, or those that target ethnic minorities in general. The model minority myth fuels the misconception that Asians are always successful in their academic endeavors. Therefore, the needs of those who do struggle with academic difficulties are overlooked, and these struggling students are not directed to appropriate resources and interventions (Leong & Gupta, 2007). As noted by Suinn (1988), however, persuading Asian students to apply for such resources may be difficult because Asian students may be reluctant to identify themselves as "ethnic minorities" due to the negative connotations the term carries. Faculty mentors ought to take note of students' apprehensions and encourage open discussion of these and other reservations.

Fifth, be aware that Asian students may have unmet mental health needs. Mental health needs among Asians deserve careful and in-depth attention. Asian women may be particularly vulnerable to emotional distress. Asian American studies scholar, Eliza Noh (2007), pointed out that suicide is a prevalent problem among Asian women, and is in fact the second highest cause of death among Asian women between the ages of 15 and 24, an age range in which most college students fall. The cumulative impact of lifelong, and at times subtle, racism and sexism can take its toll on young Asian women. Unfortunately, stereotypic perceptions of Asians may lead to their faculty mentors underdetecting mental health needs. Research on younger Asians may shed light on this matter. For example, internalizing behaviors (such as being introverted and withdrawn) among children may be indicators of depression or anxiety. Yet, teachers of children in kindergarten through 12th grade tend to perceive such behaviors among Asian students as being normal (Chang & Demyan, 2007). Similarly, university faculty and staff may fail to recognize tell-tale signs of emotional distress among Asian college students. This is of concern because Asian college students may experience more severe symptoms of depression than do students of other ethnic groups (Cress & Ikeda, 2003). The attitude of Asians seeking mental health services vary according to their level of acculturation (Atkinson & Gim, 1989). Asians may be unwilling to seek out mental health services because in many Asian cultures, it is stigmatizing to acknowledge that one needs professional psychological services. In addition, traditional Asian culture frowns upon confiding in strangers about personal problems (Noh, 2007). We recommend that faculty mentors be familiar with the mental health services available at the university or in the community, and use sensitivity when speaking to Asian students about these resources.

Finally, faculty mentors ought to advocate for an increased number of ethnic minority faculty members in their department. For Asian students majoring in disciplines that are not generally popular within their communities, having Asian faculty members in their major department serves as "living proof" that Asians can indeed succeed in that discipline, and validates that discipline in the eyes of students' families (Suinn, 1988). The presence of non-Asian ethnic minority faculty members can also be beneficial as these faculty members can be positive role models that reduce the negative connotation of the classification of "ethnic minority."

REFERENCES

Aronson, E., Wilson, T. D., & Akert, R. M. (2007). *Social psychology* (6th ed.). Upper Saddle River, NJ: Prentice Hall.

Atkinson, D. R., & Gim, R. H. (1989). Asian-American cultural identity and attitudes toward mental health services. *Journal of Counseling Psychology, 36,* 209-212.

Atkinson, D. R., Morten, G., & Sue, D. W. (1997). *Counseling American minorities* (5th ed.). New York: McGraw-Hill.

Berry, J. W. (2003). Conceptual approaches to acculturation. In K. M. Chun, P. B. Organista, & G. Marin (Eds.), *Acculturation: Advances in theory, measurement, and applied research* (pp. 17-37). Washington, DC: American Psychological Association.

Chang, D. F., & Demyan, A. (2007). Teachers' stereotypes of Asian, Black, and White students. *School Psychology Quarterly, 22,* 91-114.

Cheng, C. (1996). "We choose not to compete": The "merit" discourse in the selection process, and Asian and Asian American men and their masculinity. In C. Cheng (Ed.), *Masculinities in organizations* (pp. 177-200). Thousand Oaks, CA: Sage.

Cress, C. M., & Ikeda, E. K. (2003). Distress under duress: The relationship between campus climate and depression in Asian American college students. *NASPA Journal, 40,* 74-97.

Dinh, K. T., & Nguyen, H. H. (2006). The effects of acculturative variables on Asian American parent-child relationships. *Journal of Social and Personal Relationships, 23,* 407-426.

Dinh, K. T., Weinstein, T. L., Kim, S. Y., & Ho, I. K. (2008). Acculturative and psychosocial predictors of academic-related outcomes among Cambodian American high school students. *Journal of Southeast Asian American Education & Advancement, 3,1-23.*

Higher Education Research Institute (2007, October). HERI research brief "Beyond myths: The growth and diversity of Asian American college freshmen, 1971-2005." *Higher Education Research Institute.* [Online]. Available: http://www.gseis.ucla.edu/heri/PDFs/pubs/briefs/AsianTrendsResearchBrief.pdf.

Kawanishi, Y. (1995). The effects of culture on beliefs about stress and coping: Causal attribution of Anglo-Americans and Japanese persons. *Journal of Contemporary Psychotherapy, 25,* 49-60.

Lee, R. M., Su, J., & Yoshida, E. (2005). Coping with intergenerational family conflict among Asian American college students. _Journal of Counseling Psychology,_ 52, 389-399.

Leong, F. T. L. (1991). Career development attributes and occupational values of Asian American and White American college students. _Career Development Quarterly,_ 29, 221-230.

Leong, F. T. L., & Chou, E. L. (1994). The role of ethnic identity and acculturation in the vocational behavior of Asian Americans: An integrative review. _Journal of Vocational Behavior,_ 44, 155-172.

Leong, F. T. L., & Gupta, A. (2007). Career development and vocational behaviors of Asian Americans. In F. T. L. Leong, A. G. Inman, & A. Ebreo (Eds.), _Handbook of Asian American psychology_ (pp. 159-187). Thousand Oaks, CA: Sage.

Leong, F. T. L., & Serafica, F. (1995). Career development of Asian Americans: A research area in need of a good theory. In F. T. L. Leong (Ed.), _Career development and vocational behavior of racial and ethnic minorities_ (pp. 67-102). Mahwah, NJ: Lawrence Erlbaum.

Leong, F. T. L., & Tata, S. P. (1990). Sex and acculturation differences in occupational values among Chinese-American children. _Journal of Counseling Psychology,_ 37, 208-212.

Liu, R. W. (1998). Educational and career expectations of Chinese-American college students. _Journal of College Student Development,_ 39, 577-588.

Lotspeich, K., Fix, M., Perez-Lopez, D., & Ost, J. (2003, October). A profile of the foreign-born in Lowell, Massachusetts. _The Urban Institute._ [Online]. Available: http://www.urban.org/url.cfm?ID=410918.

Noh, E. (2007). Asian American women and suicide: Problems of responsibility and healing. _Women & Therapy,_ 30, 87-107.

Suinn, R. M. (1988). Asian Americans and psychology. In P. J. Woods (Ed.), _Is psychology for them? A guide to undergraduate advising_ (pp. 173-177). Washington, DC: American Psychological Association.

Tang, M., Fouad, N. A., & Smith, P. L. (1999). Asian Americans' career choices: A path model to examine factors influencing their career choices. _Journal of Vocational Behavior,_ 54, 142-157.

Tseng, V., Chao, R. K., & Padmawidjaja, I. A. (2007). Asian Americans' educational experiences. In F. T. L. Leong, A. G. Inman, & A. Ebreo (Eds.), Handbook of Asian American psychology (pp. 105-123). Thousand Oaks, CA: Sage.

U.S. Census Bureau. (2000). American Fact Finder. [Online]. Available: http://factfinder.census.gov.

Xie, Y., & Goyette, K. (2003). Social mobility and the educational choices of Asian Americans. Social Science Research, 32, 467-498.

Yan, W., & Gaier, E. L. (1994). Causal attributions for college success and failure: An Asian American comparison. Journal of Cross-Cultural Psychology, 25, 146-158.

CHAPTER 5
DIVERSITY RESEARCH INITIATIVES:
REFLECTION AND THOUGHTS[1]

Lin Zhan, PhD, RN, FAAN

"I am thankful for this eye-opening experience. It has
made me see what students with an ethnic background
go through on a daily basis. I have come to the conclusion
that you can't teach cultural awareness in a book. It is all
rooted in lived experiences."
—An undergraduate student

"I want to be a nurse. I had a lot of working experience as
an accountant. When I worked in a doctor's office, I felt
that being a nurse I could help others in sickness. I was
hurt when I was told that nursing was not for me."
— A Vietnamese student[2]

These voices were expressed by members of a team of undergraduate nursing students who were involved in the Diversity Research Initiative project at one urban public university[3]. This study aimed at understanding learning experience and needs of Asian American students in the College of Nursing. The research process and experience transformed nursing students and faculty — the researcher and the researched — from being strangers to becoming members of a university-wide research community, from being emotionally detached to being emotionally engaged in observed phenomena, from teacher-centered pedagogy to student-centered learning, and from being involved in a short-term project to calling for embracing diversity in all of nursing education.

The Diversity Research Initiative (DRI) team included two nursing faculty members and four nursing students (one graduate and three undergraduate). Using the University of Massachusetts Boston as a site of inquiry, the DRI team investigated the learning needs and experiences of Asian American students in the College of Nursing (CN)[4]. The impetus of understanding learning needs in Asian American students came from challenges that nursing education is facing. Nursing education in general is charged with preparing graduates who are professionally competent and ethnically representative. Of nearly 3 million nurses nationwide, only about 10% come from ethnically diverse backgrounds; and in New England, this percentage is even less. To meet the needs of rapidly increasing diverse populations locally and nationally, health care organizations are calling for increasingly diverse racial and ethnic representation in the health care workforce and for preparing health practitioners capable of rendering culturally competent care.

BACKGROUND

Approximately 39% of the students in the College of Nursing and Health Sciences are ethnic minorities. However, Asian American students' retention in nursing is problematic, and tension often exists as faculty attempt to assimilate nursing students into the profession while students struggle to be successful. Anecdotally, Asian American students reported feeling intimidated, ignored, misunderstood, and singled out for criticism. Some of them indicated that they were perceived as having "learning problems"; sadly, little information is provided regarding specific learning needs and experiences of Asian American students in nursing, or the factors that contribute to the retention "problem" and "poor academic performance." Is it because English is their second language? Do they have to assimilate into the "dominant culture" in order to succeed in the nursing program? Is diversity seen as a barrier to students' learning and success? Bearing these questions in mind, we proposed a qualitative study that used an in-depth interview technique to explore the learning experiences and needs of Asian American students in the college of nursing.

Sample

Purposive sampling was used to recruit subjects for this study. Criteria for sample inclusion were nursing students who were (1) self-identified as Asian or Asian American and (2) currently enrolled in the nursing program. Sample recruitment started with obtaining the list of Asian American students from the College's Student Office. Each Asian student on this list (N=40) was contacted via a telephone call. The initial telephone contact began with team members' introduction, information about themselves, the purpose of the study, the significance of participation, and the length and site of the interviewing. Potential subjects were told that if they participated they would join a group of other Asian American students to discuss their learning experiences, viewpoints, and perspectives. They would be ensured privacy and confidentiality; specifically, their names would not be identified in any form of research publication or information dissemination. Their participation would be strictly voluntary and they could withdraw from the study at any time, as they chose.

After obtaining a verbal consent, student researchers mailed all participants a simple demographic survey, a consent form, and a tentative interview schedule. A total of eighteen Asian American students (45% of the total population) participated in the study[5]. Characteristics of the sample were: women, 89%; living in the United States for more than five years, 94%; completion of high school education in the United States, 72%; junior level nursing students, 89%; speaking English as a second language, 99%; and holding a part-time job while attending the school, 27%. Ethnically, participants in this study comprised Chinese (N=3), Korean (N=1), and Vietnamese (N=14).

A Research Community

Two faculty members (including the author) in the DRI team recruited four nursing students representative of a mix of academic levels and racial backgrounds (two Asian Americans and two Caucasians). Students were offered 3 credits for their participation in this project. To prepare student researchers for undertaking this project, we provided a course syllabus that outlined the project goal, a tentative time line for the completion of the project, suggested readings, and the research proposal. Within the context of the research goal, we worked with these four students to formulate four major research questions:

1. How have Asian American students perceived their educational experiences in the CN?

2. What are their learning needs?

3. What are barriers to and facilitators of their learning?

4. What suggestions do they have for the improvement of their educational experience?

Immediately, we encountered challenges: how to build an effective research team, to form a research community, and to achieve research goals in a one-semester time frame. At the beginning, the four students involved in the project had not known each other, and few of them knew the faculty. In a sense, we came as strangers. Most of the students joined the group thinking this would be "just another course" to earn three credits, especially the two undergraduate students, who needed three credits to graduate that semester. We began our group process with team building, starting with students and faculty learning about each other, addressing questions raised by the group, clarifying confusion, and outlining the action plan for conducting the project. We held a research seminar weekly, either within our team or joining the university-wide research teams, where we discussed the rationale and significance for studying the learning needs of Asian American students in the CN, solicited feedback from the student researchers in terms of their views and ideas on this proposal, assessed students' research skills and their basic understanding of diversity, and emphasized the necessity of team effort and time management for the completion of this project. After the initial assessment, we found that even though all students on the project team had taken the research course, only one student had some experience in conducting qualitative and quantitative research. We all had some conception of diversity. However, none of us had conducted diversity research using our own university as a site of inquiry.

To begin with, we used racial and ethnic differences as a cultural learning basis for both student researchers and the students who were being researched. Secondly, we identified each person's skills and differences on the project team. Identification of skills and wisdom of the group members initiated the delegation of research responsibilities and tasks. Delegating was based on a skill-match and each team member was given authority to make decisions related to her/his area of responsibility. The graduate student, for example, was a clinical manager and therefore was assigned to be a leader in organizing and coordinating the project process. Another student with previous research experience was assigned to be a group leader developing the research-related questions. Delegation gave student researchers a sense of autonomy, responsibility, and accountability. We discussed the group process/stages, which helped students understand certain group behaviors, dynamics, differences, conflicts, and purposes. Student researcher pairs — one Asian and one Caucasian — were created, a strategy that set the stage for learning from each other and accepting differences. This approach also made it easier to establish rapport between the researcher and the researched, since when an Asian researcher interviewed Asian students, those being researched felt less intimidated. Finally, each group member was exposed to the basic concept of group membership and responsibility — individually and collectively — and negotiated interviewing schedules. In this stage, we were directive in order to keep the group focused while encouraging different views, opinions, concerns, and thoughts. This approach helped group members gain a sense of purpose and responsibility. To manage time effectively, the group made a master plan with a time frame for undertaking the DRI project.

As students felt more comfortable with each another, roles became more explicit; faculty became less directive, allowing students to openly exchange ideas, concerns, creations, and debates. Using both a "hands-off" and "situational" approach, we seemed to dance between giving directions/instructions and participating in the group process. Participation is more than the formal sharing of ideas and decisions. Faculty and student cooperation and dialogue in this process helped faculty learn from students, and vice versa. When group conflicts surfaced, the root of the problem was identified, and faculty worked with the group to manage conflicts. When students were uncertain about research methodology, teaching took place.

Once, in the group seminar, anxiety was generated and tension was felt among some group members when discussing qualitative research methods. Lack of certain skills and knowledge in conducting qualitative research seemed to contribute to such anxiety. Often, uncertainty creates anxiety, and minimizing anxiety requires new skills. Diversity inquiry requires researchers to have appropriate skills to communicate with people in the culture. To help the students, we detailed critical skills of qualitative research inquiry, such as how to "cue-in" to what participants would be talking about relative to the topic under discussion, what stages to go through in focus-group interviewing, how to create a climate in which the researched could express their views freely and comfortably, and how to minimize responsive bias in the interview process. To reinforce students' learning, the entire project team planned a rehearsal prior to the first focus group interview. During the rehearsal, students performed role-playing, some acting as interviewees while others acted as interviewers and observers. At the end of the rehearsal, we critiqued the process. This exercise familiarized students with critical skills in qualitative inquiry: establishing rapport, being instrumental, being a moderator, asking probing questions, interacting with the participants verbally and nonverbally, and observing the group dynamics.

Another strategy to minimize students' anxiety was to reinforce their strengths in research and ensure our support. Each student had at least one critical skill or strength to offer the project, which translated into the role of an organizer (conducting the group seminars), an interviewer (conducting interviews), a coordinator (communicating with group members and consolidating each member's feedback), and a literature searcher. Clear roles and expectations of group members affected communication and execution of our research plans, including sample recruitment, data collection and data analysis. Once it was clear that everyone on the team had something important to contribute, the group became more cohesive. This was further enhanced through a group problem-solving technique. When one student researcher had difficulty recruiting the sample by telephone, for example, the entire group — faculty and students — intervened and identified the problem, which was partly due to how the telephone message was conveyed. The group decided that rather than asking Asian American students to come to us for this study — a question that focuses on the researcher, we would say the following to focus on those being researched: "We would like to hear from you about your learning needs and experiences. Your perspectives will help the faculty provide better education for you and for students like you." The strategy worked, and the sample recruitment was successful. As the research proceeded, the group was increasingly characterized by commitment and cooperation. The faculty role was then to be mentors and facilitators, while students were in charge of the research process. Yet, as data emerged, we faced another challenge: that is, how to deepen our understanding of diversity issues.

The university-wide DRI seminars[6] and our project group seminars opened a window of opportunity for members of the DRI cohort to share its struggles, either conceptually or methodologically. These seminars enabled us to learn from one another, share our struggles and frustrations, and work together. Of equal significance, students and faculty used seminars as a platform for dialoguing and debating ideas and thoughts, and for deepening our understanding of diversity issues and their implications in higher education. At one of the DRI cohort seminars, a faculty researcher raised a critical question about "Diversity for what?", which made our project group think and rethink how to link collected data to the meaning of diversity.

On another occasion, our group presented initial data analysis to the DRI cohort. One analysis from interview data was that "Asian American students were not assertive." Immediately, this analysis generated heated discussions in the DRI cohort. Critical questions were then raised: "Whose concept of assertiveness, anyway?" "Is assertiveness valued in Asian cultures?" One researcher from another DRI group said: "If Asian students can resist harsh and discriminatory treatments, they are assertive." What a powerful statement that was! It was the hidden curriculum — ideas, opinions, debates, discussions, dialogues relating to concepts and meanings of diversity — that enhanced the ability of students and faculty to blend knowledge of research with humanity, with the art of searching, with critical thinking, with values underlying practice, and with varying social and cultural contexts. Significantly, in the process of researching, human connections were made and a research community was formed.

One student researcher described this experience in this way:

We became friends during and after the research. By the end of the semester, we felt we were so attached to each other by a special bond that we wanted to get together just to chat and relive the wonderful experiences we had. We wished we could stay and learn together again sometime in the future. We felt that we established a shared understanding and appreciation of human diversity by working and learning together during that project. We felt we grew and became stronger with the project, and we felt that we're members of the university-wide diversity community.

STUDENT-CENTERED INQUIRY

The DRI provided a student-centered learning experience. Often students learn research theory in the classroom, where they are evaluated in terms of making statistical inferences for given samples or using a step-wise, linear regression model to analyze a myriad of variables. The DRI experience de-centered the faculty and allowed students to be the center of learning. Not only did students conduct research, but they also experienced searching and researching as a gestalt, a whole, a pattern of the interrelated phenomena: Asian American students' learning experiences and educational environment, faculty perspectives on teaching diversity courses, the impact on White students taking courses on African experience/Black studies, debates around diversity in higher education and its relationship to students' learning, and meanings of diversity. These interrelated phenomena created a panorama in which students found a way to learn and to criticize what had been learned. In such learning processes, we were no longer focusing on the content, and the students were no longer needing to "do battle" with the content. Rather, we transformed the dogma of the content for either legitimate teaching or legitimate evaluation. The students invested themselves in learning and relating diversity to their realities. Reflecting on learning, student researchers noted, "I never liked research before. This experience really changed me. Research information was powerful and the research process itself was educational...I cannot believe that I was a part of that..." and "Before, I just thought to finish my three credit requirements, just another independent study. The research experience made me involved, engaged, and motivated to get the bottom of the problem. It was such a high note before my graduation."

Student-centered learning equalizes the traditionally hierarchical power of the faculty-student dynamic. In the DRI inquiry, the faculty and students worked together to advance ideas and truly understand the concept of diversity; each viewed the other as a social-cultural being embedded in interdependencies. The faculty-student relationship was then shifted to where faculty and students became co-learners, and teaching, learning, and evaluation coexisted. Students may not be able to memorize some desired answers of which method is legitimate, which measure is reliable and valid, and what corrected statistical numbers are. They did, however, catch a glimpse of other valuable human experiences and developed insights and awareness that transported them beyond simple answers to patterns in and meanings of research data. Perhaps the DRI process served as an avenue for personal growth and enlightenment, which may be just as valuable to society, to the profession, and/or to the learner.

Student researchers noted:

This experience made me more open to see realities. I found that I became more sensitive to other students' needs. I think that anyone who can speak another language is smart enough. How can we judge them [Asian students, the researched] because they have heavy accented English? It is unfair.

I am thankful for this eye-opening experience. It has made me see what students with an ethnic background go through on a daily basis. I have come to the conclusion that you can't teach cultural awareness in a book. It is all rooted in lived experiences.

"Awakening" — The Route to Experiencing Human Emotion

The DRI research project took the team members on a journey of self-reflection. Unlike the rigorous methodological approaches to empirical inquiry that often preclude interpretations of the forces that shape both the researchers and the researched, the qualitative approach used for the project led to the exploration of human phenomena and lived experiences. Researchers tend to hide themselves under a veil of neutrality or objectivity, carrying no voice, body, race, class or gender, and rarely making connection to those being researched. But to unveil the "truth" of human existence and experience, researchers must realize that what we see is not what we see but what we perceive, and the meanings of any experience will depend on the interpretation and definitions of that experience. As well, researchers cannot help but bring their human dimensions into the research processes, which disproves the notion of total objectivity in research. The complexity of human dimensions presents a special challenge to researchers when they interpret and reflect on how personal values influence those interpretations.

As noted previously, the meaning given to "assertiveness" in the group's initial analysis made all of us mindful of our own subjectivity and bias. On one Sunday, our group spent more than seven hours reexamining our own perceptions, values, biases and meanings, and how these perceptions influenced the way we analyzed data. This process shed light on how we ought to view raw data through relatively colored lenses. During the discussion, students asked themselves two major questions: 1) are we imposing our own values on the data? and 2) are we imposing the dominant culture's stereotype on the data? If so, all data then needed to be reexamined in the cultural and social context of the researched. In this hours-long meeting, we shared many of own experiences and limitations. We began to hear "voices" from the researched, Asian American students, feel their pain and suffering, and find meanings related to their learning experience in nursing. We realized that the most critical ethical obligation of qualitative research is to describe the experience of the researched as well as the researcher in the most faithful way possible.

Student researchers expressed such insight in many ways:

> As I transcribed the data, I heard voices of Asian American students; I felt so sad, depressed, and very heavy....

> I am an Asian American student and may go through the same painful experience. I felt depressed.

> How could Asian American students be treated that way in the College of Nursing? I felt their pain, so painful.

> This is the very first time I realized what students of color went through in the educational process; the first time I heard their often silenced voices... so powerful, so emotional, I wanted to cry....

> It is so easy to fall into one's own schema of thinking. When we initially analyzed data, we used our own colored lens to view data; after examining our own stereotyping and biases, we saw these data in different ways. We tried to separate our own biases from the factual data...that is what I called transformation, because I changed, and I view things differently now, not just from in my own world.

This was a moment of awakening as we realized that for diversity research, both the researcher and the researched share, inescapably, the same pervasive context: the human world. In that moment, we took a journey close to real experiences of our own humanity and emotions and began to see significance constituted through the web of languages, symbols, and institutions. In this seven-hours-long meeting, the group generated a list of key ideas, words, phrases, and actual quotes reflective of respondents' viewpoints (coding), formulated and clustered common threads in the data (recoding), identified recurrent words, phrases and themes (theme finding), and documented exceptions (variations). Furthermore, the group analyzed meanings attached to respondents' viewpoints in the ethno-cultural context. Parallel with interview data analysis, the group of students analyzed survey questionnaires that provided additional contextual information for the interview data.

FINDINGS: LEARNING NEEDS OF ASIAN STUDENTS

Three themes emerged from the data analysis of this qualitative study that were closer to the realities of Asian American students' experiences in the College of Nursing. These themes are increasing cultural sensitivity, improving teaching, and interacting encouragingly. Asian American students shared their experiences as being a) discouraged to become a nurse; b) blamed for their accented English; c) ignored when they sought help in learning; and d) judged unfairly in social and academic settings. What Asian American students in the CN called for is to have a conducive educational environment where their racial and cultural differences are understood and respected, their learning styles are considered, their interaction with the faculty is encouraged, their accented English is accepted, and their learning needs are met.

In the final DRI conference, our team's student researchers presented our study. One student researcher was quoting Asian students' narratives from the interview:

One day, my friend and I went to see a professor for help. We both failed the first exam. While I was waiting outside, the professor spoke very loud and I overheard she said to my friend "you have to withdraw from this course." I was so frightened. I knew that the professor would say the same thing to me. Immediately, I went to the registrar and withdrew myself from this course.

The presenter was in tears, but continued to quote another Asian student, saying:

I want to be a nurse. I had a lot of working experience as an accountant. When I worked in a doctor's office, I felt that being a nurse I could help others in sickness. I was hurt when I was told that nursing was not for me.

Another presenter went on:

I went to see my professor to clarify some confused concepts. My professor told me that she did not have time for meeting with me. I was refused not once, but three times. I gave up seeing her since then.

In a clinical setting, the clinical instructor told me that I had poor communication skills. I asked her why, and she replied, "You should speak like a New Englander." My patient understood me even though I speak English with accent. I felt so discouraged and was afraid of going to clinical.

The presenter stopped and could not continue. She was in tears. In this moment, the entire conference room was quiet, as if we had been "suffocated." Many were in tears, experiencing sadness, shock and anger; we were upset, touched, and outraged. At this moment, cognitive consciousness reached the level of being aware of what had gone wrong in the CN. At this moment, much attention was given to human experiences. Un-reflected consciousness, through self-reflections, emancipated cognitive interests in searching for the meaning of diversity. The author notes, "I was in tears...no words could describe how I felt, nor had I expected the data to have such a powerful impact on me." There was a long moment of silence. I saw tears in the eyes of a roomful of people. In the process of cognitive and emotional uncovering, we created new connections, identified new meanings, and searched new possibilities — all calling for changes, changes that would improve nursing education and embrace diversity and humanity.

Diversity research is more than just content. It also relives human existence and experiences. It reveals the relationship between individuals and their worlds; the relationship between what was and what can be. It uncovers the complexity of real connections between seemingly unrelated phenomena. Regardless of what is debated in higher education in terms of which realities are legitimized and which are not, which books to read, what information to process and use, what skills to perfect, what norms to follow, which culture to socialize, and what rules to execute, if we truly want to prepare for the emerging realities of our students, as we claim, we must create an environment where students and faculty embrace human diversity and develop deep, intimate relationships with one another.

One student researcher reflected on her DRI experience in this way:

> These experiences we gathered through our interviews were so true to this population that we researchers, as students ourselves, could almost experience the same pain as they did. The best part of this research effort was to show how the topic of diversity could relate to human experience and sufferings; therefore, awaken people from insensitivity. Many of us actually were experiencing a movement of awakening from our own cultural insensitivity. We took many things around us for granted. Once we heard those stories by the students, we were shocked and saddened, not just because we heard they're treated badly, but also because we were not aware of these things happening in front of our eyes. We felt sorry, not because this kind of things had happened, but because, how could we allow this kind of things to happen? It was the insensitivity that was the answer. I believe many of us cried or felt like crying for this reason. What happened should not happen. We all have the liability for not preventing it from happening.

Diversity Imperative

What have we learned from the DRI experience? Surely, we gained insight about the learning experiences of Asian American students in the CN and identified some of their learning needs. We listened to their suggestions and heard their voices. We felt their pain and the suffering of being prejudiced against, ignored, and discouraged. We connected ourselves to their experiences.

The DRI experience goes well beyond these things we have learned, however. We echo Asian American students' voices every time we disseminate the findings of our study. Our DRI team presented the project at the Fourth Annual Conference on Undergraduate Research, Scholarly, Creative, and Public Service Activities, sponsored by the Massachusetts Public System of Higher Education. The DRI report also was disseminated to all faculty members in the CN, after which a faculty retreat was held, providing an opportunity for the faculty to respond to the DRI report. In the retreat, faculty members examined the issues and concerns; shared their interactions with these and other ethno-cultural students; shared pedagogical strategies they found successful in facilitating ethnic students' learning; disclosed their own insensitivity and limitations. Some remained silent. In the face of the variety of human responses to diversity issues, two themes emerged in the faculty retreat: a sense of awareness and a sense of urgency for individual and/or institutional change.

What we learned in the DRI experience was more than how a group worked as a team, how research was conducted, how information was disseminated, and how things were done. We learned what diversity means. To search for the meaning of diversity, we must ask ourselves about the goal of the DRI and the nature of our ethical obligations. In the past, voices of Asian American students in the CN had often been ignored or silenced. The DRI project provided a powerful opportunity for these students to share their experiences, stories, feelings, worries, wishes, and dreams. This in itself is a notable achievement! Voices from Asian American students help us recognize the diversity of human dimensions, characteristics, experiences, needs, and barriers. As researchers, we have ethical obligations not only to describe and disseminate research findings faithfully, but also to unfreeze the past or "undo," in order to bring about change.

Students' voices from diversity research have important implications for nursing education. The danger in assessing and responding to any ethnic group is that of stereotyping and using such stereotyping to quickly judge and generalize cultural differences and human experiences. Social interaction between faculty and students is a continuous process by which one person communicates with another through written or oral language, gestures, facial expressions, body language, and other symbols. It also is a process by which culture is transmitted and preserved. Cultural differences as well as behaviors have a significant impact on the way we teach and the way our students learn. It is essential for faculty to assess not only students' cultural differences in learning, but also our own values and cultural perspectives, and how these values and perspectives impact our teaching and our interactions with students.

To create a conducive educational environment involves more than avoiding prejudicial statements or ethnocentric attitudes. It also requires faculty to step out of our own "comfort zone" and learn about other cultures and ethno-cultural contexts, so that we can better understand students' affects, cognitive performance, and learning styles. It is unacceptable to ignore students' requests for help. We need to reach out to students who otherwise are neglected and, even worse, discriminated against. A conducive educational environment goes beyond "cultural sensitivity." It requires multicultural and diversity education, particularly if education is to be personally meaningful, socially relevant, culturally accurate, pedagogically sound, and politically responsible. A conducive educational environment means that students must be empowered to share their diversity, to respect their own cultures, and to be a part of the educational community.

There have been growing numbers of immigrant students from Asian and other countries whose first language is not English and whose home cultures are not based on a Eurocentric model. Within the framework of the Eurocentric model, speaking English with an accent is often viewed as a major "deficit" of the students. Yet, the DRI study found that it is not language per se but the cultural insensitivity in the educational environment that becomes an obstacle to student learning. In nursing education, Asian American students are often perceived as passive learners in the classroom. Yet, our research findings indicated that they could be quite verbal and articulate if an encouraging environment and a place where they feel they "belong" was provided. They could think critically if their cultural differences were understood and their hard work was appreciated. Their articulateness, sensitivity, desire for learning, active participation in the DRI study, and insightful suggestions for the improvement of teaching are the best testimony for refuting the notion of "silent, deficient, and passive Asian learners."

Asian American students in this study reported that some clinical instructors had no patience with them and some blamed them for their accent in clinical settings where practice is based on the standpoint of only one cultural or racial group of the clients — white, and middle-class. Yet, as Asian American students reach out to diverse communities, their racial identity, cultural knowledge, and bilingual skills uniquely qualify them to care for the underserved or those who have no access to health services. Imagine a woman who only speaks Vietnamese needing emergency care. Which nurse would be more likely to provide timely and effective care: the monolingual English speaker or the bilingual Vietnamese speaker who persisted, despite being told that she/he could not become a nurse? Effective care can no longer come in a single form to fit the needs of a diverse society. Inattention to cultural diversity is no longer merely morally negligent; it is also professionally and socially irresponsible.

Students' voices in the DRI raised our social consciousness. In nursing education, ethno-culturally different students often encounter many barriers. They are expected to assimilate into the "dominant culture," but when they do this they may lose the ability to provide culturally competent care to diverse populations and communities. Many nursing textbooks make numerous stereotypical comments about nondominant ethno-cultural groups. This must stop, as students should not be dissected, analyzed, and folded into the "dominant" ideal of what it is to be a nurse. If teachers present knowledge in a way that reflects values of the "dominant culture," students from non-dominant cultures who have not been exposed to or do not value the dominant culture, may feel inferior, rejected, out of place, or perhaps, hostile. Assimilation of one culture into another disconnects the critical relationship between individuals and their worlds, worlds that are full of meanings, significance, and realities. Such disconnections make students feel that they do not belong in or to the educational institution, as noted by those researched: *"I feel neglected by professors because they are from a different culture." "Being a minority made me feel inferior to others."* Such disconnection disables our fundamental tenets of education: a sense of agency, a sense of responsibility and accountability, and a sense of connection (Moccia, 1989). Education is the process that Greene (1988) describes in *The Dialectic of Freedom:*

> *It is through and by means of education many of us believe that individuals can be provoked to reach beyond themselves into their intersubjective space. It is through and by means of education that they may become empowered to think about what they are doing, to become mindful, to share meanings, to conceptualize, to make varied sense of their lived worlds. (p.12)*

The second danger that nursing students encounter lies in nursing education itself. Nursing has already been made painfully aware that its education, being primarily education for women, has suffered from the social, historical, and political forces against women in society. Nursing education has been oppressed due to the nurse-equals-woman-equals-nurse phenomenon. Perpetuated oppressions directly impact nursing education and, even worse, there is a tendency for oppressed groups to oppress others, as was made evident by imposing a psychological damage to Asian American students, who were told: "Nursing is not for you." Whose right is it to make such a judgment? If we allow perpetuated oppression, we thereby socialize students into a system of oppression and control, which is often perpetuated to maintain the status quo. As nursing calls for increasing ethnic variety within its ranks, so must it integrate cultural competency into its educational experience (Zhan, 1996, 2001). What researchers and the researched called for in the DRI inquiry was an approach to education and practice that frees human potential and liberates human thinking; that allows one to develop rational and moral capacities as well as emotional, expressive, intuitive, esthetic, and personal capacities; that brings one's full sense of self to bear with one's life work — in this case, caring for those with health needs.

The purpose of higher education for nurses is not only to align nursing with other academic fields, improve its research and theory base, or advance it as a profession. It also is to blend humanities and liberal arts with the science of nursing. Nursing is concerned with human responses to health and illness, and human responses are diverse, and culturally and socially embedded. Nursing curricula, however, are primarily based on a model of behavioral objectives, which do not allow seeking for meanings, for the intangibles of caring, for the depth of human existence and experience (Bevis & Watson, 1989) and for political sophistication. The DRI experience described here offered an opportunity for students to blend diversity knowledge with science, with multiple ways of knowing, with individual reflections and emotions, and with understanding the relationship between individuals and their worlds. To truly endorse nursing's philosophical underpinning — humanity — diversity has to be embraced within the core of the nursing curriculum. Existing ideologies of domination and oppression must be examined critically to develop vital consciousness among nurse educators, administrators, and students (Zhan & Cloutterbuck, 1997).

One year after the DRI project, I received a note from one student researcher:

> After I graduated from nursing school, I started working at a world-renowned hospital in Boston, Massachusetts. In my first week of work I had five Spanish-speaking patients. It was very difficult communicating with these people. I relied on their family members and the unit assistant to translate to me. This is the first time I became aware that I had a handicap. The following week I overheard a physician ask his Russian patient "Why don't you speak English?" This angered/infuriated me.... My professional goal is to become a transcultural nurse. As a professional nurse it is my responsibility to meet the needs of patients from diverse backgrounds.

What nursing education could learn from the DRI experience is to revisit nursing as a human science; to practice nursing with humanity and caring; to integrate nursing's unique contributions, ethics, epistemology, and esthetics into its education; to use a student-centered paradigm; and to embrace diversity. As we search for the meaning of diversity, we have much to learn from the Asian American students in this project, who bravely shared their educational experiences, their feelings, and their insights. Most importantly, they want to be encouraged to hold on to their dreams, dreams that have been built through human suffering and painful life journeys. As one student said: *"...I came to the United States by boat, with nothing...I started to work in a community as a volunteer. I began to realize that my dream is to help people in sickness. I want to be a nurse."*

Nurse educators are charged to prepare future nurse leaders, individuals who bear the responsibility of ensuring that all people are cared for, health is restored, hopes are fulfilled, visions are realized, futures are constructed, and dreams are built! We ourselves, then, must model humanity, caring, and civil liberty in the educational process. We have a unique societal mission: to care for the vulnerable, many of whom are ethnic minorities, poor, disabled, sick, and aged. To fulfill our mission, nursing must form a partnership with people from diverse backgrounds. Diversity in nursing, therefore, is a *must!*

Conclusion

Diversity education is imperative for all nursing faculty, administrators, and students. As the United States becomes ever more diverse, we have both a social and professional responsibility to understand diverse populations for whom we care and with whom we work. American society today is really a connection of intertwining cultures, each bringing its own character and palpable contributions to the nation (Zhan, 1999). Higher education is no exception. How we deal with this interconnectedness has significant implications for the quality of life for all.

My teacher and dear friend, Em Olivia Bevis, a distinguished nurse educator and leader, and an extraordinary human being, inspired us all through her voice and her commitment to the betterment of nursing education. I remember what she said when she visited me in Boston:

We need to enlarge our vision in nursing education instead of reduce it.

We will not objectify students but will respect them as subjects.

We will liberate students and not oppress them.

We will educate rather than instruct.

We will enable instead of facilitate.

References

Bevis, E. O., & Watson, J. (1989). _Toward a caring curriculum: A new pedagogy for nursing._ New York: National League for Nursing Press.

Greene, M. (1988). _The dialectic of freedom._ New York: Teachers College Press.

Moccia, P. (1989). Preface. In E. O. Bevis & J. Watson, _Toward a caring curriculum: A new pedagogy for nursing._ New York: National League for Nursing Press.

Zhan, L. (1996). Rethinking nursing research: Health of populations and outcome measures. _Health and Policy: Prism._ 4(2),1.

Zhan, L. (1999). _Asian voices: Asian and Asian American health educators speak out._ Sudbury, MA: Jones and Bartlett.

Zhan, L. (2001). _Cultural competency: Asian voices._ Speech given at Massachusetts General Hospital's Cultural Competence Conference (February 26), in Boston.

Zhan, L., & Cloutterbuck, J. (1997). Nursing: A new day, a new way. _New England Journal of Public Policy,_ 13(1), 11-33.

Footnotes

1 Part of this chapter is replicated from _Asian Americans: Vulnerable populations, model interventions, and clarifying agendas_ (Zhan, 2003). Permission for partial replication was granted by Jones and Bartlett, publisher and copyright owner, Sudbury, MA.

2 This student now is a registered nurse working in one of Boston's hospitals.

3 This research study was conducted in spring 1998, as part of the campus wide Diversity Research Initiative. The project was funded by the Ford Foundation.

4 Today, the college of nursing is termed College of Nursing and Health Sciences.

5 Nonparticipating students gave the reason as schedule conflicts or other commitments during that semester

6 In addition to our weekly group seminar, three DRI teams held seminars together during that semester.

Special Acknowledgment

Gratitude goes to the Ford Foundation for providing the opportunity to conduct the DRI inquiry; to all DRI team members — students and faculty alike — for offering insights and support throughout this challenging and sometimes painful process; to student researchers for their ability to explore a previously invisible and untouchable area; to Jain Rong Liu, a very special student researcher, for her leadership in helping us remain in touch with human dimensions; and to all student participants for their bravery in sharing their experiences in higher education, for reminding us as educators of our commitment and responsibilities to all students.

CHAPTER 6
CHINESE AMERICAN CHILDREN, FAMILIES, AND SPECIAL EDUCATION
Lusa Lo, EdD

Undeniably, the demographics of the U.S. population continue to change rapidly. Since 1980, the rate of increase in the number of people from diverse cultures has been dramatic: Whites 22%; Blacks, 41%; Hispanics, 198%; and Asians, 270% (U.S. Census Bureau, 2006). As projected, over one-third of the total population will be from diverse cultures by 2050 (U.S. Census Bureau, 2004). The changing demographics have greatly impacted the demographics of the U.S. student population. Between 2005 and 2006, diverse students comprised 43% of the public school student population (National Center for Education Statistics, 2007), including students in special education.

The overrepresentation of diverse students in special education has captured the attention of researchers (Artiles, Harry, Reschly, & Chinn, 2002; Green, 2005; Hosp & Reschly, 2004), but that attention has rarely focused on the Asian/Pacific Islander (API) group that has been underrepresented, due in part to lack of data. Existing national data, however, revealed that the number of API students with disabilities, as compared with other ethnic subgroups, has been increasing since 1998 (see Table 6-1). Existing data may underestimate the number of API students with disabilities since a number of the disabled students may not be identified and ultimately they may not receive much-needed services (Robertson, Kushner, Starks, & Drescher, 1994).

Table 6-1. Number of Students Served Under IDEA, Part B, Ages 3-21, by Race and Ethnicity

	1998	1999	2000	2001	2002	2003	2004	2005	2006	Growth 1998-2006
American Indian/ Alaska Native	75,721	89,017	88,427	92,417	94,827	98,667	100,509	101,196	101,055	33%
Asian/Pacific Islander	105,775	111,699	121,014	123,553	130,313	137,596	144,387	149,954	156,905	48%
Black	1,193,730	1,199,380	1,259,110	1,288,463	1,310,690	1,334,509	1,354,771	1,346,177	1,278,712	7%
Hispanic	788,480	821,102	877,649	928,993	980,609	1,036,039	1,081,743	1,119,140	1,150,899	46%
White	3,859,817	3,806,832	3,957,574	3,976,420	4,015,252	4,035,710	4,043,770	4,003,933	3,893,108	1%

Source: U. S. Department of Education, Office of Special Education Programs. (2007). Individuals with Disabilities Education Act (IDEA) Data. http://www.ideadata.org.

In order to ensure that children with disabilities receive free and appropriate education and special needs services, parents are required to serve as their decision-makers and advocates. For children with disabilities before the age of majority, parents undertake the decision-making role and work closely with the school to develop appropriate educational programs. For those with severe disabilities, parents' decision-making roles extend to their adult life. Existing literature consistently suggests that families from diverse backgrounds are less likely to be equipped to take on these roles (Salas, 2004; Tellier-Robinson, 2000; Zetlin, Padron, & Wilson, 1996). A lack of knowledge and understanding of the special education system, cultural and language barriers, and a lack of culturally appropriate services are identified factors contributing to these families who have difficulty ensuring their children receive the support and services to which they are entitled. Limited studies to date have examined what challenges Asian American families may experience when serving as their child's advocates (Park & Turnbull, 2001; Park, Turnbull, & Park, 2001). Therefore, the purpose of this chapter is to share the experiences of three Chinese American families who had to navigate the special education system and the challenges they experienced during the process.

Connecting to the Families

The author, as an assistant professor in the field of special education, had the opportunity to meet the Siu, Tam, and Wong* families three years ago. These three families are different in their socioeconomic status, educational level, and English proficiency (see Table 6-2). Each of the three families adopted different strategies to overcome the hurdles they came across while navigating the special education system, but all were aimed at achieving one common goal – to ensure that their children received appropriate education and services. Here are their stories.

Table 6-2. Demographics of the Families

Family	Highest Educational Level	Socioeconomic Status	Level of English Language Proficiency	Number of Children with Disabilities	Types of Disabilities
Siu	Master's degree	High	Fluent	3	Autism spectrum disorder
Tam	High school graduate in home country	Low	Limited	1	Hearing impairments
Wong	Fifth grade in home country	Low	None	1	Cerebral palsy

* All names are pseudonyms.

The Siu Family

Mr. and Mrs. Siu met in China. After they got married, both of them moved to the United States in 1990 to begin a new life. Their first daughter, May, was born in 1996. Everything went according to plan. Mr. Siu obtained his master's degree in computer engineering at a prestigious university and found a high-paying job at an investment company as the principal network system engineer. Mrs. Siu chose to be the homemaker, to stay home and take care of May. As May grew older, Mr. Siu began noticing that her skills were regressing. She gradually lost eye contact. Mr. Siu was worried and shared his observations with their family doctor. However, the doctor disregarded his concerns, told them that May was developing very well, and sent them home. Owing to their respect for the doctor's professionalism, Mr. and Mrs. Siu thought that they might be overreacting and that they should believe the doctor's diagnosis, as "doctors knew best." When May turned three, she appeared to lose all the skills that she had learned, such as eating, walking, and lifting. Mr. Siu could no longer ignore the obvious and once again took May to see the same doctor. This time, the doctor was willing to conduct a series of tests, and the test results indicated that May had Rett syndrome. Mr. and Mrs. Siu were devastated by the news. He couldn't help but wonder, "Could this have been avoided if the doctor had listened to my initial concerns?" Mr. and Mrs. Siu left the hospital with more questions than answers. "What is Rett syndrome?" "Why did May have Rett syndrome?" "What do we do now?" "Can we have more children?" When the doctor did not provide any concrete answers to their questions, Mr. Siu began searching on the Internet and in books for information regarding the disorder.

In 2000 and 2001, their second and third children, David and Andrew, were born. As the two sons developed, Mr. Siu noticed that both of them had difficulty maintaining eye contact. Due to his prior experiences with May, he could not afford to waste even a second, so he visited the same family doctor and insisted on having his sons evaluated. After a series of evaluations, Mr. Siu was told that both of his sons were diagnosed with autism spectrum disorder.

In 2002, because of the high level of assistance May required, Mr. and Mrs. Siu were forced to make a difficult decision: to send May to a residential care facility. Despite this series of devastating incidents, Mr. Siu remained optimistic. He called his life an "adventure" and felt that he was "luckier" than other parents because he had three children, even though they had disabilities. He never asked, "Why me?" Mr. Siu was very proactive. Despite the lack of culturally appropriate support for Chinese families of children with disabilities, his high educational and English proficiency level enabled him to try various ways to search for information about his sons' disabilities and "cure." In the process, various physicians who claimed that they could "cure" autism got his attention. In 2006, Mr. Siu chose a doctor who claimed that his sons' disabilities could be "cured" with appropriate diet and vitamin supplements. In spite of the costly remedy, including a $200 hourly consultation charge and laboratory costs of over $1,000 per session, he felt that he could not afford to miss the opportunity. Mr. Siu said,

> I am different from my wife. She is very conservative. She feels that we should just deal with the disabilities. I have a different philosophy. I feel that we need to give everything a try and make an effort. You will never know what works and what doesn't, unless you try. While I can still afford it, I will keep trying. Try this one. Oh, it doesn't work. Move on to other things. Don't give up. ... When I look back in my life, I want to be able to say that I have done my best to help my children.

After a 3-month treatment period, David and Andrew showed improvement in maintaining eye contact and in speech development. However, as no further gain was observed after six months, Mr. Siu decided to stop the treatments.

Mr. Siu was very involved in his sons' academic performance. Every day after work, he spent hours working with them – reading with them, helping them with homework, and reinforcing the skills they had learned in school. He told the author that he was very disappointed and felt frustrated with the school system and the professionals because they had very low expectations of his sons. "Every time in IEP [Individualized Education Program] meetings, they asked for my concerns. I told them, but they simply ignored them," said Mr. Siu. When David, the oldest son, was in second grade, Mr. Siu noticed that he was capable of learning single digit addition and subtraction because he had tried that with him at home. Therefore, he requested the school to teach David these skills. Despite Mr. Siu's insistence that his son had progressed, the professionals refused to include these skills in his IEP, claiming that David was not yet ready.

Another challenge Mr. Siu encountered was the language barrier. Although he was able to communicate with professionals fluently, he found the IEP documents and evaluation reports very difficult to understand because they were full of technical terms such as "percentile," "KABC-II," and "ABA." Annoyed by the professionals' attitudes and losing faith in the school system, Mr. Siu chose not to argue with the professionals. Instead, he assumed the teacher's role. He used computer reading and mathematics programs as teaching tools to support his sons and tracked his sons' learning progress. In order to prove to the professionals that his children could learn, Mr. Siu presented them with the computer progress reports. This strategy worked most of the time. The professionals were usually willing to compromise by giving his sons appropriate special education services and teaching them particular learning skills as needed. However, all the successes relied heavily on Mr. Siu's persistence and hard work. He said,

They [the professionals] are just like robots. When you push a button, then they will move a little. If you don't, they just stay where they are. This is very frustrating. My background is in computer engineering, not in education. I don't know much about the curriculum in the U.S. As a matter of fact, I should not be expected to know about all this. This is their job. I should not be the one telling them how to do their job.

In order to educate himself about the teaching methods in school so that he could teach his sons at home, Mr. Siu requested to observe his sons in class sessions numerous times. Without providing any explanation, the teachers either denied or ignored his requests, repeatedly, refusing to return his phone calls and emails. In order not to create more conflict with the school, which Mr. Siu thought would do more harm than good to his sons, he chose not to pursue the matter further.

In 2005, Mr. Siu began participating in a parent support group, which enabled him to meet other Chinese families of children with disabilities, acquire mutual support, and attend a training session on how to prepare for an IEP meeting and understand the IEP document. Mr. Siu felt that the training session was extremely useful and applicable. It informed him how to act appropriately and how to make proper requests in team meetings. He said,

There is a shortage of this kind of training in the Chinese community, especially when the training is done in Chinese. I am sure that all Chinese parents of children with disabilities would benefit from this. I don't understand why schools and government agencies do not offer a similar kind of training to parents of children with disabilities.

Mr. Siu's struggle working with the professionals continued. The school refused to allow his children to be integrated in general education classrooms, not even for nonacademic subjects. Mr. Siu finally gave up on battling with his sons' schools and decided to move the entire family to a community that had a better school system, to a school district that offered full inclusion to all students with disabilities.

During the author's recent visit, Mr. Siu was very pleased with the current school and his sons' learning progress. Considering the promising accomplishments of his sons, Mr. Siu is now in the process of searching for after-school programs so as to enhance their development. He said, "My wish is that both David and Andrew will be able to graduate from college."

The Tam Family

Mr. and Mrs. Tam moved to the United States in 1989. They have two children, Daniel and Lucy. Daniel was born with a hearing impairment. He has no auricle on either ear and has a deformity in both middle ears. After a series of surgeries, Daniel now needs to wear hearing aids. He relies on a frequency modulated (FM) system in the classroom, in which the teacher speaks into a microphone, and the system transmits the voice directly to his hearing aid.

Mrs. Tam always blames herself for Daniel's disability because she needed to take Western medicines to treat a horrible stomachache during the fifth month of her pregnancy. She said, "Every time I see Daniel's condition, my heart aches. It was entirely my fault. I didn't know I was pregnant when I took those medicines." In order to give Daniel the best care, Mrs. Tam chose to be a full-time housewife. Thus, the family financial burden fell on Mr. Tam, who earns $10,200 annually.

The hearing disability hindered Daniel's speech learning progress. He could only speak using simple words when he was three, whereas most children can speak simple phrases by that age. In the same year, Daniel started school in a special education classroom with children who are hearing impaired. Mrs. Tam expected that the school would provide a good learning environment and that Daniel would be able to understand and speak fluent English. However, a year later, Mrs. Tam realized that Daniel had not made any progress. However, when Daniel was spending time with other children without disabilities, Mrs. Tam noticed that he was able to pick up simple vocabulary very quickly from these children. Why was he not making progress in school for the entire year? Mrs. Tam decided to drop by Daniel's classroom. Repeatedly, she found that the teacher only taught simple ABCs most of the time, and that the students were spending a majority of the school time playing and coloring. This situation made her anxious and worried. She understood that the classroom environment could be the main factor that was hindering Daniel's academic development.

Therefore, in the subsequent IEP meeting, she requested to have Daniel transferred to a different school and be placed in a general education classroom that had children without disabilities. According to Mrs. Tam, her request was accepted in the IEP meeting, but it was never stated in the IEP document. She thought the verbal agreement was equally important in such meeting. However, the school never processed the transfer and Mrs. Tam felt betrayed. She faced great challenges "fighting" with the school for an appropriate placement for Daniel, which made her tired both physically and mentally.

Mrs. Tam later realized that if she wanted to be a successful advocate for Daniel, she had to learn English, so she began attending adult ESL classes. She also used what she had learned in these classes to teach Daniel at home. As expected, Daniel progressed significantly, proving to the school that Daniel's cognitive and learning ability was no different from that of a child without disabilities. Mrs. Tam once again requested to have her son transferred to another school. However, her requests were repeatedly denied by the school because the team felt that general education classes were for children without disabilities and that the setting would be inappropriate and too overwhelming for Daniel.

Not giving up, Mrs. Tam contacted as many parties as she could think of, including those in the public school district, charter schools, and private schools. Using limited English and gestures, she tried her best to communicate what she wanted. After a year, Daniel was assigned to a school by the public school district. Although it was very far from home, Mrs. Tam considered it worthwhile because Daniel could finally be in a supportive learning environment. The distance between Daniel's and Lucy's schools exhausted Mrs. Tam every morning. Without a car, Mrs. Tam had to take public transportation, drop Daniel off at his school, take another bus, and drop Lucy off at her school. Mrs. Tam said,

> I am not afraid of hard work. I am willing to sacrifice as long as my children are learning and getting what they need. I know my strategies of seeking help may not be appropriate, but there's nothing I can do. I don't know anything. I am doing the best I can.

Three months later, Mrs. Tam learned that Daniel was not receiving any speech therapy support, a special education service that Daniel received at the previous school. According to the new school, he would no longer receive such service because she had signed a document in the public school district office indicating that she no longer wanted Daniel to receive any special education services. Mrs. Tam felt that her son once again suffered because she was limited in English and was unaware of the school system. To reacquire the services for Daniel, Mrs. Tam learned from her friend that she could request an evaluation from the new school. The result indicated that Daniel was qualified for speech services. At that team meeting, Mrs. Tam received more bad news. The team suspected that Daniel had attention deficit hyperactivity disorder (ADHD). Mrs. Tam told the author sorrowfully that, "Although I do not know what ADHD is, I know that it's not good. I do not understand why Daniel was so unlucky; all the bad things happened to him." Because of his behaviors in the classroom, Mrs. Tam had received several complaints from the school. She also learned that Daniel had been bullied at school because of his disability and the school did not attempt to resolve the issues. For those reasons, Mrs. Tam felt that it was time to have Daniel transferred to a school that was much closer to home.

Mrs. Tam's utter devotion to Daniel triggered jealousy in Lucy because she felt neglected. One night, Lucy told Mrs. Tam that she hated Daniel because he "stole" her mom. Lucy said, "You no longer love me. All your attentions are on Daniel only." Mrs. Tam was heartbroken. She never noticed that she had hurt Lucy because of what she did for Daniel. Thereafter, Mrs. Tam decided to spend an hour each evening with Lucy, asking about her day, reading to her, and playing games with her.

Mrs. Tam's encounter is only the tip of the iceberg of what a low-income Chinese family with children with disabilities experiences in the United States. A year ago, realizing Chinese families' helplessness and the lack of government and community supports in special education, several professionals in the local community established a coalition. Its mission was to provide Chinese parents with training opportunities, at no cost. Mrs. Tam said,

All the training programs were extremely helpful for me as they were targeted to our needs. I really thank all the contributors who devoted their own time and energy to provide us with free workshops. They gave us the warmest and most practical support. I learned how I should work collaboratively with schools. Simply arguing with them won't help. If these workshops were available when Daniel was first diagnosed, I am sure I would be able to act differently and attain a win-win situation.

The Wong Family

The Wong family moved to the United States from China in 2003 with two daughters, Mary and Jenny. Mary was born without any disability. However, when she was a few months old, she had a fever that damaged her brain and resulted in hemiplegia. Due to her disability, both her kindergarten teachers and classmates discriminated against her. Mary was upset and refused to go to school while she was in China. Mrs. Wong then removed Mary from school and kept her at home until they moved to the United States. After they arrived, Mary was further diagnosed with cerebral palsy and epilepsy. Like Mrs. Tam, in order to take good care of her child, Mrs. Wong chose to be a full-time homemaker. Mr. Wong became the only breadwinner of the family with a monthly income of $780.

A few months after moving to the United States, Mary was enrolled in a local middle school, which she enjoyed very much. Six months afterward, Mrs. Wong received an IEP meeting invitation letter. Because Mrs. Wong was a non-English speaker, she relied on Jenny, who was 10 years old, to translate the document for her. Even though Mrs. Wong didn't know what an IEP meeting was, her intuition told her that it had to be important and that she had to attend. At the meeting, an interpreter was not provided by the school and Mrs. Wong could not understand what the professionals were discussing. The highly respected status of scholars in Chinese culture led Mrs. Wong to believe that the school would not do any harm to Mary, so she accepted all the special education services proposed in the IEP plan. At that time, Mary had a Chinese bilingual teaching assistant working with her. Mrs. Wong was very pleased with the arrangement and delighted to see that Mary could once again attend school. She felt that the U.S. school system was much more supportive of Mary's needs than the system in her home county.

In 2005, Mary was transferred to a nearby high school. Toward the end of that school year, Mrs. Wong received Mary's new IEP. Once again, her daughter Jenny, a 6th grader, acted as the translator. This time, however, she was confused by the terminology on the documents, so she was only able to translate a limited amount of the IEP content for her mother. According to the document, Mary would no longer receive the physical therapy services recommended by her physician. Mrs. Wong was devastated by the arrangement. In addition, she realized that Mary was starting to lose interest in attending school because she could not understand what the teacher was saying. Although the IEP established in her previous school had stated that there would be a Chinese bilingual teaching assistant working with her, none was available in the current school and the school did not attempt to hire one. All these problems overwhelmed Mrs. Wong greatly. Coming from a traditional Chinese background, she was afraid to confront the school. She also wasn't sure whether or not she had the right to request the services Mary needed. "Should the school be the ultimate decision maker? If I reject the IEP, would Mary be treated badly afterward?" Despite Mrs. Wong's anxiety, her husband encouraged her to refrain from questioning the system, saying, "We have to be grateful for what the school has done for Mary. We should not make too many requests." Mrs. Wong decided not to pursue the issue and signed the IEP, thus agreeing with what the school had suggested.

In 2006, while attending a workshop organized by her support group, Mrs. Wong learned that once Mary turned 18, she would lose the right to make decisions for her daughter unless she was Mary's legal guardian. She attempted to contact one of the state agencies that could help her with the guardianship process, but none of the staff members in the area office spoke Chinese. Unable to communicate, Mrs. Wong felt helpless and didn't know what to do. Fortunately, with the assistance of the workshop presenter, Mrs. Wong was introduced to and guided by another family who had gone through a similar process.

Recently, Mrs. Wong informed the author that, due to the lack of funding, her support group no longer provided the parents with any training. She wished there were someone who could guide her through the process, so she would know how to prepare Mary for a successful adult life.

IMPLICATIONS FOR POLICY MAKERS, EDUCATORS, AND SERVICE PROVIDERS

The birth of a child with a disability is a major challenge for many families. These families not only have to be familiar with their child's developmental stages, but also have to learn new vocabulary related to their child's disability. In order to ensure that their children with disabilities receive free and appropriate education, these families also have to be familiar with the current special education laws and regulations. Without knowing the school system and unable to speak fluent English, the diverse families of children with disabilities are clearly at a disadvantage. The experiences of the three Chinese American families in this chapter reflect a number of inadequacies of the current special education system for diverse families. Some of them are typical, and some of them are unique. Several inferences can be drawn from these families' experiences.

First, parent education training is crucial for all families of children with disabilities. As suggested by many studies (Hughes, Valle-Riestra, & Arguelles, 2002; Park & Turnbull, 2001), families, especially the ones from diverse cultures, are often unfamiliar with the special education process, particularly the complicated IEP process. There is a need for school and community to collaborate and offer families information regarding various types of disabilities. If schools are unable to offer educational workshops to families of children with disabilities, they should provide these families with resources regarding where they might seek support, especially where they might find the organizations that specifically support families who do not speak English fluently.

Parent Training and Information (PTI) centers across the nation play a critical role in supporting families of children with disabilities. In Massachusetts, there are two PTI centers, but none of their workshops is offered to Chinese American families in their primary language, Chinese. Chinese American families who are limited- or non-English-speakers have no means of obtaining resources and information. With the dramatically increasing Asian population in the United States, of which Chinese Americans occupy the largest subgroup, the impact of the special education system on this minority and their needs should not be neglected. Every year, federal funding opportunities are available to PTI centers. Priority of such funding should be given to centers that provide support and training to underrepresented and underserved families.

Second, the lack of trained, bilingual Asian American educators and service providers continues to be a concern in the education field (Bracey, 2001; Perlstein, 2000; Rong & Preissle, 1997). Similar to English language learners, bilingual children with disabilities require assistance from bilingual professionals in the classroom. In middle school, Mary Wong had been given help by the Chinese bilingual teaching assistant, but when she was transferred to the high school, none of the professionals were bilingual in Chinese. In the United States, 41% of the students receiving special education services are from diverse populations (U.S. Department of Education, 2007), but only 14% of the special education teachers are from diverse cultures, and just 1% of them are Asians (University of Florida, 2003). A similar dilemma is faced by government agencies (V. Hernandez, personal communication, November 12, 2007). The recruitment methods that are currently used by the school districts, university teacher training programs, and government agencies need to be reevaluated.

Third, the language barrier is one of the major hurdles that prevent many diverse families from being equal partners with the schools (Lee, 1995; Salas, Lopez, Chinn, & Menchaca-Lopez, 2005; Sohn & Wang, 2006). The three families described in this chapter experienced varying degrees of challenges regarding this obstacle. Mr. Siu, described as a fluent English speaker, found it difficult to understand the evaluation reports, which were full of technical terms. This prevented him from understanding whether or not the IEP plan that was proposed by the school was the best for his children. Mrs. Tam, a limited English speaker, signed a document that she did not understand, resulting in the removal of Daniel's special education services. Mrs. Wong, a non-English speaker, failed to understand every letter sent by the school and what was discussed in the IEP meetings. This prevented her from becoming an appropriate advocate for her daughter. All these challenges could have been avoided by hiring qualified interpreters and translators who (a) have knowledge of both English and the target language(s), (b) are able to convey information, knowledge, and culture for the targeted language users, (c) have knowledge of terms and concepts in special education, and (d) are able to match the comprehension level of the material with the targeted audience (Santos, Lee, Validivia, & Zhang, 2001). Without these professionals, the communication gap between schools and diverse families continues.

Finally, the importance of support groups should not be overlooked. Over the last two decades, research has suggested the value of using parent support groups to provide emotional and psychological assistance and information to families of children with special needs (Bull, 2003; Crnic, Greenberg, Ragozin, Robinson, & Basham, 1983; Koroloff & Friesen, 1991; Pilon & Smith, 1985). Furthermore, by speaking with other members of their own group, parents can learn how to develop positive relationships between themselves and the schools (Allen, Brown, & Finlay, 1992). Throughout the course of my interviews, the three families commented that it was extremely difficult for them to locate support groups, especially the ones specifically for Chinese families of children with disabilities. The shortage of funding also makes it difficult for the established support groups to continue operating. Funding opportunities for these small-scale, local support groups are necessary.

Information is the key to understanding. The author salutes the Chinese American families described in this chapter for their effort, love, and life-long devotion to their children. Although this chapter depicts only the experiences of three Chinese American families, their experiences are shared by many Chinese American families of children with disabilities in the United States. Their experiences offer valuable insights to policy makers, educators, and service providers. Without addressing the challenges these families experience, barriers between schools, government agencies, and those families will continue. The ones who suffer the most will be our children.

REFERENCES

Allen, M., Brown, P., & Finlay, B. (1992). Helping children by strengthening families: A look at family support programs. Washington, DC: Children's Defense Fund. (ERIC Document Reproduction Service No. ED365410)

Artiles, A. J., Harry, B., Reschly, D. J., & Chinn, P. C. (2002). Over-identification of students of color in special education: A critical overview. Multicultural Perspectives, 4, 3-10.

Bracey, G. W. (2001). Why so few Asian American teachers? Phi Delta Kappan, 83, 14-15.

Bull, L. (2003). The use of support groups for parents of children with dyslexia. Early Child Development and Care, 173, 341-347.

Crnic, K. A., Greenberg, M. T., Ragozin, A. S., Robinson, N. M., & Basham, R. (1983). Effects of stress and social support on mothers of premature and full-term infants. Child Development, 54, 209-217.

Green, T. D. (2005). Promising prevention and early intervention strategies to reduce overrepresentation of African American students in special education. Preventing School Failure, 49, 33-41.

Hosp, J. L. & Reschly, D. J. (2004). Disproportionate representation of minority students in special education: Academic, demographic, and economic predictors. Exceptional Children, 70, 185-199.

Hughes, M. T., Valle-Riestra, D. M., & Arguelles, M. E. (2002). Experiences of Latino families with their child's special education program. Multicultural Perspectives, 4, 11-17.

Koroloff, N. M., & Friesen, B. J. (1991). Support groups for parents of children with emotional disorders: A comparison of members and non-members. Community Mental Health Journal, 27, 265-279.

Lee, F. Y. (1995). Asian parents as partners. Young Children, 50, 4-9.

National Center for Education Statistics. (2007). Table 2. Public school student membership, by race/ethnicity and state or jurisdiction: School year 2005-06. [Online]. Available: http://nces.ed.gov/pubs2007/pesenroll06/tables/table_2.asp.

Park, J., & Turnbull, A. P. (2001). Cross-cultural competency and special education: Perceptions and experiences of Korean parents of children with special needs. Education and Training in Mental Retardation and Development Disabilities, 36, 133-147.

Park, J., Turnbull, A. P., & Park, H. S. (2001). Quality of partnerships in service provision for Korean American parents of children with disabilities: A qualitative inquiry. *Journal of the Association for Persons with Severe Handicaps,* 26, 158-170.

Perlstein, L. (2000, February 1). Few Asian Americans attracted to teaching. *The Washington Post,* B1.

Pilon, B. H. & Smith, K. A. (1985). A parent group for the Hispanic parents of children with severe cerebral palsy. *Children's Health Care,* 14, 96-102.

Robertson, P., Kushner, M., Starks, J., & Drescher, C. (1994). An update of participation rates of culturally and linguistically diverse students in special education: The need for a research and policy agenda. *The Bilingual Special Education Perspective Newsletter,* 14, 3-9.

Rong, X. L., & Preissle, J. (1997). The continuing decline in Asian American teachers. *American Educational Research Journal,* 34, 267-293.

Salas, L. (2004). Individualized education plan (IEP) meetings and Mexican American parents: Let's talk about it. *Journal of Latinos and Education,* 3, 181-192.

Salas, L., Lopez, E. J., Chinn, K., & Menchaca-Lopez, E. (2005). Can special education teachers create parent partnership with Mexican American families? *Multicultural Education,* 13, 52-55.

Santos, R. M., Lee, S., Validivia, R., & Zhang, C. (2001). Translating translations: Selecting and using translated early childhood materials. *Teaching Exceptional Children,* 34, 26-31.

Sohn, S., & Wang, X. C. (2006). Immigrant parents' involvement in American schools: Perspectives from Korean mothers. *Early Childhood Education Journal,* 34, 125-132.

Tellier-Robinson, D. (2000). Involvement of Portuguese-speaking parents in the education of their special-needs children. *Bilingual Research Journal,* 24, 225-239.

University of Florida. (2003). *Percent of service providers from different racial groups, by type of service provider.* [Online]. Available: http://ferdig.coe.ufl.edu/spense/scripts/tables/ ChooseReport.asp.

U.S. Census Bureau. (2004). *Table 1a. Projected Population of the United States, by Race and Hispanic Origin: 2000 to 2050.* [Online]. Available: http://www.census.gov/ipc/ www/usinterimproj.

U.S. Census Bureau. (2006). _2006 American community survey data profile highlights._ [Online]. Available: http://factfinder.census.gov/home/saff/main.html?_lang=en

U.S. Department of Education, Office of Special Education Programs. (2007). _Table B2C. Number and percent of population served, by race/ethnicity and age group (3-21, 3-5, and 6-21): 1998 through 2005._ Retrieved February 23, 2008, from http://www.ideadata.org

Zetlin, A. G., Padron, M., & Wilson, S. (1996). The experience of five Latin American families with the special education system. _Education and Training in Mental Retardation and Developmental Disabilities, 31,_ 22-28.

CHAPTER 7

BRIDGING THE BROKEN NARRATIVE: HOW STUDENT-CENTERED TEACHING CONTRIBUTES TO HEALING THE WOUNDS OF TRAUMA

Nancy J. Lin, MA
Karen L. Suyemoto, PhD

[Our grandmother] would tell about how she gave birth
to all these children... "This one's dead, he was a police
officer. He got shot during the Khmer Rouge... These two
didn't survive. They were walking... in the jungle and
stepped on a landmine." ...You would feel the pain that
she had, and then she would just start crying... So we just
left it as it is...we would hug her and say she's fine...
She'll wipe her tears and say, "We'll talk about it later."

We begin with this quote by a young man who wanted to know what life was like for his family back in their town in the Battambang Province of Cambodia. As his grandmother attempts to describe the past, it becomes clear that there can be no separation between their family's stories and the Cambodian genocide. When horrifying events in history take on personal significance, learning "the facts" is anything but neutral. What is the best way for educators to reach students who have personal and familial experiences with sociocultural trauma[1]? How can health service educators convey information in personally and socially sensitive manners that will help students negotiate their own experiences and be able to utilize the information to develop best practices?

As health service educators, we are in a position to influence our students in at least two ways: how they develop as individuals and who they will become as health professionals. For students who have personal or familial experiences with trauma, these two areas of influence are not disconnected. Aiding students' personal development and helping them to heal from trauma inherently contribute to the health of the communities of which students are members; they are also necessary in order for students to integrate meanings of their personal and familial experiences with their professional training such that they can be efficacious and empathic as health care providers. Finally, teaching about trauma in ways that attend to the personal and professional development of students from refugee backgrounds who have first-hand or familial experiences with trauma can enable these students to contribute to the education of other students in order to positively affect all students' empathy, understanding and resulting ability to provide good health services to individuals, families, and communities who have experienced trauma.

This chapter discusses how a student-centered teaching pedagogy can be used to most effectively teach students who have personal or familial experiences with trauma about trauma and related services. A student-centered teaching approach entails awareness by the instructor of the personal and social contexts of students, explicit intention to integrate personal experiences of students and the skills to do so effectively, and understanding of the interactions between personal engagement, education, and professional development. Addressing the social, political and transitional issues that are relevant to refugee communities is necessary for training aspiring health professionals from refugee backgrounds because the task of effectively serving those who have experienced trauma requires an awareness of how one's own experiences of trauma have shaped one's beliefs and worldviews. In this chapter, we first explore the consequences of the absence of a community's trauma history from the mainstream discourse in society. We then discuss how this social silence can be perpetuated within the affected communities by entwined cultural norms and attempts at psychological coping. We explore how these silences have intergenerational effects and may therefore be an important context for students in health service classrooms who not only have experienced trauma but also who come from these familial backgrounds.

In teaching issues of psychological trauma to students of refugee backgrounds, health service educators can address issues of representation and social injustice and provide opportunities for self exploration. We discuss the ways in which the learning experience can lead students of refugee backgrounds to grow and influence their relationships outside of the classroom. By exploring some of the moments in which families acknowledge the past, we introduce the educator's role in helping students to break the silence in order to promote healing in their communities and improve their professional efficacy. We conclude by describing four principles for student-centered pedagogy for students of refugee backgrounds and offer some practical steps that illustrate and operationalize these principles.

Throughout the chapter, we draw from our experiences teaching psychology and Asian American Studies courses with Southeast Asian refugee students and from our research on intergenerational effects of and communication about trauma in second generation Cambodian American refugees (Lin, 2005). Thus, we utilize a focus on Cambodian American students and experiences to illustrate our points. Although we use the Cambodian American experience as an illustration, we believe the principles and practical suggestions are useful in teaching about trauma to students with personal and familial experiences with trauma, such as students from refugee families from Vietnam, Laos, Somalia, Sudan, and the Congo, for example.

MEANINGS AND IMPACTS OF SILENCE

After a trauma such as genocide, silence often enshrouds the survivors, their families and communities, and the larger society in which they live. Silence has a far reach. The larger society resists discussion of what happened; in this country, refugee communities have generally received little recognition for the struggles they have survived. Within refugee communities themselves, survivors resist talking about their experiences, remaining silent even with their own children; hence, often neither students who were refugees themselves nor those who were raised by refugee parents have explored the meaning of trauma. Health service educators are charged with preparing students of refugee backgrounds to serve traumatized communities as future health professionals. Fostering competence to do this difficult work requires health professionals to have an awareness of how their own lives have been shaped by trauma. Hence, in preparing students of refugee backgrounds to become health service providers, educators have the task of breaking the silence and helping students bridge their family's broken narratives. Gradually, students can develop an understanding that their life contexts are relevant to the process of becoming effective health professionals and that the path to their success as health professionals necessitates more than memorizing clinically relevant facts without engaging with the lived experience of trauma.

The Impact of Under-representation of Traumatic Histories in Education and Social Discourse

In the United States, we acknowledge the murder of six million Jews in the last century and the horror of atrocities committed by humankind against itself (Power, 2002). We teach about it in our public schools and keep the memory of those events alive in our cultural consciousness. The swastika continues to be a symbol that engenders gut level reaction, making the statement, "Never Again," an anthem requiring little explanation. In health and mental health classes, we talk about damage done to survivors of the Nazi work camps and we have a shared image of their gaunt skeletal bodies resulting from chronic starvation, endless hard labor, and inhumane living conditions. We acknowledge that the Holocaust had long term intergenerational effects that continue to be felt today. Although the acknowledgement of genocide is a far cry from a complete healing of the wounds for survivors and their families, it nonetheless enables the healing to commence. Through the coming together of individuals, families, and societies to explore, argue, and co-construct what it means to be a survivor, victim, aggressor, or bystander, and what we can learn in order to change for the better in the future, the pain and shame of genocide can be brought into the light and made accessible – the healing of those affected directly and through networks of relationships and identities can be facilitated.

However, history does not give a fair account of all events. For example, despite the efforts of three generations of Armenian Americans, only recently have there been serious attempts within the United States Government to officially recognize the death of nearly one million Armenians in Turkey in 1915 as genocide (Hulse, 2007). Even when the offense is not genocide, we may resist revisiting moments of blatant group-based oppression in history, especially when our own society is implicated. For example, it was only in 1976, thirty years after the end of the Second World War that an official apology for the unjust incarceration of American citizens was made by the United States Government to the remaining survivors of the Japanese American concentration camps (Presidential Proclamation 4417, 1976).

Similarly, although we in the United States are taught as a matter of course about the reign of Hitler, the reign of Pol Pot is hardly mentioned. Few Americans know that only thirty years ago, Pol Pot and his followers, the Khmer Rouge, caused the death of nearly one-fourth of the population of Cambodia and that today, over ninety percent of people of Cambodian heritage around the world have lost one or more family members due to starvation, overwork, treatable illnesses and government sanctioned murder during his rule (Kiernan, 2004). Most Americans have no knowledge of Operation Breakfast, through which President Nixon authorized a four-year aerial bombing campaign of Cambodia without a declaration of war, resulting in the deployment of over half a million tons of explosives and the deaths of countless innocent villagers; undermining the credibility of the Cambodian Government; and contributing to the rise to power of the rebel Khmer Rouge

(Chandler, 1991; Hood & Ablin, 1987; Shawcross, 1987). Although it would be a gross inaccuracy to conclude that American policies led directly to genocide in Cambodia, our country's complicity in these events likely contributes to our silence about them, including the silence in our public schools.

Silence has meaning. And silence has effects. The inequity of social acknowledgment is not simply a regretful and accidental omission but becomes an injustice that has implications for health and mental health. Without being taught about the American contribution to the war leading up to the Cambodian genocide and the events of the genocide itself, the average American stands little chance of understanding the plight of Cambodian Americans in their midst, much less recognizing that there may be reasons to feel remorse over the actions of our country rather than self-righteousness in our generosity of accepting Cambodians as refugees. The heaviest burden of our silence undeniably rests on the shoulders of the Cambodian American community, and therefore on the Cambodian American students in our classrooms. Silence influences the way in which Cambodian Americans are able to talk about, mourn, create meaning from, and heal from their experiences of horror and injury and the subsequent anger, anxiety, and sorrow when questions such as "Why us?" and "Could my loved ones still be alive somewhere?" cannot be answered. Without social acknowledgement, it is difficult for the older generation to create its own narrative of survival and pass it on to their American-raised children. Hence, the younger generation is taught not to care about the past, learning about their family's legacy of war only through the older generation's rebukes, accidental outbursts, and overheard conversations (Lin, 2005). When we participate in social silence, this process of meaning making and questioning is attempted in isolation. The memories themselves remain unacknowledged by the larger society and seem to be distant and untouchable. Without a larger context in which to place these bits and pieces of information, the younger generation is left with a tangle of meaning that is confusing and begs the organizing hand of guided learning to help make sense of it. Hence, for an educator to teach about Cambodia and the era surrounding the genocide is not only a way for students to learn accurate history but also an act of resisting silence in a manner that personally engages students and helps them become health service providers who understand the sociopolitical etiology of illness and especially psychological trauma.

On multiple levels, the consequences of silence in society and in the classroom are great while the potential for personal growth leading to healing and clarity of purpose when silence is broken are greater still. In educating future health professionals from these communities, health service educators are situated in a position of power to influence the health, mental health and quality of care to communities that have suffered from war and other tragedies. However, in order to effect positive change, health service educators must understand not only the systemic injustice that perpetuates silence as described above but also understand how and why community members may themselves maintain silence and how students from second and later generations may be affected by trauma and silence. This understanding forms the contextual foundation for student-centered pedagogy that enables students from refugee backgrounds to personally grow and best contribute professionally to serving individuals and communities affected by trauma. The following section describes how and why Cambodian Americans often resist talking about their legacy of trauma, illustrating the ways in which students from other refugee backgrounds may similarly have come to understand their own community's psychological trauma as taboo.

Silence within the Community:
Coping, Protection, and Intergenerational Impacts

Breaking any silence has its risks. In particular, sharing and learning about personal and familial traumas can be fraught with consequences to long-held understandings and patterns of relating. The mother, brother, aunt or grandfather who survived the betrayal and deprivation of the Cambodian genocide and contemplates breaking the silence risks negatively affecting their own mental health or self-image and negatively affecting relationships with children and other family members. Breaking the silence may challenge cultural norms; it may remove thin scabs of protection to reveal deep psychological wounds that remain unhealed and that are overwhelming; it may cause harm to loved ones or change relations with them as hidden identities are brought to light. Thus, there are multiple reasons why community members may silence themselves and others about shared trauma. But, just as social silence affects those from families who have experienced it, familial and community silence affects the children of those who have directly experienced the trauma who may be students in health service classrooms. Understanding community, interpersonal and personal dynamics related to silence is important for health educators who aim to understand students from refugee backgrounds and effectively engage in student-centered teaching. It is also important for health service providers generally, in terms of understanding what questions patients from traumatized communities may have difficulty answering honestly and what areas require sensitive follow-up to facilitate more effective communication.

Silence and the role of cultural rules. In relation to cultural norms, maintaining silence is the status quo because to speak is generally discouraged by Cambodian (and other Asian) cultural and religious understandings of propriety, morality, and respect. In our own research, review of literature and teaching, Cambodian Americans and other Asian Americans have spoken of several important cultural principles that guide their behavior, including: *Speaking of evil is not good karma... The darkness of the past should not be brought into the present and allowed to contaminate the future... It is disrespectful for children to question their elders... Taken together, children ought to be protected from perils of the past, requiring older generations to use good judgment on their behalf to shield* *the young from their own dangerous curiosity* (e.g. Chao, 1992; Lin, 2005; Uba, 1994). Cultural rules vary from culture to culture, as does the tightness of adherence to those rules by individuals. However, although not all Cambodians and Cambodian Americans may abide by these rules, for many individuals and families, these types of cultural principles strongly discourage intergenerational sharing of painful family history.

Silence and coping with trauma. Among Cambodian Americans and others from traumatic refugee backgrounds, silence is not only related to cultural rules. At least equally important is the need for victims of trauma to develop ways to cope with their traumatic experiences and protect themselves from re-experiencing the injuries of the past that are often far too close to the surface for comfort. Sack and colleagues (1994, 1995) assessed Cambodians who had just arrived in the United States and found rates of diagnosable levels of posttraumatic stress disorder (PTSD) as high as fifty-five percent among mothers and thirty percent among fathers. One of the hallmark symptoms of PTSD is the avoidance of activities that serve as reminders of past trauma (APA, 2000). For a Cambodian American experiencing PTSD, an important part of an avoidance strategy may be to change the subject or tell only a partial truth when, for example, a son asks about some aspect of the traumatic past. However, relying for too long on avoidance as a strategy can create a private world constrained by numerous fears and maintained at high costs to social relationships. If parents are unable or unwilling to break the silence, they risk alienating their children not only from themselves but from a significant piece of family and community history that has played a large role in defining the context of the present-day lives of both parents and children. This information may be vital to later generation Cambodian Americans in understanding their own identities as Cambodian Americans and what it means to be a member of their particular families and community.

In addition to avoidance, a second hallmark symptom and coping strategy of individuals with PTSD is emotional numbing (APA, 2000). Cambodian American individuals who suffer from PTSD may show few emotions about the past, may be more detached from emotional responses generally, or may feel detached from other people. Silence about past events may enable emotional numbing and detachment. Depending upon how an individual expresses emotional numbing, younger family members may misinterpret these reactions and come to believe that the experiences the older generation endured are unimportant and not worth mentioning, that the older generation is generally unfeeling or stoically able to endure everything, or that there is little love or affection for them from the older generation (Lin, 2005). Hence, emotional numbing, combined with silence related to avoidance of memories, can lead not only to the frustration of intergenerational communication but also hurtful and inaccurate conclusions about the behavior of older generation family members.

Silence, trauma and the experiences of the younger generation. Having discussed the role of trauma in the lives of the survivor generation and how it motivates the maintenance of silence, let us now turn to the role of the younger generation. The younger generation is also a participant in maintaining silence, although perhaps a lesser partner. Familial trauma has multigenerational effects, perhaps particularly when it is sociocultural trauma that affects the entire community and the meaning of being a member of that community. In the studies by Sack and colleagues (1994, 1995), it was found that forty-one percent of children could be diagnosed with PTSD when both parents had PTSD. Thus, there are times when children's own PTSD may contribute to silence in ways similar to those described above. But even when children of trauma survivors do not themselves develop trauma related symptoms, there are profound effects of the trauma and the silence surrounding it. These effects (some of which are discussed above) can contribute to the younger generation participating in maintaining silence.

According to our qualitative study of how young adult Cambodian Americans learn about their family's trauma history, the younger generation is aware of the risk of hurting the survivor generation and often approaches this intimate learning with a mixture of guilt, awe, fear of causing injury, and feelings of being overwhelmed as to how to integrate these revelations into their family relationships, sense of self, and understanding of the world (Lin, 2005). Children would sometimes overhear conversations between older adults as they reminisced about the past. In those families that regard the past as taboo and avoid talking about it, children learn to maintain silence as protection through the older generation's discomfort with some topics and incomplete telling of certain stories indicating something terrible happened (e.g., a grandmother's sudden silence while talking about gathering firewood with her daughter in Cambodia makes the child realize something bad happened to that aunt). In those moments when there is an opportunity to talk about the past, it is as if each generation is engaged in an awkward and delicate dance, each wanting intimacy but focused on trying to avoid injuring the other while fulfilling their roles properly. To speak is difficult work, while maintaining silence is often much easier in practice and gives the illusion of safety.

The younger generation's caution may be reinforced by their experiences of how the silence is sometimes broken in ways that further damage, rather than bridge, the broken narrative. Despite the efforts of some Cambodian American families to keep the genocide a secret from their children, many in the younger generation nonetheless learn about it in other ways. Cambodian American young adults in our study reported that their parents would sometimes blurt out details of their own past experiences (e.g., running through the jungle barefooted, having to do schoolwork by candlelight in hiding) when they were rebuking their children (e.g., for being lazy or not getting good grades). Others described learning about familial trauma when parents argued and hurled insults at one another regarding who had suffered the most, inadvertently revealing secrets to their children.

In learning about the past in these accidental moments, young adults in our study reported that they felt that they could only grasp bits and pieces of the information and were frequently confused about how to weave the information together into a coherent story (Lin, 2005). The walls guarding family secrets were porous, but children rarely understood the context of these unintentional revelations. Some young adults described feeling shutdown or made so uncomfortable by witnessing their parents' displays of negative emotion that they felt no desire to learn more about it. Few reported feeling comfortable enough to ask their parents and elders for explanation or elaboration, most often because they did not want to risk causing more upset to their family members whose emotional reactions indicated to the children that they were still injured. Others felt so little connection to their families and Cambodian culture that they did not care to know more.

The Role of Educators in Breaking (or Perpetuating) the Silence

Given the scope of challenges facing the Cambodian American community, it may seem as if the situation is hopeless. However, our research shows that there is positive communication occurring in some families and communities that contributes to healing the effects of trauma. Our research and teaching experiences lead us to conclude that education plays an important role in facilitating this communication. Some Cambodian American young adults in our research and classes reported feeling enough curiosity about the silenced experiences that they were motivated to research on the Internet, read books or talk to their siblings or Cambodian American age mates about stories they had heard as a way to fill in the gaps. Sometimes this curiosity was catalyzed by experiences in classes that discussed refugee experiences or traumatic experiences. Some young adults do ask the older generation to share more about their journey, but when they do, they are careful to make sure there was a clear reason or context for doing so. Rites of passage such as birthdays, marriage, and other significant events were times when both the younger and older generations felt it was appropriate to ask some questions (e.g., *Where exactly was I was born? What was your wedding day like? Did I cry a lot when you carried me through the jungle as a baby?*). However, our research and teaching experiences indicate that by far the most intimate and detailed stories are told when children approached their family members to ask about their journeys for the purpose of school assignments.

In our research, Cambodian American young adults talked particularly about Asian American studies courses that utilized student-centered approaches to encourage students to learn information about culture and explore their own cultural, family, and socioeconomic backgrounds in relation to course material. By utilizing student-centered pedagogy, professors created opportunities for Cambodian American students to learn their own history in supportive, culturally and contextually sensitive environments that enabled students to overcome the legacies of silence within themselves. Furthermore, through assignments that encouraged personal connections, Cambodian American students could approach their elders with culturally valid "reasons" to learn about their personal journeys through Pol Pot's Cambodia, the refugee camps, and finally to America, thus overcoming the legacies of silence within their families and communities. Elders generally respected teachers and educational attainment and could hence feel they were taking a risk by telling their narratives towards an honorable purpose while students could readily defend their questions by displacing potential feelings of intrusion to the demands of school, not a desire to injure or pry. Respect for education presents an opportunity for educators to shift the systemic, cultural and family dynamics that prevent discourse about the Cambodian genocide, hinder the healing process, and frustrate the younger generation from understanding what happened and how it impacts them. This respect is shared to varying degrees among many immigrant and refugee communities, thus offering an opening for health service educators to take what we have learned from the Asian American studies context to help students from diverse refugee backgrounds to develop the awareness and skills needed to be of greatest service to their communities.

Our research suggested that the process of intergenerational communication catalyzed by education enabled students to co-create (with their families, classmates, professors, and other community members) new meanings for what it is to be Cambodian and what it means to be a survivor, thereby contributing to the community's process of healing. Our findings suggest that young adult Cambodian Americans experienced positive psychosocial development and a strengthening of intergenerational relationships in their families by being enabled by their Asian American Studies classes and professors to take in the history of the war and genocide as personally significant events (Lin, 2005). Students were encouraged to make further connections outside of the classroom with the Cambodian community and their own families. For some, this culminated in a new sense of Cambodian identity and ethnic pride and a commitment to serve the community. We believe that these findings are relevant not only for Asian American Studies educators but for all educators whose students include those from refugee backgrounds. Because health service courses include issues of working with trauma and with individuals and communities who have experienced trauma, we believe that health educators are in a unique position to contribute to healing individuals and communities directly and through the training of health service providers from refugee backgrounds who may be in a unique position to serve their own communities.

STUDENT-CENTERED APPROACHES FOR STUDENTS FROM REFUGEE BACKGROUNDS LEARNING ABOUT TRAUMA

Traditional educational approaches focus primarily on conveying "the facts" and may conceptualize education as a task focused on specific learning goals primarily relevant to the classroom or to the discipline/profession. Given the systemic under-representation of Cambodian history, health service educators teaching about trauma would be making contributions simply by exposing their students to the idea that there was a Cambodian genocide, focusing on just the facts. Although on the surface it may seem that this is the approach to teaching that poses the lowest level of emotional challenge to students, there are several consequences to consider. First, adhering to the facts without exploring the emotional pull of this material can be damaging to Cambodian American (as well as other) students if in aiding them to avoid pain, the health service educator inadvertently conveys that emotional reactions are shameful and unacceptable as responses. When we choose to be distanced from the emotional impact of course material, we may also be telling our students that we are uncomfortable with helping them manage their own feelings and would rather not see them express themselves in class. This can not only silence students and make some of them feel as if their experiences are not valid, but also can model an avoidance of emotional reactions that students may generalize to their interactions with patients in their service provisions. This approach to teaching in many ways replicates aspects of avoidance and numbing and results in further perpetuating silence both in the classroom and in the community.

Furthermore, our teaching and research experiences suggest that education can have significant impacts beyond the classroom and the specific conveyance of information and skills that are discipline specific. We believe that these impacts are worth striving for and are particularly relevant to those in health service professions whose disciplines aim to contribute to personal and social healing and health. Thus, we propose that a student centered approach is more effective in meeting the goals of health education, particularly when the topic is about trauma and services to individuals and communities who have experienced trauma to students from refugee backgrounds. A student centered approach sees learning as a co-constructive process rather than a one-way dissemination of information from educator to learner. It emphasizes pedagogical approaches that actively consider the interactions of students' personal (and familial and community) contexts and experiences with the content and process of learning in the classroom.

This section discusses some of the ways in which health service educators can take an active role in breaking the silence by using the student-centered approach to teaching issues of psychological trauma to students of refugee backgrounds. At the core of the student-centered approach are four foundational principles: 1) learning is related to students' contexts, 2) learning is relational and interactive and requires taking relational risks, 3) learning involves trust and respect, and 4) learning is personal and changes students and the way they see others. These principles guide student centered teaching in ways that enable students from refugee backgrounds to engage in self-reflection and personal growth around issues of trauma, and craft opportunities for students to practice behaviors that reflect positive changes in their attitudes and knowledge and act as foundations for good service provision.

Principle 1: Learning Is Related to Students' Contexts

Student centered learning is learning that is sensitive to the particular personal, familial, community, and sociohistorical contexts of students. This is one reason why we spent the first part of this chapter discussing the legacies of trauma and silence. For health service educators, understanding how community and familial narratives are broken by trauma and the legacy of silence contributes to the ability to engage students from refugee backgrounds through student-centered learning. For example, understanding legacies of silence helps educators understand why students from refugee backgrounds may not know their own family histories, may themselves feel discomfort in discussing these issues in class, or may be reluctant to address them in service provision. Health service educators can then develop strategies to incorporate these contexts into the classroom.

Make contexts explicit. Understanding cultural rules enables health service educators to name them and make them explicit, assisting students from refugee backgrounds to understand not only their own cultural, personal, and familial experiences but also the rules of the cultures of the communities they will serve (this latter point is helpful for all students). These cultural rules also affect who is culturally sanctioned to speak on taboo issues like trauma and under what circumstances. Understanding these rules helps health service educators enable students to bridge the broken narrative within their families and communities by creating a reason or a context for sharing that is culturally sanctioned (a point that will be discussed in more depth below), creating a potential role for health service educators in the community's healing process.

Helping students of refugee backgrounds understand familial and community contexts of trauma and healing can also prepare them for the realization that learning about trauma may be emotionally difficult but necessary for further personal and professional growth. By encouraging discussions of personal contexts to frame discussions of trauma, educators normalize students' experiences and guide them to use their own stories as a way to understand those of others. By practicing in the classroom skills such as listening while tolerating strong emotions and making connections between similar experiences, students develop the foundations for becoming empathetic health professionals.

Principle 2: Learning Is Relational and Requires Taking Relational Risks

In traditional classrooms that focus on learning as a one-way dissemination of information, students may not develop an explicit relationship with their teacher or other classmates because their role is largely to be information recipients. In contrast, in the student-centered classroom, educators are asked to surrender some control over the learning process to the students by co-creating the classroom experience through encouraging the sharing of personal opinions, experiences, reactions and interpretations. Students are entrusted with putting forth effort in participation, being genuine in their responses, and above all, treating each other respectfully. Health service educators employ modeling, re-define roles, attend to students' in-class reactions and introduce challenges gradually to successfully implement student-centered teaching.

Redefine roles: All students participate in a learning/teaching community. In traditional teaching, the primary role of educators is information provider while the role of students is information recipient. In a typical lecture-style environment, teachers are expected to arrive with knowledge to disseminate while ideally, students listen in rapt attention. In student-centered pedagogy, students and teachers co-create the learning process by engaging in discussions of personal opinions and experiences that frequently and necessarily involve disagreement, alliance-building and emotional responses. These moments are not endpoints of learning but part of the process and critical as opportunities for students of refugee background to connect to the learning process by sharing their experiences, opinions, and reactions with fellow classmates. Learning does not stop with the sharing of ideas but continues as students experience the support or skepticism of others and are challenged to understand the contributing factors underlying long-held beliefs. By being asked to communicate how their experiences influence their understanding of trauma, students of refugee background can develop their self-understanding and their voice.

The reality inside some traditional health service education classrooms may be that there is a group of students who are actively responding to us standing in the front of our classroom and apparently engaged in the learning process while another set of students consistently sit in the back of our classroom not raising their hands and giving us little evidence as to whether they are hearing what we are saying. Unfortunately, too many students of refugee background find themselves in the latter category, present but passive. The motivation to be passive learners among students of refugee background may include the legacies of silence, feeling invisible, or feeling misunderstood because their experiences have been so grossly underrepresented throughout their learning process that they have not learned how to fully engage in the classroom. Other reasons may be related to being refugees but not to trauma and silence, per se, such as previous experiences of ridicule or feeling unsure of whether or not they have fully understood the educator due to language issues or different classroom culture, or family and economic demands that limit energy. Given these and other motivators for passive learning, imagine how much harder it may be for students from refugee backgrounds to actively engage in the learning process when the topic of learning is trauma. Students who are the survivor generation of refugee trauma may feel that their coping strategy (i.e., avoidance of those memories) is threatened by class attendance. Some may disengage from learning by sitting in the back of the class and not really listening, emotionally numb. Others may choose to cut class or drop out altogether if their trauma symptoms are too severe for engaging in learning about this topic. When these students are asked as to why they are not participating, they may shrug their shoulders and truly not understand themselves, often times experiencing their trauma as a trigger for severe anxiety or varying degrees of dissociation (sometimes labeled as "boredom" but in reality, a far more serious inability to engage in the tasks at hand). Among students whose parents were refugees, they may similarly disengage in order to avoid thinking about painful family dynamics that have shaped their lives, or fall silent at finally beginning to understand that what they have lived has been heavily influenced by a sociocultural trauma and should not have been blamed on particular individuals. Unfortunately, the roles defined by most traditional classrooms do not lend themselves well to talking about emotionally-loaded private experiences and hence would not encourage students to talk to their teachers or to one another about their reactions.

In contrast, when one walks into a student-centered classroom, among the first things one may notice is that the participants in the class (including the instructor) are seated in a circle and facing one another. In this style of environment, all seats confer equal status and are indicative of the roles each member plays in the classroom. Unlike a lecture-style class in which seating arrangements underscore learning as a unidirectional dissemination of information by the instructor to the students, the student-centered learning itself is the discourse between all participants. Hence, the goal of health service educators in a student-centered class is not to simply tell students information about psychological trauma but rather, to offer some ideas to initiate a process in which students incorporate their lived experiences to co-create with others what psychological trauma means to them. Through this process, students of refugee background can explore the nature of their trauma and begin to heal from its effects.

For example, in a course that teaches about the Cambodian genocide, sitting in a circle allows participants to notice each other's reactions and engage in a class conversation about those reactions. The educator's role is to foster discussions that help students to reflect on each other's responses and participate themselves by offering observations and noticing how members of the class are responding to the topic and to one another. She invites all students to connect some of their own personal narratives and family histories to the discussion and points out parallels or counterpoints with the material she is teaching (i.e., Cambodian experience of the genocide). The fluidity of the student-centered approach is especially important to students of refugee backgrounds in learning about psychological trauma because it engages the class with their personal lived experiences and through discussion, validates the refugee student's understanding of trauma. Through discourse, that understanding of trauma is allowed to shift as the class incorporates new understandings (i.e., the experience of others and course material) and reinterprets the information from new vantage points.

Attend to students' emotional reactions in class. Allowing class discussions to flow in the direction of student needs and interests can be especially important when teaching students of refugee backgrounds about trauma. First of all, the psychological trauma is a very personal experience, one that is impossible to generalize and teach as "the experience." The student-centered learning process engages participants to share their diverse lived experiences while creating space for voicing less well-represented refugee experiences by students whose families have gone through it. Hence, the meaning of trauma emerges as the co-construction of those many experiences. Secondly, when teaching about a topic to an audience that is likely to react to the learning process in a deeply emotional and somewhat unpredictable manner, the educator's role in the student-centered learning process is to contain those emotions and make the classroom a safe space for students to express themselves. In order to create safety, health service educators serve not only as people on whom the student can count for support but also as moderators who encourage students to support each other. In this way, the educator models the kind of support that future patients might need from health professionals and offers students guided opportunities to practice clinical skills in the classroom. In other words, students of refugee backgrounds not only share their own stories and learn how to receive and give support; they learn through those experiences how to encourage and support future patients to break their silence and embark on the healing process.

Use a gradual approach to achieving student participation. In order for student-centered learning to be effective, health services educators have the task of putting students in the mindset that they are all participants in the learning process and that they are responsible to each other to actively participate themselves and allow each other to be heard. Hence, the goal is not to please the educator through participation but to become a member of a class community that values each student's voice. This is especially important for students of refugee backgrounds learning about trauma because one of the most important skills they need to develop is the ability to find a balance between the need to protect themselves and the need to engage with others in order to meet other life goals. In order to foster this sense of community, health services educators must think about introducing the foundations to understand trauma and building relationships within the class as equally important first goals. Regularly incorporating class activities that can foster interactions between small groups or pairs of students is very useful. Beginning with a small number of people, students of refugee backgrounds can begin to practice widening their circle of mutual trust.

In teaching about refugee experiences, one activity that can serve both as an icebreaker and introduction to the context of fleeing war asks students to imagine they are fleeing by foot from Cambodian to Thailand and they as a "family" must negotiate what five things they will bring with them. As the discussions progress, each family is asked to take progressively difficult actions such as leaving an item behind or splitting up. The purpose of this activity is two-fold: relationship-building (i.e., for students to become accustomed to working with one another to negotiate group goals) and content-learning (i.e., understand the real challenges that Cambodian refugees have faced). By incorporating both process and content, students of refugee backgrounds are given the chance to express something about themselves and their values in a hypothetical situation while also making the connection with their classmates that the choices that they may have faced as refugees were impossible choices, difficult for anyone to choose. After each class activity, the educator using a student-centered approach checks in with students to provide the opportunity for students to learn from one another *(How was each family different in making decisions?)*, challenge students to think beyond the concrete demands of the activity (*What would be the hardest thing for you if you were truly in this situation?*), and monitor students' emotional health by paying attention to signs of individuals who seem withdrawn or upset by some aspect of the activity. This is especially important for students who have suffered trauma because it may be challenging for them to anticipate when and what conditions may evoke difficult emotions as well as how to handle their reactions. We will discuss specific techniques of checking in with upset students in a later section.

As students become more and more accustomed to working in small groups, it may be helpful to transition into larger groups for some in-class activities and also begin to ask students to work in pairs and small groups outside of the classroom in group projects. The purpose in varying group size and activity is to help students practice speaking up and make use of the natural tendency of familiar people to stick together to foster constant relationships between particular students as well as challenge students to build working relationships with people with whom they are less familiar. For students of refugee backgrounds, both types of relationships are important to developing a level of trust and sense of community with the members of the class because discussions on charged topics related to refugee trauma will otherwise feel too exposing and unsafe. In particular, future health professionals of refugee backgrounds will need to learn how to build relationships with a variety of people and would be well served to practice the skill of determining whom to trust, how much they can be trusted, and again, how to balance the need to protect oneself while accomplishing other life goals. Often times, a class will have a student who is eager to contribute and takes up much of the discussion or activity. Educators who point out whose voices are over- or under-represented, remind students of their role as co-participants and use the group dynamic as a lesson in power and privilege to teach the importance of both having a voice and being an ally to give others a voice.

PRINCIPLE 3: LEARNING INVOLVES TRUST AND RESPECT

If we expect students to take the kinds of risks in class that are needed in the student-centered approach, students must feel reassured that others in the class have good intentions towards them and that what they share in class will also be understood in the context of mutual respect for each person's uniqueness. They need to feel confident that classmates will not attack them or use their words against them. To confer unfamiliar classmates with these qualities may be particularly difficult for students who have been refugees or were raised by refugees -- when survival is in part enabled by being very cautious of the intentions of others, trust comes slowly. Hence, students will differ in how readily they can trust one another, with students of refugee backgrounds likely to be less trusting initially. Educators can demonstrate their sensitivity towards these and other individual differences by giving students opportunities to learn about each other, together define some explicit group rules (i.e., allowable behavior) and gradually introduce activities that allow them to become more intimate with one another. For example, educators can shape class discussions and assignments that take into consideration different levels of comfort for speaking in class, engaging in emotionally difficult material, and demonstrating ability to tolerate ambiguity or contradiction. Through combinations of speaking to the class and conversing in smaller groups, writing journal entries and sharing poems or songs, there are many vehicles through which students can express themselves. By offering choices, educators allow students to control what and how much they share with the class. For students of refugee backgrounds, being given these choices teaches them that it is important to think about the learning process as opportunities to find creative ways for self-expression that meet their needs.

Model positive risk-taking. In a classroom setting, students generally learn whether or not to trust their instructor and one another by observing the outcome of taking risks. For example, a student of refugee background may watch and listen to how people react when another student gives a controversial opinion about a sensitive topic or reveals something personal. How do other students react? What does the educator do? In these moments of vulnerability, students of refugee backgrounds learn what is safe and what is dangerous. As health educators, we are in a position to influence the dynamic of our class by taking the risk ourselves and showing the class what it means to be supportive and respectful while staying engaged in the material. Hence, if I take the first step by offering something of myself to the class (e.g., revealing my own ethnic background and sharing my family's experience fleeing China), the class will begin to understand what level of personal engagement is acceptable and how personal context contributes to the discourse of the class. Also, by sharing my particular background, I underscore that we are all participants through which students of refugee background might be encouraged to participate as experts in their own experiences.

Maintain safety for students. In a class discussion, if a student behaves in a manner that is perceived as attacking, disparaging or otherwise damaging to another student, how should a student-centered educator react in order to restore a sense of safety in the classroom? This issue is especially of concern to students of refugee backgrounds because they are in the position of being personally acquainted with trauma, either directly or through their families, and may thus be more emotionally sensitive to others' comments or feel that the comments of others who do not have refugee experiences are misguided. Hence, for different reasons, students of refugee background may take on the role of perceived victim or perceived aggressor. For example, a Cambodian American health service student who spent four years of his teenage years in a refugee camp may become angry at a fellow student who makes a remark about "what a relief it must be to finally have the U.N. take care of you," perceiving the statement as an insult. In some instances, following up on general remarks by asking the perceived aggressor to explain what they mean, encouraging the perceived victim to express *why* the statement makes them feel upset, or inviting other students to comment on their reactions and thoughts can move the discussion in a more enriching direction. However, in cases in which students blatantly attack or are under attack, the willingness of health service educators to clearly intervene by identifying the attack and its negative consequences on the victim and putting an end to such behavior is extremely important to the safety of students. For students of refugee background, their experiences with trauma makes them especially vulnerable to feeling great shame and self-blame for things that are entirely out of their control. Hence, educators who clarify the conflict at hand and intervene when necessary protect students from harm and also model positive ways for students of refugee background to trust their own voices and defend themselves when they feel attacked or misunderstood both inside and outside the classroom.

PRINCIPLE 4: LEARNING IS PERSONAL AND CHANGES STUDENTS AND THE WAY THEY SEE OTHERS

Student focused learning focuses on changing how people understand themselves and their world around them. Unlike traditional types of learning that tend to focus on assimilating content into an existing framework, student focused learning often demands a critical assessment of the framework itself. Hence, for some students, student focused learning can be transformative. Many students of refugee background have been silenced about their life experiences for such a long time that they have learned to compartmentalize their personal narratives into a corner to experience in isolation. One of the important gifts that health services educators can give to these students is a structure for personal reflection, connection with others who have similarly lived through refugee experiences, and an audience of eager and empathetic listeners of their personal narratives. This process of reflection, hearing, and being heard allows health service students to come out of isolation and join not only with others of their own ethnic community but also with students of other refugee backgrounds as well as students who can identify with many of the challenges they may have faced, such as growing up in poverty, racism, or being immigrants.

As the sense of community becomes larger, many students begin also to broaden their sense of identity beyond their national origin or ethnicity. This may be both a relief as well as a burden, because such changes challenge longstanding allegiances and boundaries. When students have come to this country as refugees, they have left a situation in which their very identity put them at great physical risk. For example, among Cambodian refugees who survived Pol Pot's purge of the professional class, to be challenged in America as having experienced privilege because one's parents had been professors can feel unfair and provoke a furious response. Likewise, many refugees can have very strong feelings about their current or former identities and may experience varying levels of distress when they are asked to think through their beliefs in a critical manner. Health educators who anticipate that their students may be navigating a changing landscape of identity can support students in this process by giving them the message that it is alright to change their mind, feel differently or be conflicted about themselves and their worldview.

Educators can support their students of refugee background through their identity shifts by underscoring learning as a dynamic process that is complicated and has no endpoint. Practical ways to implement this in the classroom include commenting on, highlighting, and praising students for trying to articulate a different perspective. For example, health service educators can ask students to take the position of devil's advocate or assign different points of view to students in discussions and debates so as to make it clear to the class that they are relieved of the burden of ascribing to particular beliefs. Such exercises teach students of refugee background about different perspectives that they might encounter as future health professionals operating within a dominant health service framework that may or may not value their cultural sensitivity. Giving students opportunities to take different perspectives helps them to develop the ability to hold multiple and competing truths in making health service decisions. They can begin to see themselves as professionals that can effectively serve the needs of refugee patients while balancing the demands of larger systems.

On a more personal level, future health service professionals taking part in student-centered learning need tools to raise their self-awareness. Reflection journals can serve as written records of students' opinions and beliefs throughout the course term, allowing them to see their own progress and changes. In addition, health educators can guide and monitor their students' changes or effect change in others when students are asked to share journal entries regularly. Health service educators may ask students to read to the class (or some acceptable variation on sharing) in order to bring the class into a discussion of issues raised by that student's journal entry. In this way, journals can act as a tool for further growth in the class, validate the experience of the student who wrote it, as well as serve as a form of gradual participation for students who might otherwise be silent in the classroom. Reading students' journal entries must be done with sensitivity to the students' needs and desires for anonymity. Special care must be taken when students of refugee backgrounds are asked to share their work because their experiences may include traumatic content, placing them in a very vulnerable position. Health services educators should carefully consider whether or not there is a sufficient level of trust between all participants in the classroom and choose material judiciously before approaching students of refugee background with the proposal of reading their work out loud. When accomplished respectfully, such techniques can lead to mutual support and interesting discussions that can synergize personal growth among students.

At the same time that health services students from refugee backgrounds begin to recognize changes in their own beliefs about psychological trauma, they may begin to relate to their community members differently. One of the new behaviors that Cambodian American students in Asian American studies courses report is talking more to their family and other community members. For some students, their growing interest in Cambodian culture and their family's experiences during the war leads them to begin asking questions about it. Health educators can design their courses in manners that take into account students' developmental process. As their course brings students to higher level of awareness about the lived experience of trauma in refugee communities, health services educators can incorporate assignments into their course that involve students interviewing community members of refugee backgrounds or, in the case of students from refugee backgrounds themselves, intereviewing their family members. This brings their learning to a full relational circle and situates students of refugee background in the topic of what it means to come from their background and have this legacy of trauma.

Just as student centered learning creates change within and between students, so health services educators should anticipate interviews of family and community members to shape the interviewee and the relationship between the student and their family and/or community member. In this regard, health service educators can underscore the importance to students of approaching the interview with the wellbeing of their interviewee close to heart. Practicing on other classmates may help especially anxious students of refugee backgrounds to approach their interviewee. How to introduce the topic (as an assignment or in relation to one's own personal growth and desire to understand more) and learning clinical skills such as actively listening, allowing silences and displays of strong emotion to have a meaning other than termination of dialogue, calmly asking if the interviewee would like to continue telling her story or stop for the time being: these are all important clinical skills, and for students who come from refugee backgrounds, also personal skills that enable them to be more effective as family and community members.

As students progress in the course and experience changes in the way they understand trauma, health services educators may need to remind students that others who have not participated in such courses may not have the same impetus for change that they may now have. In particular, when it comes to future patients who may be more conservative about communication and continue to deal with issues of trauma through avoidance, health services educators can help students imagine what interactions may feel like and how they might go about engaging in difficult conversations. Helping students to practice with one another or with supportive community members who are healthy enough to share their own narratives for the purpose of education are effective ways to help future health professionals prepare for the world outside of the classroom.

CONCLUSION: BRIDGING THE BROKEN NARRATIVE

The goal of this chapter is to highlight the importance of choices that health educators make in the environment of their classrooms that teach about trauma and traumatized communities to students of refugee backgrounds. Health service educators' choices have impacts on future health service practitioners from refugee backgrounds and whether or not they will be adequately prepared to effectively serve their own communities or other refugee communities. We explored the damaging effects of silence which often accompanies trauma, drawing attention to how and why silence is perpetuated by the larger society, the survivors' community, and by the survivors and their families as well. However, in looking more closely at the moments in which these silences are transgressed, we shared our observation on an important opportunity for educators to break the silence, bridge the narrative, and contribute to the healing process in their students, and through them, their communities. We then described how student-centered learning can teach students of refugee background about trauma in a manner that promotes their healing and personal growth, enabling them to become effective health service practitioners for their communities. Although we utilized the Cambodian American experience as an example to illustrate four principles of student-centered teaching, we believe that student centered approaches to teaching about trauma can be an opportunity for psychological growth and healing not just in Cambodian American students but also students from other refugee backgrounds learning to become future health professionals serving their communities.

As conflicts around the world continue and families come to this country to seek refuge, health services educators continue be on the frontline of integrating individuals from diverse cultures and life paths into the fabric of our country and preparing these individuals to serve their own communities and others as effectively as possible. Whether or not we seek it, we are crucial partners in co-creating our students' new professional and personal identities and hold great sway in how refugee communities in this country will be served by the health service professions. We can contribute to bridging the broken narratives and contribute to healing or we can stand by as others have in the past.

REFERENCES

APA (American Psychiatric Association). (2000). Diagnostic and statistical manual of mental disorders (4th ed., text revision). Washington, DC: Author.

Chandler, D. P. (1991). The tragedy of Cambodian history. New Haven, CT: Yale University Press.

Chao, C. M. (1992). The inner heart: Therapy with Southeast Asian families. In L. A. Vargas & J. D. Koss-Chioino (Eds.) Working with culture: Psychotherapeutic interventions with ethnic minority children and adolescents (pp. 157-181). San Francisco: Jossey-Bass.

Hood, M. & Ablin, D. A. (1987). The path to Cambodia's present. In D. A. Ablin & M. Hood (Eds.), The Cambodian agony (pp. xv-lxi). New York: M.E. Sharpe, Inc.

Hulse, C. (2007, October 18). House Speaker now unsure if Armenian genocide motion will reach a vote. New York Times. Retrieved February 25, 2008, from http://www. nytimes.com/2007/10/18/washington/18cong.html

Kiernan, B. (2004). How Pol Pot came to power: Colonialism, nationalism, and communism in Cambodia, 1930-1975. New Haven, CT: Yale University Press.

Lin, N. J. (2005). Legacies of trauma: The Cambodian American experience. Unpublished master's thesis, University of Massachusetts, Boston.

Power, S. (2002). A problem from hell: America and the age of genocide. New York: Basic Books.

Presidential Proclamation 4417, President Gerald Ford, Confirming the Termination of the Executive Order Authorizing Japanese-American Internment During World War II. Federal Register, Vol. 41, No. 35 (February 20, 1976). Retrieved February 29, 2008 from the Ford Library website: http://www.fordlibrarymuseum.gov/library/speeches/760111p.htm

Sack, W. H., Clarke, G. N., Kinney, R., Belestos, G., Him, C. D., & Seeley, J. (1995). The Khmer adolescent project: II. Functional capacities in two generations of Cambodian refugees. Journal of Nervous Mental Disorders, 183, 177-181.

Sack, W. H., McSharry, S., Clarke, G. N., Kinney, R., Seeley, J., & Lewinsohn, P. (1994). The Khmer adolescent project: Epidemiologic findings in two generations of Cambodian refugees. Journal of Nervous Mental Disorders, 182, 387-395.

Shawcross, W. (1987). *Sideshow: Kissinger, Nixon, and the destruction of Cambodia.*
New York: Simon & Schuster.

Uba, L. (1994). *Asian Americans: Personality patterns, identity and mental health.* New
York: The Guilford Press.

FOOTNOTE

1   We are differentiating here between personal trauma and sociocultural trauma. Personal trauma includes
traumatic events that happen to an individual or a family that occur in a relatively stable social and political
context in which the trauma is not explicitly related to the social context itself. Examples of personal trauma might
include childhood abuse or rape of a woman within a society not currently characterized by widespread social
upheaval or war (e.g., the current U.S. society). In contrast, sociocultural trauma is trauma that is experienced
by a large group or entire society due to war, oppressive governmental regimes, genocide, etc. Examples of
sociocultural trauma might include the experiences of peoples in Cambodia and Vietnam during the Vietnam War
and its aftermath, the Armenian people during the genocide, the Southern Sudanese people during the civil war
of the 1980s and '90s and Jews during the Holocaust, etc. These peoples have multiple experiences of specific
traumatic incidents (including assault, murder, rape, incarceration, attacks by pirates, etc.), as well as witnessing
trauma, that are qualitatively different than personal trauma due to the sociocultural context. In this chapter,
when we discuss students who have experienced trauma, we are referring to students who have personal or familial
experience with sociocultural, rather than personal, trauma.

CHAPTER 8

COMMUNITY CULTURAL DEVELOPMENT AND EDUCATION WITH CAMBODIAN AMERICAN YOUTH

Shirley Suet-ling Tang, PhD

Introduction

In Dalama...'the end'n is just the beginning' — the music CD that took Cambodia by storm in 2006 — praCh Ly, a second-generation Cambodian American rapper who grew up in California and Florida, captures the fury and frustration of many Southeast Asian American youth in defiant hip-hop tones: "people die over a buck, the government don't give a fuck/.../it's a war on the streetz/I gotta survive.../so I go to sleep with an open eye[1]." Such lyrics critique a society that marginalizes urban youth and negates opportunities for their educational achievement and community development. Ly raises questions about the failure of the juvenile justice system, effects of declining wages on poverty-stricken communities, families struggling to overcome war trauma, and resource-poor urban schools. In the track, "wars on the streetz," he is vehemently explicit about schools as distressing places that compound the problems of their community — "teacher illiterate, counselors throw'n fits, students are criminals, principal an idiot."

The educational and economic crises encapsulated in Ly's music are particularly resonant for a generation of Khmer (Cambodian)[2] and other Southeast Asian American youth. From West Coast to East Coast, Southeast Asian American rappers and poets, spoken word and graffiti artists, filmmakers and photographers, performance and multimedia artists, are producing new sounds, words, images and other media that transform their righteous anger into creative art expressions (May & praCh, 2004). Responding to the inequality and injustice they experience in their schools and neighborhoods, Southeast Asian American youth are creating new cultural terrain for powerful learning and social change. As Ly describes his creative productions: "it's not just musix, it's a movement."

A basic question Ly and others are asking is whether educational reforms alone can radically transform the structure and culture of inequality experienced by urban students and families in socially marginalized communities in the United States. Strategies for raising levels of academic achievement during the past decade, for example, have targeted high stakes testing and student/teacher/school assessments, improving school personnel quality, and implementing accountability-monitoring systems. But, as educational researcher Jean Anyon has argued, "As a nation, we have been counting on education to solve the problems of unemployment, joblessness, and poverty for many years. But education did not cause these problems, and education cannot solve them" (Anyon, 2005, p. 3). Recognizing the limitations of current educational reforms in dealing with urban poverty and racial injustice that are directly and indirectly maintained by federal and regional policies, Anyon echoes praCh Ly in proposing "a new social justice movement" that brings together educators, community organizers, parents, neighborhood residents, and young people in multi-constituency political coalitions to address not only educational injustice, but also broader issues of social inequality that continue to hinder lasting, positive development in urban communities. Moreover, for those of us in higher education, we need to reflect more fully on how our roles, responsibilities, and resources can engage not only those populations who have already gained access to our institutions, but also those whom we do not see or hear because they are not directly in our sites/sights/cites. In this chapter, I will focus on exactly this group of young people, who are not directly in our academic institutions but who are in the so-called "pipeline." I will also analyze "alternative learning communities" in which they have participated and worked to co-construct. The experiences of Southeast Asian urban youth in nontraditional learning settings offer insights about the current educational status of Southeast Asian students as well as models of engagement that intersect directly with their needs and issues. Rather than locating my focus on current college students or higher education sites, I intentionally draw attention to Southeast Asian American youth and their nontraditional learning environments in order to highlight both the problems represented by strikingly low college graduation rates of Southeast Asian American students (see next two sections for details) and the opportunities represented by alternative learning practices (the focus of this chapter).

Educational reforms alone do not enable youth to survive racism, poverty and police harassment; nor do they offer fresh ways of conceptualizing and confronting street-level challenges that have been significantly shaped by rapid global transformations. In my study of Khmer American community development in the small city of Revere, Massachusetts, for example, educational reforms designed during the 1970s period of Black-White racial desegregation have become less relevant due to the influx of refugees and immigrants especially from Southeast Asia and Latin America that have redefined the racial, cultural, and linguistic profiles of the city's neighborhoods (Tang, 2002). Furthermore, global/transnational realities such as wars, migrations, and deportations directly impact the (re)construction of refugee/immigrant families and communities in local neighborhoods (Kiang & Tang, 2006). Southeast Asian refugee parents, for example, continue to deal with trauma-related illnesses and endure hardships and discrimination in the United States, while their children who were born or grew up here have few opportunities to learn about those experiences either at home or in schools. Intergenerational conflicts caused by a lack of mutual understanding then severely disrupt many family units. Both young people and their elders keep their distance and retreat into further isolation, not knowing the causes and solutions of the ruptures in their families — or where exactly to find home.

For social movements in the making, therefore, the legacies as well as possibilities of progressive political activism that Anyon (2005) describes in terms of rights-based advocacy for reforms within the domains of housing, labor and education can be complemented by fresh strategic interventions that engage directly with people's lived experiences in relation to cultural discontinuities, social dislocation and displacement. Southeast Asian American youth, for example, not only seek opportunities to learn more about the histories, cultures, spiritual traditions, and political events in their homelands, but they also participate in cultural productions and innovations that represent or even reimagine their local/global contexts of displaced homes, fragmented identities, and resilient survival. Quite simply, Anyon's movement needs praCh.

In this chapter, I explore cultural activism as a new terrain for social change created by this younger generation of Southeast Asian Americans. Specifically, I analyze the construction of alternative learning communities led by youth and young adults. Instead of focusing on individual artists like Ly, however, this study analyzes the long-term, collective cultural development of young people in an out-of-school community arts program over a period of nine years. The program, Youth-Art-In-Action (YAIA), partnered urban youth from the Coalition for Asian Pacific American Youth (CAPAY), a pan-Asian youth leadership network in Massachusetts affiliated with UMass Boston's Asian American Studies Program and college students at the School of the Museum of Fine Arts in Boston. From 1997 through 2005, YAIA youth participants were primarily low-income young women of color from refugee/immigrant families, most of whom lived in the adjoining cities of Revere and Lynn, Massachusetts. Most identified as Khmer (Cambodian) and many, like their peers across the country, had dropped/stopped out of school as well.

SOUTHEAST ASIAN AMERICANS AND EDUCATION

According to the U.S. Census Bureau's most recent American Community Survey (ACS), the Asian American population continued to outpace all other racial groups in Massachusetts from 2000 to 2005 — increasing by 23% compared with Latinos and Blacks, who grew by just 14.5% and 6%, respectively, and Whites whose numbers actually declined by 4%[3]. Such dramatic and sustained Asian American growth locally and nationally throughout the last three decades has resulted in ever greater ethnic, socioeconomic and language diversity for this population, which now includes recent immigrants and refugees of more than 40 different ethnicities, together with those who have lived in the United States for generations. Limitations in how population and related data on educational achievement have been both collected and interpreted, however, have too often led to the portrayal of Asian Americans as a homogeneous group, marginalizing important voices and perspectives in the population.

Despite three decades of critique (Fong, 1998; Lee, 1999; Prashad, 2000), Asian Americans are still too often referred to as a "model minority," a label that distorts the rich diversity, complex realities, and critical challenges facing many segments of this population. Although aggregate data may seem to show that Asian Americans excel educationally and economically, when such data are disaggregated by ethnic group, it is clear that certain communities, especially among Southeast Asian ethnicities, have some of the highest poverty rates of any group locally or nationally (U.S. Government Accountability Office, 2007). Indeed, the Asian American population occupies both ends of the socioeconomic spectrum: while some rank among the country's most highly educated and highest income wage earners, others are among its most poorly educated and impoverished.

Nationally in 2000, for example, roughly 9% of Cambodians, 7% of Hmong, 7% Lao, and 20% of Vietnamese adults had college degrees, compared with nearly 25% of Americans overall[4]. Vietnamese Americans had an average per-person income of just over $15,000, compared with over $21,000 for the U.S. population overall. Cambodians and Lao had average per-person incomes below $12,000 and Hmong Americans had the lowest average per-person income of any ethnic group described by the 2000 Census: $6,613. In 1999, over 29% of Cambodian, 37% of Hmong, 19% of Lao, and 16% of Vietnamese in the United States lived under the poverty line, compared with just over 12% of the U.S. population overall (Niedzwiecki & Duong, 2004).

Locally, the profile is similar, as Cambodians in metropolitan Boston have considerably lower levels of educational attainment compared with other Asian Americans (Watanabe, Liu, & Lo, 2004). For example, of the population 25 years old and older, nearly 40% of Cambodians have less than a ninth grade education compared with 22% of Vietnamese, 15% of Chinese, and just 4% of Indians. Similarly, nearly 50% of Indians and 30% of Chinese in metropolitan Boston have a graduate or professional degree, compared to 4.4% of Vietnamese and just 2.9% of Cambodians. Too often, the lack of disaggregated Asian American data has hidden specific profiles of Southeast Asian American communities, which, in turn, has led to disparities for those communities in relation to funding, services, and other relevant resource allocations (Liu, Tran, & Watanabe, 2007).

KHMER AMERICAN STUDENT NEEDS

Large numbers of Cambodian refugees settled in Massachusetts throughout the 1980s, drawn by employment opportunities, progressive social welfare policies, and, importantly, some of the first Cambodian Buddhist temples in the country (Kiang, 1994). Many Cambodians found semi-skilled factory jobs available in plants that assembled electronics, computers, and medical supplies. Revere and Lowell have served as historic Cambodian mixed commercial-residential hubs for the local Cambodian American population, while the city of Lynn currently has the fastest-growing Cambodian American population in Massachusetts. After Long Beach, California (Gorman, 2007), Lowell and Lynn represent the second and fifth largest concentrations of Cambodian Americans in the United States.[5]

During the early years of resettlement in the 1980s, Cambodian refugees in Revere faced intense racial violence, ranging from vandalism and harassment to firebombings and murder. As threats and attacks continued into the 1990s, Khmer American gang activity emerged in Revere and later Lynn as an adaptive response by youth to claim identity and gain protection in school and on the street. Local violence, then, compounded the traumas already survived by Cambodian refugee families from war, forced migration, and displacement through refugee resettlement (Wehrly, 1988; Welaratna, 1993). Reflecting both the demographic realities of the refugee population, and the shape of continuing educational and economic inequality, one-third of Lynn's Asian Americans between 18 and 64 years of age and 6 out of 10 over the age of 65 are not proficient in English. Contrary to popular stereotypes, 36% of Asian American adults in Lynn (25 years and older) have less than a ninth grade education, compared to only 7% each for Whites and Blacks and 26% for Latinos[6].

Reflecting this reality in recent testimony to Congress on behalf of Southeast Asian American groups nationally, KaYing Yang and Max Niedzwiecki pointed out that the four most important factors leading to the achievement gap between Southeast Asian Americans and other students are: "limited English proficiency; systematic miscommunication between students, parents, and teachers; discrimination; and widespread feelings of alienation from mainstream schools" (Yang & Niedzwiecki, 2003). Similarly, political scientist Khatharya Um argues that the problem results, in part, from Southeast Asian American youth being systematically "pushed out" of the educational system at the middle- and high-school levels (Um, 2003). She writes, "Under-representation in higher education is symptomatic, in critical aspects, of the numerous and compounding impediments that Southeast Asian youth encounter in the earlier stages of their educational experience and that deter their pursuit of higher education. Given their "political histories — of war, dislocation, and dispossession — many Southeast Asian students and their families already start from a position of grave disadvantage" (Um, 2003, p. iii). This position of disadvantage is further exacerbated by additional challenges in the resettlement process, including "poverty, daily encounters with delinquency and crime, family dysfunction, and racism both at school and in society" (Um, 2003, p. iii).

Conceptual and Methodological Approach

In this chapter, I highlight an alternative, out-of-school intervention that was created specifically with engagement by urban Khmer American youth as a core commitment. Though not discounting the necessity and importance of educational reforms to strengthen existing school systems, my own research and on-the-ground experiences have led me to participate in the development of alternative sites and strategies.

Given a well-established body of educational research showing urban schools and school systems in general to have an absence of caring relationships (Poplin & Weeres, 1993), and to be sites of struggle for Southeast Asian American students in particular (Kiang & Kaplan, 1994; Kiang, Nguyen, & Sheehan, 1995; Le & Wallen, 2006; Lee, 2005), practitioners and some scholars have turned to community-based spaces/sites and out-of-school time as alternative learning communities, supported by caring, culturally responsive adults (Bodilly & Beckett, 2005; Danish & Gulotta, 2000; Eccles, & Gootman, 2002; Gordon, Bridglall,

& Meroe, 2004; Heath & McLaughlin, 1993; Weis & Fine, 2000). A small but compelling body of literature highlights the educational, sociocultural, and civic added value(s) of such after/out-of-school programs for urban youth and communities, particularly those that provide opportunities beyond academic support or recreation to include heritage arts, media literacy, and other expressions of youth-centered cultural development (Ball & Heath, 1993; Davis, Soep, Maira, Remba, & Putnoi, 1993; Heath & Smyth, 1999; Roffman, Suarez-Orozco, & Rhodes, 2003).

The focus on alternative learning communities created with youth at the center (Ellis, 2001) offers a useful counterpoint to consider how schools, organizations, and communities respond to educational inequalities facing many youth of color, including Khmer Americans in Revere and Lynn. These are young people from marginalized groups whom, beginning in the 1980s, public discourse demonized as delinquent and school systems labeled as at-risk, disruptive, and typically in need of special education (Datnow, Hubbard, & Woody, 2001; Losen & Orfield, 2002). The learning communities investigated in this study are distinct from the alternative education programs in schools or special programs designed to connect youth involved in the juvenile justice system with coordinated networks of social services, though there is evidence to show that some of these models have been effective (Atkins, Bullis, & Todis, 2005). Rather than address the debates over ideology, methodology, and impacts of alternative education programs in general (Vigil, Nguyen, & Chang, 2006), I am interested in a many-centered, holistic approach to build and sustain alternative learning communities that connect schools, streets, indigenous institutions, and other public spaces. Such alternative learning practices have received limited scholarly attention or public investment, but deserve recognition as a significant educational strategy.

In the only book-length ethnographic study of Southeast Asian American youth in a community-based, after-school arts program, Angela Reyes (2007) documents important aspects of cultural/linguistic and identity development as well as critical thinking and community-building through a media literacy and video production program in which she served as a staff member and participant observer over a four-year period. Though primarily intended as a study of Southeast Asian American youth discourse analysis, Reyes found that "the after-school video-making project provided under-served Southeast Asian American teenagers with a vital site for exploring and expressing their identities. This finding has implications not only for Asian American youth but for other racial, immigrant, and linguistic minorities whose needs are also often overlooked in schools" (p. 151).

Similar in values to the program described by Reyes, but distinct in terms of program setting and structure, community context, cultural repertoire, multigenerational relationships, duration, and research focus, the following sections offer an analysis of grassroots cultural productions generated during the past nine years by the Youth-Art-In-Action (YAIA) program. My own involvement with YAIA began while I was working as a youth/

community organizer in Revere from 1997 to late 1999. Since then, I have maintained relationships with old and new program participants while also serving as a Humanities Scholar for YAIA from 2000 to 2005. In this role, I helped design the curriculum for the documentary research components of YAIA's public art/public history projects (Goldbard & Adams, 2001, 2002; Hayden, 1995).

Through those nine years of involvement, I regularly interviewed teaching artists, surveyed youth participants, observed at the studio and at community events, and facilitated informal and formal discussions with participants at art exhibitions and other venues each year. I also reviewed and evaluated curriculum materials and exhibition content as well as reflective writings by/with youth participants and written comments by event participants. My analysis reflects long-term, methodological, and programmatic commitments to grounded theory and critical ethnography in following the holistic development and life stories of these young people and their communities (Kiang, 2002; Kiang, Suyemoto, & Tang, in press; Tang, 2008).

NEW CULTURAL TERRAIN

Young people in the Youth-Art-In-Action program have turned to cultural activism to generate vital knowledge, ideas, creative expressions and practices with which to understand and address how they — and their communities — make concrete meanings of "migration," "home," "justice," and "global/local connections." Cultural activism opens an imaginative and reflective space, an inviting terrain for critical thinking, and an engaging environment for active, participatory learning that many young people are denied in mainstream urban schools. Contradicting popular perceptions that urban youth are academically weak and unsuited for traditional classrooms, Southeast Asian American youth artists demonstrate that they are highly motivated, responsible learners. They are successful in constructing authentic learning communities through which they meaningfully contest dominant representations of Southeast Asians and powerfully craft their own local/global narratives of place and belonging. They develop ways to assess community issues and indigenous resources in local neighborhoods, to revive and transform cultural and spiritual traditions, to engage diverse publics to question and resist the effects of the dominant culture, and to challenge and nurture groups and institutions to make space for their cultural production. They create a new public sphere grounded in the multilingual, multigenerational and multiethnic realities and collaborations of local neighborhoods as well as transnational networks, frequently sharing responsibility with all participants to address differences and divergences through direct interactions, to envision what they collectively want, and to give their imaginations real and determinate shape.

MAPPING SPECIAL PLACES AND COMMUNITY RESOURCES

In one of several examples to be detailed here, small groups of youth in YAIA conducted historical and ethnographic research in the Khmer American neighborhood in Revere for a project they titled, "Mapping Places," in 2001. One group of youth participants focused on the Revere Beach area, and uncovered a common experience of racial harassment and police repression experienced by many urban youth of various racial and cultural backgrounds. They created a book of writings, photos, drawings, and digitized images to present young people as "normal kids" who simply wanted to "have a good time" and interact with their peers on the beach — highlighting their shared experience to claim space and identity in the city. A second group explored "the Four Corners" on Shirley Avenue — a busy commercial intersection within the neighborhood that showed dramatic demographic changes during the past two decades. By tracing the evolution of physical sites at that intersection, they discovered some of the critical stages of community development in their neighborhood, and found that Cambodians had contributed significantly to the city's development process since they began resettling there in the early 1980s. Through their interviews, they began to grasp the historic significance of a fundraising carwash organized by Khmer American young women half a generation earlier in 1996 to raise money and community awareness following the murder of a Khmer American young man next to the Four Corners. The group's Four Corners art installation used sculpture, photography, text, and architectural design to present the historic emergence of an earlier generational cohort of Khmer American young women in the mid-1990s, who pooled resources among themselves and organized their version of a public demonstration against the city's blatant neglect of problems facing Khmer Americans.

By foregrounding the historical legacies and cultural commitments of Khmer residents across generations, youth artists were intervening in the networks of communication and information-exchange that shaped public perceptions of Khmer Americans. Their art installation was created to motivate a diverse audience to recognize the deep commitments shared and represented by Khmer Americans in the city. Moreover, in juxtaposing their review of official accounts of economic development and land redevelopment in the city with their own mapping of "special places" and community resources, they also drew critical attention to indigenous community visions for creating a more peaceful, multicultural neighborhood and a more just, equitable society.

What was the significance of bringing awareness to the cultural inheritance of Khmer Americans in 2001? YAIA's intention, in part, was to document and analyze the experiences of Revere's Khmer community at a time when it seemed unable to survive against economic and political forces associated with land redevelopment. Housing prices and land values had already become too expensive for most Khmer American residents and small businesses to remain in the city. YAIA's art installation was thus created to not only assert a strong visual presence of Khmer Americans within the city of Revere, but also to question what "displacement" and "dispossession" meant for Khmer Americans. It was hoped that through the cultural production process, a range of voices would come forward, and important lessons would emerge for everyone to remember. Indeed, for a refugee population already forcibly dispersed from their homeland by war, the meaning of displacement in this setting that they had claimed home for nearly twenty years was not abstract or academic. Through the Mapping Places project, YAIA artists showed that "development" did not have to be defined or imposed from the outside. Rather, through interaction, shared experiences, and active learning, young people identified and analyzed issues that were important for themselves, and engaged others in public dialogue and actions, to make sense of their own community, and to re-visualize and re-create it, both in their imaginations and on the street.

REVIVING AND TRANSFORMING CULTURAL AND SPIRITUAL TRADITIONS

With goals of creating a shared public space for participants from diverse backgrounds and strengthening their collective visions of what cultural production means in contemporary life, YAIA artists turned to their community's traditional arts, language, and spiritual commitments to establish a solid foundation for their work. At the same time, they adopted and fused a mix of cultural insights and practices to create art in composite and hybridized forms. In 2002, youth participants built a miniature model of the Sanghikaram Wat Khmer Buddhist temple in Lynn — celebrating it as a center of cultural practice and preservation for both the old and young generations, and also envisioning its potential to address current challenges of life in the United States. For many Khmer adults and elders, the Buddhist temple serves as the most important cultural and spiritual influence in their lives. The temple is the center of Khmer culture locally and serves as a site of communal solidarity and information sharing (Carini, 2005; Graff & Howard, 1993; Smith-Hefner, 1999). For example, the temple in Lynn has consistently provided opportunities for staff from Lynn's mainstream health agencies to outreach to community members and provide discussion or counseling sessions. In addition, the temple has also offered Khmer-language classes to support intergenerational communication within the community.

Recognizing the Buddhist temple as an important community site, YAIA decided to make it a focal point of their intergenerational art project. The group identified 1.5 and 1.8 generation[7] community leaders who had gained the trust of the oldest generation to act as "bridges" to introduce the young people to the elderly and the monks at the actual temple site in Lynn. Through a series of temple visits, young people collected migration and resettlement stories of the elderly women and men and the monks. While at the temple, the youth also learned about religious rites and cultural symbols.

With the guidance of Master Artist Yary Livan, the only surviving master of traditional Khmer ceramics and kiln building, YAIA artists ultimately produced an original architectural model of the temple that combined traditional heritage and American adaptations to present their visions of cultural survival and community reconstruction. When building the miniature temple, Livan advised the young people to include traditional architectural structures that had been destroyed during the wars and the Khmer Rouge era[8]. Through their own historical research they quickly learned that many of Cambodia's artists had died during this period and in subsequent years. They concluded that if the younger generation did not inherit the skills of surviving elders, then their traditional arts heritage would soon disappear. They decided not only to embrace Livan's advice about temple design, but also added to the existing building's layout a number of new spaces of their own design, including a traditional arts and dance room, a classroom for Khmer language instruction, a kitchen for traditional cooking and an open space for community gatherings. They also created figurines of people who represented a wide range of ages, ethnicities, and occupations to place within their model. Young people asserted that the Buddhist temple was a source of cultural pride, while it also had the potential to serve as a site for developing culturally responsive curricula in schools, and for facilitating healthy communication and meaningful interaction between parents, teachers, students, and community members who were typically separated by language and culture barriers.

In the years that followed their production of the temple model, YAIA artists continued to emphasize the importance of simultaneously embracing and transforming cultural and spiritual traditions. Their cultural work sparked significant conversations about how second-generation young women negotiate between new and old cultures in their everyday struggles. In the project *Four Generations* (2005), for example, youth artists created a sculpture intended to serve as a focal point for intergenerational dialogue in the Khmer American community exploring the questions: "Who were we?", "Who are we?" and "Who are we going to become?". These questions had emerged from several years of documenting and analyzing different voices and experiences in the community. The four sides of their sculpture visually represented these voices and experiences: a traditional elderly woman representing Khmer ancestors; a contemporary elderly woman representing today's older generation; a younger woman (the Apsara) representing the younger generation; and an infant symbolizing hope for a brighter future. YAIA's young women artists — again with the artistic and cultural mentorship of Yary Livan — used the traditional art form of bayon sculpture to create this contemporary sculptural piece, demonstrating their commitment to engage older generations effectively in dialogue by connecting through an art form that would be most familiar to them, even as they reinterpreted and re-created it to address issues relevant to their own lived experiences.

MULTIPLE PUBLICS, NEW LEARNING SPACES, AND LOCAL/TRANSNATIONAL LEARNING COMMUNITIES

YAIA regularly presented art exhibitions and installations including *Mapping Places* (2002), *Buddhist Temple* (2002), and *Four Generations* (2005) in multiple public spaces. The quality, innovation, and impact of the artwork produced and exhibited by the program moved diverse participants and audiences on many levels across boundaries of culture, race, gender, age, and geography. At a community's traditional Khmer New Year celebration, for example, the *Mapping Places* art exhibition generated powerful responses throughout the day from everyone who walked by — ranging from children and elders to store-owners and agency workers to street-involved youth and even the Revere police on duty. This was an additional, deliberate act of community cultural development intended to connect the past with the collective identity, experience and vision of current generation. In typical Khmer New Year celebrations, the dominant forms of female creative expression are confined to Khmer traditional dance, popular music, karaoke, and fashion shows that feature traditional costumes. The YAIA art exhibition, however, created a new cultural context for multiple publics to explore the community's development (Revere Beach, Four Corners, etc.) over time, to recall and share stories, and to participate in a public dialogue about how to envision inspiring, new possibilities for Khmer American community and cultural development within the city.

Exhibiting their successful cultural productions has also typically inspired fresh ideas to develop new learning spaces and reach new audiences. YAIA's *The Journey Box* (2000) project, for example, was initially launched in 2000 to provide a lens to discover the hopes, dreams, passions and concerns of refugee youth and to share them with a larger local public. The youth artists who participated in the original production were all local children of recent refugees/immigrants from Bosnia, Vietnam and Cambodia. As these young people continued their own life journeys, moving from urban cities to college or jobs outside their neighborhoods, they suggested taking *The Journey Box* to a regionwide level to create a larger forum for dialogue that would encourage young people to think about the legacies of wars around the world and what is important in life beyond their individual selves. Since then, *The Journey Box* has become a traveling/collecting project that moves throughout the region to youth programs, schools and public events, where diverse youth audiences explore the common and varied life journeys reflected in the collection, and also add to its contents. The collection now holds a documentary video, a youth dance performance video, a CD by Khmer Dynasty Cambodian rap artists, a photo transfer collage quilt, 30 black-and-white photographic essays, numerous paintings, drawings, sculptures, and handmade books. Past destinations in metropolitan Boston for *The Journey Box* have included: Khmer Youth and Family Center in Lynn, Revere High School, B2K Cultural Heritage Festival at the Boston City Hall Plaza, the "Making Art, Making Change: Community Identity, Peace and

Justice" event at the Cambridge Center for Adult Education, the "CreAsian Festival" at the Boston Center for the Arts, and Roca Inc.

Furthermore, as other YAIA artwork increasingly gained attention from older generations of Khmer American artists and community leaders, young people began exhibiting their work alongside more established artists who were actively involved in creating transnational networks to preserve traditional Khmer art forms and to encourage contemporary artistic expression and exchange. Four Generations and other YAIA projects, for example, were presented side by side with creative work by recognized artists in Lowell, Massachusetts — the second largest Khmer community in the United States — during the annual Cambodian Expressions Film and Arts Festival. The events of the festival were widely publicized and discussed across the state and within the transnational networks of artists and community leaders who frequently travel back and forth between Cambodia, the United States and other countries (Reid, 2004). Artistic production thus played a central role in enabling greater cultural exchange in the region and across national borders, further enlarging the learning communities with which young people could engage and share.

INSTITUTIONAL SPACES FOR CULTURAL PRODUCTION, EXHIBITION, AND EDUCATION

YAIA has succeeded in garnering support from mainstream institutions to make space for their cultural production because of social change commitments of particular individuals working within these institutions and the long-term relationships that YAIA teaching artists have cultivated with these individuals. Constant advocacy by founding Program Director and Lead Artist Marge Rack and Master Artist Yary Livan contributed significantly to the process of promoting the artistic expressions of urban youth artists and, over time, securing a space for YAIA within these institutions. For example, after nine years of continued effort, YAIA was invited to exhibit their artwork at the Museum of Fine Arts Boston. For this groundbreaking month-long event, YAIA created a 5 x 20 foot painting of Angkor Wat to represent Khmer people and culture. They also produced a multimedia slide show that documented the extended process of collaboratively creating and mounting the large-size painting. This art project for the museum did not draw direct attention to issues facing youth in schools or in the community such as those highlighted in the Mapping Places or The Journey Box projects, but by claiming space within one of the world's elite art museums, based on the compelling quality and vision of their cultural productions, YAIA presented a valuable contrast to the everyday depictions of failure and fiasco that dominated public discourse about urban youth.

In addition to exhibiting their art in the museum, YAIA also engaged other kinds of mainstream institutions, such as middle and high schools in local neighborhoods as well as community colleges and regional universities with sizable populations of Southeast

Asian students to create opportunities for remembering and respecting their community's rich culture and history. In 2002, for example, YAIA participants and students in the Asian American Studies Program at UMass Boston organized an oral history/story-sharing event at a local Khmer restaurant on Shirley Avenue in Revere, where community members across three generations recounted their experiences in Revere over the past 20 years. Based on follow-up interviews and archival research inspired by the restaurant story-sharing, young people then produced a storybook that documents the early years of refugee resettlement in Revere. Real Life Real Stories was told from the perspective of a young daughter of a Khmer refugee family who experienced racial violence but hopes for a brighter future for her family and the community. The story highlights the historic 1987 Enough Is Enough rally — recognized as the first demonstration for racial justice by Cambodians in the United States — when local residents were joined by pan-Asian organizations, civil rights leaders, and other multiracial groups to support the Cambodian community's demands for justice and peace following a Christmas 1986 arson that destroyed a triple-decker house in Revere where 21 Cambodian refugees were living (Asian American Resource Workshop, 1987; Kiang & Tang, 2006; Tang, 2002).

The storybook project came full circle when, in spring 2004, YAIA participants and students from UMass Boston presented Real Life Real Stories at the James A. Garfield School in Revere, engaging middle school students of diverse backgrounds as well as older students from Revere High School's Asian Club. The Garfield School event was a pivotal moment for preserving history in the community, especially in marking the role that schools can play within communities that face injustice. One of the central images in the storybook shows young children with markers and poster boards preparing signs at their school for a march against anti-Asian violence in the community. This image is important because it documents what actually happened at the Garfield School, when, at the urging of the school's principal, students from diverse backgrounds made bilingual signs and other visual materials in English and Khmer for the upcoming Enough Is Enough rally. Children from the Garfield School, along with their families and school staff, actually represented a significant contingent at the rally on January 10, 1987. Several school board officials spoke at the rally about the importance of education in fighting racism. The participation of local school officials, teachers, students, and parents in the rally — particularly from the Garfield School — was a splendid moment to be remembered in Revere's history, especially given the critical role that school-based learning environments play in shaping children's attitudes, values, and knowledge regarding equality and justice.

After seeing YAIA's Real Life Real Stories presentation at their school in 2004, the young Garfield students responded to the storybook presentation enthusiastically. When asked to reflect on an image/idea from the discussion that they thought was important to remember, many Khmer American children wrote about their relationships with their parents or with their non-Khmer classmates/neighbors. The content of their writings revealed the continued prevalence of inter-ethnic tensions in the school and neighborhood, and, more importantly, reminded us of the stressors and conflicts that children in local Khmer American communities continue to endure, even at young ages, with little intervention by adults.

Because they wished to make a longer-term commitment to the educational achievement of Southeast Asian American students, YAIA engaged schools at other levels as well. In 2003, for example, YAIA's finished temple model was presented at the annual Khmer New Year celebration held at North Shore Community College in Lynn. Like other YAIA projects, this project came full circle when the elderly men whom the young women had initially met at the temple then offered to exhibit the model permanently at the Lynn temple after seeing it themselves at the New Year event. From 2003 to 2004, the temple model was also exhibited in the Robert Ford Elementary School in Lynn, thus offering an opportunity for teachers, staff, students, and parents of various backgrounds to gain better understanding of Khmer traditions and culture. Each time the temple traveled to exhibitions, YAIA youth artists accompanied the artwork and engaged various audiences in dialogue about their purpose, process, and further possibilities.

CONCLUSIONS

Grassroots artistic creations in Lynn and Revere represent a new cultural terrain that is nurturing an emerging movement toward the articulation and representation of cultural identity and community cultural development (Goldbard & Adams, 2001, 2002). With powerful implications for urban education and social justice (Anyon, 2005), this movement has based its strategies of social change on generating capacity for marginalized urban youth to construct their narratives of home and belonging, creating transformative learning communities that reach diverse participants within and beyond the local neighborhood, and shaping artistic interventions in public spaces. At the center of this work of community cultural development is the unique cultural inheritance of the Khmer people, locally and transnationally. YAIA's projects have deeply explored the multilayered experiences of Khmer elders' entangled pasts, while stemming directly from the lived conditions and complex realities that face the younger generation — particularly those who grew up in the United States during the late 1980s and 1990s.

YAIA's richly expressive cultural productions augment an older generation's articulations of haunting war memories and idyllic pasts, to reflect two decades of changing geopolitical conditions — globalization of the market-driven economy, privatization and increased concentration of wealth, persistent poverty and increased racial profiling in inner cities, massive cutbacks in government funding for education and community services, and the rise of Hip Hop and other youth movements to counteract such forces — all against the backdrop of deindustrialization and demographic changes in the post-civil rights and post-Vietnam era, and all of which have dramatically altered the meanings of home, identity and development for themselves and for many other urban, diasporic populations. Rather than claiming a fixed home or a monolithic identity, YAIA artists explore new possibilities for imagining symbolic home and community meanings within a wide spectrum of contradictions and juxtapositions, in life and in art. The people and spaces with which they engage are diverse and complex, as are the artistic and cultural media that they adopt/adapt in their production. Their projects demonstrate an array of multiethnic and multigenerational collaborations, suggesting that some of the problems facing the younger generation can potentially be addressed by cultural and political alliances that use art as an organizing tool, efforts that deal directly with such widely shared experiences as displacement, disempowerment and dislocation.

As geopolitical conditions affect changes in community cultural development, schools and communities must find creative ways to meet new cultural demands and social needs. YAIA artists, their adult mentors, professional artists, and the diverse publics that they engage through the cultural production process exemplify dynamic learning communities that contrast sharply with their urban school experiences. Contrary to popular perceptions, Southeast Asian American young people consistently express an active intention to learn. But their issues of interest and ways of knowing are often marginalized or overlooked in schools (Ko, 2001). The cultural production process supported by YAIA, however, shows that when given the opportunity to connect with a network of high-skilled and caring teachers and artists, young people can grow and mature culturally at a profound level. When guided and mentored, they develop a public consciousness and exhibit a strong capacity to work for a positive future, both for themselves and for their communities.

A critical difference between YAIA and the innovative, after-school, Asian American community-based video production program described fully by Reyes (2007), for example, is the unique, ongoing, multidimensional participation of Yary Livan as not only a Cambodian national treasure and Master Artist, but also as a powerful, humanistic teacher, and loving, Khmer-speaking elder/uncle/father throughout the conception, production, and exhibition of many of the YAIA projects described above. Ellis (2001) notes in her research about youth-centered arts learning that "teaching artists are often missing from the picture, whether in analysis of economic impact studies or planning for arts education advocacy. Yet this is where some of the most fruitful learning takes place: teachers who are artists, artists who deeply understand teaching, peers who develop an artistic and cultural life with each other, parents who get involved, and individuals working to make a difference. These people mattered in the research and could be better supported" (p. 244). This is certainly the case for YAIA's teaching artists, Yary Livan and founding director Marge Rack.

By emphasizing the dynamic and fluid movements of young people across multiple spaces — from street corners to the Buddhist temple to art museums to citywide public forums to middle and high schools and even college settings — YAIA has also intensely challenged conventional notions of "street life" that continue to draw boundaries around where urban youth should belong and segregate them from the rest of the society, including higher education. The broader community cultural development context thus draws attention to holistic interventions that are grounded in multilingual, multigenerational, multiethnic and multisectoral realities and visions.

Consistent with this insight, the Urban Institute and Wallace Foundation (2005) concluded in their research report based on a national survey of cultural participation, "for those who study or wish to expand cultural participation[, t]he most fundamental implication is that arts research, policy, and management should be re-oriented to pay greater attention to the diversity of cultural participation. For researchers, that will mean probing more deeply into motivations and experiences, and exploring variations within, as well as across, disciplines" (p. 11). While speaking to the domain of cultural work, such a recommendation could easily be applied to urban education at different levels as well.

Clearly, educational policy makers and practitioners must design relevant programs to address significant educational disparities that exist within the Asian American population (U.S. Government Accountability Office, 2007). These should include increasing the cultural competence and linguistically appropriate service delivery of teachers, counselors and other school personnel who work with Khmer American students and parents. Bilingual/bicultural Khmer American teachers and staff should also be actively recruited, trained and supported[9], and programs should enable Khmer American parents to participate in local and state advisory councils/consortiums and planning groups. Moreover, state and local jurisdictions should analyze the alarming failure rates of Khmer American students on state-enforced high-stakes tests, and allocate programs, strategies, and funds to address specific needs in communities that are most affected — actions that are mandated by federal No Child Left Behind legislation, but not enforced or targeted. Disaggregated data must be collected and analyzed to ensure that educational programs, services, and interventions — from school to home to the street — are effectively reaching Khmer Americans.

While educational advocacy and reform at the national, state and local levels are clearly necessary, my study suggests that an additional, critical factor is the involvement and empowerment of community participants, particularly the younger generation, through opportunities, capacities, and structures that actively connect their commitments and visions with long-term community cultural development. Drawing on holistic approaches, the alternative learning communities described in this chapter engage people with distinctly different backgrounds on the front lines of such possibilities. Ultimately, such alternative learning opportunities mean to be transformative for individuals, families, schools, and communities.

When Southeast Asian American artists practice cultural activism, create learning communities, and engage multiple publics and spaces for community cultural development, they show us the potential of a new source of social power. For those of us in higher education, we need to understand that this new source of power is what may drive our students — and many others who are still struggling to access our institutions — to fulfill their potential, personally and intellectually. Like Anyon with praCh Ly, we need more.

REFERENCES

Anyon, J. (2005). _Radical possibles: Public policy, urban education, and a new social movement._ New York: Routledge.

Asian American Resource Workshop. (1987). _To live in peace: Responding to anti-Asian violence in Boston_. Boston: Author.

Atkins, T., Bullis, M., & Todis, B. (2005). Converging and diverging service delivery systems in alternative education programs for disabled and non-disabled youth involved in the juvenile justice system. _Journal of Correctional Education,_ 56(3), 253-286.

Ball, A., & Heath, S. B. (1993). Dances of identity: Finding an ethnic self in the arts. In S. B. Heath, & M. W. McLaughlin (Eds.), _Identity and inner-city youth: Beyond ethnicity and gender,_ (pp. 69-93). New York: Teachers College Press.

Bodilly, S., & Beckett, M. (2005). _Making out-of-school time matter: Evidence for an action agenda_ (pp. 11-30). Santa Monica, CA: RAND Corporation.

Carini, F. (Producer). (2005). _Temple of the heart_ (posted on TownOnline.com on May 6 and viewable at that time at: http://www.buddhistchannel.tv/index. php?id=60,1131,0,0,1,0). [Film].

Danish, S., & Gulotta, C. (Eds). (2000). _Developing competent youth and strong communities through after-school programming._ Washington, DC: Child Welfare League of America Press.

Datnow, A., Hubbard, L., & Woody, E. (2001). _Is single gender schooling viable in the public sector? Lessons from California's pilot program._ Final report prepared for the Ford and Spencer Foundations. [Online]. Available: http://www.oise.utoronto.ca/depts./tps/ adatnow/research.html. (ED471051)

Davis, J., Soep, E., Maira, S., Remba, N., & Putnoi, D. (1993). _Safe havens: Portraits of educational effectiveness in community art centers that focus on education in economically disadvantaged communities_ (pp. 151-179, 182-192, 212-220). Cambridge, MA: Harvard Project Zero, Project Co-Arts.

Eccles, J., & Gootman, J. (2002). _Community programs to promote youth development._ Washington, DC: National Academies Press.

Ellis, D. M. (2001). An emerging youth-centered framework for arts learning. _Journal of Arts Management, Law, and Society,_ 31(3), 231-251.

Fong, T. (1998). _The contemporary Asian American experience: Beyond the model minority._ New York: Prentice-Hall.

Goldbard, A., & Adams, D. (Eds.). (2001). _Creative community: The art of cultural development._ New York: Rockefeller Foundation.

Goldbard, A., & Adams, D. (Eds.). (2002). _Community, culture and globalization._ New York: Rockefeller Foundation.

Gordon, E. W., Bridglall, B. L., & Meroe, A. S. (2004). After-school programs, youth development, and other forms of supplementary education. In E. W. Gordon, B. L. Bridglall, & A. S. Meroe (Eds.), _Supplementary education: The hidden curriculum of high academic achievement_ (pp. 35-62). Lanham, MD: Rowman & Littlefield.

Gorman, A. (2007, July 18). Cambodia town is now on the map. _Los Angeles Times,_ B1.

Graff, N. P., & Howard, R. (1993). _Where the river runs._ Boston: Little, Brown.

Hayden, D. (1995). _The power of place._ Cambridge, MA: MIT Press.

Heath, S. B., & McLaughlin, M. W. (Eds.). (1993). _Identity and inner-city youth: Beyond ethnicity and gender._ New York: Teachers College Press.

Heath, S. B., & Smyth, L. (Directors). (1999). _ArtShow: Youth and community development_ [Video]. Washington, DC: Partners for Livable Communities.

Kiang, P. N. (1994). When know-nothings speak English only: Analyzing Irish and Cambodian struggles for community development and educational equity. In K. Aguilar-San Juan (Ed.), _The state of Asian America: Activism and resistance in the 1990s_ (pp. 125-145). Boston: South End Press.

Kiang, P. N. (2002). Stories and structures of persistence: Ethnographic learning through research and practice in Asian American studies. In Y. Zou & H.T. Trueba (Eds.), _Ethnography and schools: Qualitative approaches to the study of education_ (pp. 223-255). Lanham, MD: Rowman & Littlefield.

Kiang, P. N., & Kaplan, J. (1994). Where do we stand: Views of racial conflict by Vietnamese American high school students in a Black-and-White context. _The Urban Review,_ 26(2), 95-119.

Kiang, P. N., Nguyen N. L., & Sheehan, R. L. (1995). Don't ignore it!: Documenting racial harassment in a fourth-grade Vietnamese bilingual classroom. Equity and Excellence in Education, 28(1), 31-35.

Kiang, P. N., Suyemoto, K. L., & Tang, S. S-L. (2008). Developing and sustaining community research methods and meanings in Asian American studies course work. In T. Fong (Ed.). The handbook of research methods in ethnic studies. Lanham, MD: Rowman & Littlefield.

Kiang, P. N., & Tang, S. S-L. (2006). Electoral politics and the contexts of empowerment, displacement, and diaspora for Boston's Vietnamese and Cambodian American communities. Asian American Policy Review, 15, 13-29.

Ko, S. J. (2001). Examining the contribution of ethnic attitudes, collective self-esteem, and spirituality to delinquent behavioral outcomes among Cambodian adolescents: An exploratory study. Unpublished doctoral dissertation, University of Massachusetts Boston.

Le, T. N., & Wallen, J. L. (2006). Youth delinquency: Self-reported rates and risk factors of Cambodian, Chinese, Lao/Mien, and Vietnamese youth. AAPI Nexus, 4(2), 15-44.

Lee, R. (1999). Orientals: Asian Americans in popular culture. Philadelphia: Temple University Press.

Lee, S. J. (2005). Up against whiteness: Race, school and immigrant youth. New York: Teachers College Press.

Liu, M., Tran, T., & Watanabe, P. (2007). Far from the Commonwealth: A report on low-income Asian Americans in Massachusetts. Boston: University of Massachusetts Boston, Institute for Asian American Studies. [Online]. Available: http://www.iaas.umb.edu/publications/general/LowIncRep.pdf.

Losen, D. J., & Orfield, G. (Eds.). (2002). Racial inequity in special education. Cambridge, MA: Harvard Education Publishing Group.

May, S., & praCh. (2004). Art of faCt: An interview with praCh. In F. Stewart & S. May (Eds.), In the shadow of Angkor: Contemporary writing from Cambodia. Manoa, 16(1), 73-89.

Niedzwiecki, M., & Duong, T. C. (2004). Southeast Asian American statistical profile. Washington, DC: Southeast Asia Resource Action Center (SEARAC).

Poplin, M., & Weeres, J. (1993). *Voices from the inside: A report on schooling from inside the classroom.* Claremont, CA: Institute for Education in Transformation, Claremont Graduate School.

Prashad, V. (2000). *The karma of brown folk.* Minneapolis: University of Minnesota Press.

Reid, A. (2004, April 18). Sights, sounds of a culture: Cambodians hold monthlong event. *Boston Globe*, B3. [Online]. Available: http://www.boston.com/news/local/ massachusetts/articles/2004/04/18/sights_sounds_of_a_culture/.

Reyes, A. (2007). *Language, identity, and stereotype among Southeast Asian American youth: The other Asian.* Mahwah, NJ: Lawrence Erlbaum.

Roffman, J. G., Suarez-Orozco, C., & Rhodes, J. E. (2003). Facilitating positive development in immigrant youth: The role of mentors and community organizers. In F.A. Villarruel, D. F. Perkins, L. M. Borden & J. G. Keith (Eds.), *Community youth development: Programs, policies and practices* (pp. 90-117). Thousand Oaks, CA: Sage.

Smith-Hefner, N. J. (1999). *Khmer American: Identity and moral education in a diasporic community.* Berkeley: University of California Press.

Tang, S. S-L. (2002). *Enough is enough!: Struggles for Cambodian American community development in Revere, Massachusetts.* Unpublished dissertation, University at Buffalo, State University of New York.

Tang, S. S-L. (2008). Community-centered research as knowledge/capacity building in immigrant and refugee communities. In C. R. Hale (Ed.), *Engaging contradictions: Theory, politics and methods of activist scholarship* (pp. 237-264). Berkeley: University of California Press.

Um, K. (2003). *A dream denied: Educational experiences of Southeast Asian American youth: Issues and recommendations.* Washington, DC: Southeast Asia Resource Action Center.

Urban Institute and Wallace Foundation. (2005). *Motivations matter: Findings and practical implications of a national survey of cultural participation.* Washington, DC & New York: Authors.

U.S. Government Accountability Office. (2007). *Information sharing could help institutions identify and address challenges some Asian Americans and Pacific Islander students face* (GAO-07-925). Washington, DC: GPO. [Online]. Available: http://www.gao. gov/new.items/d07925.pdf.

Vigil, J. D., Nguyen, T. H., & Chang, J. (2006). Asian Americans on the streets: Strategies for prevention and intervention. AAPI Nexus, 4(2), 1-14.

Watanabe, P., Liu, M., & Lo, S. (2004). Asian Americans in metro Boston: Growth, diversity, and complexity. Boston: Institute for Asian American Studies, University of Massachusetts Boston.

Wehrly, B. (1988, January). Cultural diversity from an international perspective. Journal of Multicultural Counseling and Development, 16, 3-15

Weis, L., & Fine, M. (Eds.). (2000). Construction sites: Excavating race, class, gender, and sexuality in spaces for and by youth. New York: Teachers College Press.

Welaratna, U. (1993). Beyond the killing fields. Palo Alto, CA: Stanford University.

Yang, K. Y., & Niedzwiecki, M. (2003, June 17). Southeast Asian Americans and higher education. Testimony prepared for Evaluation of Asian Pacific Americans in Education Congressional Forum. Washington, DC: Southeast Asia Resource Action Center.

FOOTNOTES

1   See: www.mujestic.com.

2   In this article, I use "Cambodian" and "Khmer" interchangeably

3   The 2005 American Community Survey (ACS), conducted by the U.S. Census Bureau, is a nationwide survey that collects information on the U.S. population similar to the long form used in the 2000 Census. See: www.census.gov/acs/www/index.html and www.iaas.umb.edu/research/acs2005/.

4   Census data in this section are compiled from documents released by the Southeast Asia Resource Action Center. See: Southeast Asia Resource Action Center (SEARAC): Southeast Asian American

5   Statistical Profile Based on the Data from 2000 Census, 2004. http://www.searac.org/seastatprofilemay04.pdf

6   Institute for Asian American Studies, "Community Profiles: Asian Americans in Lynn," University of Massachusetts Boston, June 2003; see: http://www.iaas.umb.edu/research/census/community_profiles/preliminary.shtml.

7   The 1.5 or 1.8 designations refer to the generations who were born in Cambodia (or refugee camps in Thailand or the Philippines) and came to the United States as teens or as children — giving them linguistic and cultural skills and sensibilities with which to communicate effectively with the refugee/immigrant first generation while also understanding and experiencing the sociocultural realities of growing up in the United States as the second generation.

8   Yary Livan originally studied at the Royal University of Fine Arts, Phnom Penh. He survived the Khmer Rouge genocide, and received political asylum in 2002 after migrating to Massachusetts. He has been a potter for over 30 years. See: http://khmerwave.com/Pasite/home.html.

9   Ironically, however, bilingual education in Massachusetts was essentially eliminated by a statewide voter referendum in 2002, and several Khmer-speaking teachers in Lowell were then fired, based on their failure to pass an English-proficiency teacher test. The fired teachers filed a discrimination case in 2003 with the support of the Asian American Legal Defense and Education Fund, and an arbitrator ruled in 2006 that they had to be reinstated by the Lowell Public Schools. See: Maria Cramer, "Lowell Teachers Ordered Reinstated," Boston Globe (March 30, 2006), 2, B2; and Jenna Russell, "Lowell Teachers Say Test Is Racist," Boston Globe (July 20, 2003), B5.

CHAPTER 9

Cá Trí Nho: Roles of Vietnamese American Studies and Education Post-Katrina

James Đien Bùi, MSW
Peter Nien-chu Kiang, EdD
Shirley Suet-ling Tang, PhD
Janet Hong Võ, BA

INTRODUCTION

Nearly three years have passed since Hurricanes Katrina and Rita devastated the Gulf Coast region of the United States in fall 2005. Yet, the processes of rebuilding for the Gulf's displaced communities are still far from completed. How these communities reconstruct themselves — and are restructured by others — will greatly affect the status, sustainability, and future of the Gulf Coast economically, environmentally, and politically, as well as culturally, linguistically, and racially (Campanella, 2006; Catania, 2006; Donato & Hakimzadeh, 2006; Dyson, 2006). This includes historic and significant Vietnamese Americans communities across the Gulf region from Bayou La Bâtre, Alabama to Biloxi, Mississippi to New Orleans, Louisiana. Vietnamese American residents from the neighborhood of New Orleans East (also known as Versailles, Versai, Village de L'est, and Vi t Village), in particular, have returned in large numbers to reclaim and rebuild, despite both the hardship caused by Katrina and Rita, and the relatively minimal support provided by relief agencies and the local/state/federal bureaucracies (Green, Kleiner, & Montgomery, 2007; Leong, et al., 2007; Nguyen, 2007).

Many factors are involved in the (re)development of the Gulf Coast region, including the presence, capacity, and vision of Vietnamese American communities, such as those located in New Orleans East and East Biloxi. Although efforts to rebuild these communities have understandably focused on land, housing, public health, and economic revitalization (Kromm & Sturgis, 2007), an additional sector of redevelopment needing greater attention is the education system, including both K-12 schools and local higher education institutions. Public education represents an essential dimension of the rebuilding process — both because of the specific educational roles that schools and colleges play for communities and because of their interplay with other critical sectors of development. For example, it is difficult to attract health professionals back to the region to adequately staff a local hospital if local schools are not open or functional for the children of those doctors, nurses, and other health care personnel to attend. Although Vietnamese communities had little influence on the local K-12 and higher education systems pre-Katrina, there is an opportunity post-Katrina to reshape the education system and develop innovative educational models that can more fully serve and represent the diverse populations of the Gulf Coast, including Vietnamese Americans.

The following case study outlines insights we have gained regarding the reciprocal roles of education and community rebuilding in Gulf Coast Vietnamese community settings following the 2005 hurricanes. The coauthors of this chapter are each affiliated, in part, with the Asian American Studies Program at the University of Massachusetts Boston — an urban public university located far from the Gulf Coast but adjacent to the fifth largest Vietnamese American community in the United States. Each coauthor has participated actively in the shaping of teaching/learning opportunities and student/faculty/community collaborations in the areas of Southeast Asian American and Vietnamese American Studies, particularly at the local level in metropolitan Boston (Kiang, 2004). In the aftermath of Katrina and Rita, however, the challenges of Vietnamese community rebuilding also deeply drew our attention as researchers, practitioners, organizers, and teachers/students.

Our study begins with an overview of post-Katrina Gulf Coast community and educational contexts for Vietnamese located in two distinct settings: New Orleans East and East Biloxi. We then connect the process of Vietnamese American community rebuilding with a broader conceptualization of education that reaches from K-12 to higher education and that concretizes the role and value of Vietnamese American Studies. We conclude with a brief description of directions for continued work in these areas. Our integrative methodological approaches — about which we have written extensively elsewhere — reflect our mutual groundings in the fields of community organizing, asset-building, and community cultural development (Bùi, Tang, & Kiang, 2004; Kiang & Tang, 2006; Tang, 2008a; Vo, 2007b) and our interests in models of culturally responsive service learning and community-centered instruction that enable students to apply and extend what they learn from the classroom to critical issues and activities within local community settings (Kiang, 2003; Kiang, Suyemoto, & Tang, 2008a; Tang, 2008b).

VIETNAMESE AMERICAN COMMUNITY CONTEXTS IN NEW ORLEANS AND BILOXI

Although Vietnamese American communities were well rooted economically and socially in the Gulf Coast region for a quarter century before Hurricane Katrina, their existence was little known to the public, beyond depictions in Louis Malle's 1985 Hollywood film, *Alamo Bay,* Robert Olen Butler's (1992) Pulitzer Prize winning short story collection, *A Good Scent from a Strange Mountain,* and Zhou and Bankston's (1998) study on education and acculturation of youth. Post-Katrina, however, in response to the breathtaking failure of local and federal government agencies and the mainstream media to recognize the impact of the storm on these communities, regional and national Vietnamese American and Asian American ethnic media and advocacy organizations intervened to highlight the struggles and needs of Vietnamese Americans, particularly in New Orleans East and East Biloxi (Kao, 2006).

There were approximately 10,000 Vietnamese American residents living in New Orleans East before the storm forced the evacuation of the residents to neighboring states (Tang, 2006). A majority of these residents had a shared history as refugees who resettled in Louisiana following the fall of the South Vietnamese government in April 1975. This highly concentrated Vietnamese population also shared local village and religious relationships with each other, pre-dating their refugee migration to the United States (Nguyen, 2007). After their relocation due to Hurricane Katrina, a large number of residents reestablished connections through their robust Mary Queen of Viet Nam (MQVN) church network, and began to return collectively to rebuild their homes, communities, and congregation (Leong et al., 2007; Nguyen, 2007). Although, the rate of return to New Orleans East during the first year post-Katrina was high, it appeared that individuals between the ages of 25 and 35 were less likely to resettle and reinvest their futures in these communities — perhaps because the quality of the education system and opportunities for economic success still seemed relatively poor for their generation (Vo, 2007b).

Meanwhile, in East Biloxi, the Vietnamese American community had established itself during the early 1980s because of economic opportunities in the seafood industry. By 1985, there were an estimated 15,000 Vietnamese residents in the Southern Mississippi Gulf Coast area, working mostly in shrimping and fishing-related businesses (Schmidt, 1995). However, by the late 1980s, stricter shrimping and fishing regulations had forced half the Vietnamese population to seek employment elsewhere, forcing families to relocate to different states across the country. By the early 1990s, Biloxi had begun to usher in a new economic development plan, which called for casino development that essentially dis-/replaced former shrimping facilties along the harbor, including the docks, warehouses and canneries. Many Vietnamese who remained in Biloxi retooled themselves into the low-income casino workforce, mainly because the vast majority of them were Limited English Proficient (LEP). For those Vietnamese shrimpers who remained in the seafood industry, matters only got worse in the 1990s when global economic policies brought in cheaper seafood imports, ironically from Southeast Asia, while the cost of fuel climbed steadily to make the costs of shrimping too high for many to sustain. For example, in 1985, it cost $1.00 in fuel to produce $3.00 worth of shrimp, but by 2005, prior to Hurricane Katrina, the ratio had essentially reversed, so that $3.00 of fuel was needed to produce $1.00 worth of shrimp, signaling the economic downward spiral in the shrimping industry and the resultant economic disenfranchisement of the Vietnamese community (Ratliff, 2006). Without viable alternative economic opportunities, the Vietnamese in Biloxi remained in the shrimping industry because it "had been the backbone for the community for nearly three decades, employing up to 15 percent of the adult population" (Tang, 2006, p. 23). As East Biloxi's local economy shifts further toward gaming and tourism and away from the traditional livelihoods of the Vietnamese, it is unlikely that additional former residents will return to their homes and community unless substantial intervention is provided (Le, 2006).

The post-Katrina era was marked not only by the total physical destruction of Gulf Coast cities like Venice, LA, and Bay St. Louis, MS, but the plight of Vietnamese Americans being further marginalized by the lack of inclusive planning efforts across the entire Gulf Coast region. Many instances from the Bring Back New Orleans Commission in New Orleans to the Living Cities Plan in Biloxi had categorically excluded Vietnamese American communities. Outreach and language access issues were not seriously considered by planners or politicians. In some cases, direct efforts to exclude Vietnamese Americans were also evident. In New Orleans East, the city had permitted a controversial landfill to open barely one mile away from the heart of the Vietnamese American community. Fortunately in August 2006, community efforts to shut down the operation were successful. For East Biloxi, Vietnamese Americans are being displaced by casino expansion and the industry's appetite to reserve parcels of land for later development, even though many Vietnamese Americans are still living in trailers. In fact, the casino business had reached an all-time high only two years after Katrina, with profit increases well above any year pre-Katrina.

For example, during one author's trip to East Biloxi in March 2007, there were still many parcels of land that remained unclaimed, while others along the waterfront were being developed as casinos and hotels. The owner of Pho 777 in East Biloxi stated, for example, that her new business was opened specifically to cater to the tourists and construction workers who are rebuilding the new Biloxi (Vo, 2007b). Shrimping, however, is no longer an option for many. Beyond the current status and future prospects of Vietnamese Americans in relation to jobs and relevant economic opportunities in both the short and long term, other factors such as the profile and prospects of the local education system are in need of significant attention if community recovery and revitalization are to occur (Warnke Community Consulting, 2006).

PUBLIC SCHOOL CONTEXTS IN NEW ORLEANS AND BILOXI

The process of reestablishing and redesigning educational structures and opportunities is essential to the long-term rebuilding of sustainable, asset-rich communities. Yet, many families from New Orleans and Biloxi still have not returned to their homes unless they have had compelling reasons to rebuild and reclaim their properties. In some cases, those who return are motivated specifically by job opportunities, but many others who fled from the flood waters in 2005 have already enrolled their children in more stable and viable school systems in Houston, Mobile, or other settings, and will not uproot their children to attend school in a system such as Orleans Parish if it is not stable or if its quality is weak. As Hill and Hannaway (2006) observe in their assessment of public education in New Orleans:

> In the first three years or so after the hurricane, K-12 education in New Orleans will be a trailing phenomenon, dependent on how fast the economy and housing are rebuilt...the location, size, and instructional orientation of schools will depend on developments in the economy and housing (p. 2).

For example, as of April 30, 2008, a total of 82 schools were functioning in New Orleans, 53 of which had been placed under the administration of the Recovery School District and 42 of which were newly structured as charter schools (Greater New Orleans Community Data Center, 2008a, 2008b). At the time of our analysis, we were unable to assess the state of the K-12 public education system in the Gulf Coast communities of Biloxi and New Orleans because the institutional data for achievement proficiency and rates for the first full academic year, post-Katrina (2006-2007), had not yet been reported (Vo, 2007b).

Long before Katrina, however, the public education system in New Orleans was already viewed as one of the worst in the nation, reflecting realities of poverty and racial injustice as well as a political economy of profound corruption (Adamo, 2007). Pre-Katrina School Performance Scores (SPS) — which factor in student-level LEAP21/GEE 21 tests, Iowa Tests, attendance and dropout rates — from the 2003-2004 academic year, for example, show that of 117 schools rated in the Orleans Parish, only one had the high rating of Five Stars (SPS 140.0 or above). Only 8% of the schools had a performance range between Four to Three Stars (SPS 139.9-100) while 27% of the schools had Academic Warnings (SPS 45.0-59.9) and 47% were Academically Unacceptable (SPS below 45) (Louisiana Department of Education, 2005).

Many details about the families with school-age children who have returned to New Orleans or reenrolled are still unclear, so it is not yet possible to assess Katrina's specific educational effects. Funding priorities of the Bush administration, however, supported the establishment of charter schools rather than traditional public schools in New Orleans (Kromm & Sturgis, 2007), based in part on the assumption that charter school status and privatization would offer greater flexibility in school structure and facilitate faster reopenings. The positive and negative dimensions of this reliance on charter schools as an engine of educational reengagement have not been fully examined, but it is clear that a dramatic restructuring of the education system in post-Katrina New Orleans is under way. Interestingly, this emerging charter-centered school system may offer a discrete opportunity for reenvisioning what K-12 education can mean and do in relation to Vietnamese community rebuilding in New Orleans East. The lack of a critical mass of local Vietnamese American teachers, educational administrators, and other education professionals who are prepared to take on such a responsibility, however, represents a significant limitation in community capacity. Furthermore, the lack of powerful models of transformative educational practice with Vietnamese American populations anywhere else in the United States also represents a substantial challenge for those who are committed to the rebuilding and development of the Versailles-New Orleans East Vietnamese community.

In the smaller city of Biloxi, the K-12 school system functioned fairly well pre-Katrina with Asian (Vietnamese) students enrolled predominantly in three of the district's seven elementary schools and in one high school. In the 2004-2005 school year, for example, Biloxi High School was rated as a Level 5 school in the State of Mississippi, reflecting superior performance (Mississippi Department of Education, 2008). Like New Orleans, post-Katrina school achievement levels in Biloxi were not yet reported at the time of our analysis, and no clear accounting of how post-Katrina population shifts have affected school enrollments in Biloxi was yet available. Of note historically, however, are records kept by the

Biloxi school board and school district administration that refer specifically to the influx of the Vietnamese refugee/immigrant population to the city during the 1980s (Skelton, 2000). To respond to the English language instructional and social service needs of the newcomer Vietnamese student population, the Biloxi School District received major federal bilingual education grants that were among the largest grants ever received by the school district (Skelton, 2000). Thus, from the perspective of the school district, the presence of Vietnamese in Biloxi historically can be considered as an asset in generating resources for the system rather than as a burden that drained resources from the system. Echoing Tang's analysis of schools and community development involving Cambodian refugees in Revere, Massachusetts during the same historical period, this precedent from the 1980s may be useful to recall as Biloxi's Vietnamese American community begins to activate its social capital more fully in relation to education, public schools, and community rebuilding.

Similarly, in the Orleans Parish public school district of New Orleans, it may be time to develop a more comprehensive agenda for Vietnamese community rebuilding that directly connects with the transformation of the city's schools and/or the design and implementation of new, culturally responsive, community-based models of charter schools, especially in light of the reality that many young children from New Orleans East during the first two years since Katrina have had few options but to travel on unreliable buses to attend other charter schools at a distance. Such an educational agenda might lead, for example, to designing a curriculum that not only addresses state and federal testing mandates required by the No Child Left Behind Act, but that also engages with the Vietnamese American community's historical, cultural, and linguistic contexts and capacities and its visions for rebuilding and development.

Though there are few models for this at the K-12 level, such instructional and curricular practices are well-articulated across the fields of Asian American studies and ethnic studies. Unfortunately, however, there are no strong models of Vietnamese American studies or Asian American studies locally in any of the Gulf Coast schools, colleges, or universities. Thus, there is a need not only to identify relevant curricular and instructional models, but a need also for skilled, culturally responsive practitioners who can facilitate the development of such models concretely in the local context.

Engaging a Reverse Brain Drain

While the traumatic forced relocation and resilient return of former residents are central themes in the story of post-Katrina Gulf Coast Vietnamese community rebuilding (Chen et al., 2007; Leong et al., 2007), an important back-story involves the short- and longer-term visits and commitments by Vietnamese American and other Asian American university students and younger generation professionals from throughout the country who have come to the Gulf Coast to apply their knowledge and skills in rebuilding the Vietnamese community through service, advocacy, research and education. This post-Katrina dynamic of individuals with higher education who have opted to work, at least temporarily, in Gulf Coast community development as an alternative to corporate or professional fields in their own cities and regions has been termed by Bùi in this chapter as a reverse brain drain.

Though this phenomenon was initially individually defined and ad hoc, it has become structured, intentional and collectively organized, primarily through the National Association of Vietnamese American Service Agencies (NAVASA), which established a long-term collaboration in 2005 with the newly formed Mary Queen of Vietnam Church–Community Development Corporation (MQVN CDC) — a nonprofit community organization that itself grew out of the core community rebuilding efforts led by the Mary Queen of Viet Nam Church in New Orleans East. NAVASA's Gulf Coast work is defined by three guiding principles:

1. Creatively build local institutional capacity to carry out long-term (re)development work

2. Pragmatically develop programs, projects and systems tethered to a community-driven agenda

3. Practice critical thinking inside and out — reflecting the Freirian philosophy of praxis by engaging local leadership with "reverse brain drain" activists to mutually share/shape work through transparent dialogue and action.

With MQVN CDC serving as a base of operations for grant-funded, community-based projects, services and staffing, NAVASA also established a national service program known as the Dan Thân Corps (Dan Thân translates as "be the change"— a reference to Gandhi's oft-quoted challenge to "be the change we wish to see in the world"). Dan Thân fellows, most of whom are bilingual Vietnamese Americans in their early 20s, have come from other areas throughout the United States to work for a period of time at the MQVN CDC or elsewhere within local Gulf Coast Vietnamese American communities.

For example, Mai, a Vietnamese American originally from Orange County, CA, has been working in New Orleans since May 2006 following her graduation from George Washington University. Mai initially signed up for the Dan Thân fellowship for one year. After eight months, however, she decided to extend her fellowship and continue indefinitely because she was learning and contributing meaningfully to important rebuilding efforts (M. Dang, personal communication [with J. H. Vo], May 2, 2007). Individuals like Mai who choose to relocate to New Orleans and Biloxi — communities with which she and others like her had no previous relationship — represent significant new assets that have enhanced the local region's short- and medium-term capacity.

Another example, Mary, a Vietnamese American born and raised in New Orleans East, joined the Dan Thân Corps in November 2005 after volunteering at the Mary Queen of Viet Nam Church. Prior to Katrina, Mary's interest was in medicine, but exposure to the opportunity to change/build her community compelled her to pursue a nonconventional profession as a community development professional. She candidly admits that she never knew what a nonprofit organization was, let alone a community development corporation. Her previous education in school (K-12 and higher education) and within her community never exposed her to the realities of social injustice and the historical disenfranchisement of Vietnamese Americans. With NAVASA support and training, she has been pursuing the community's priority to build an affordable senior housing project.

Bùi, who has directly supported and supervised more than a dozen Dan Thân fellows and other staff while serving as Gulf Coast regional director for NAVASA, describes the impact of this remarkable reverse brain drain in the following way:

> The droves of young Vietnamese American progressive students and activists who have come to New Orleans East over the past year to not only support the rebuilding effort, but also take part in what some consider an unprecedented grassroots movement [are] a sign of what may be on the horizon for Vietnamese American politics (Tang, 2007, p. 38).

The work of NAVASA and the Dan Thân fellows locally through MQVN CDC illustrate a powerful medium through which students and young adults have successfully connected their personal and political commitments to culture, identity, and justice with local processes of community building, development, and advocacy. Further evaluation of the Dan Thân Corps model will help identify and enhance what motivates this generation's engagement with underresourced communities.

THE ROLE OF VIETNAMESE AMERICAN STUDIES

One way to extend and deepen the "reverse brain drain" concept is through connecting Vietnamese American Studies theory/practice with the curriculum of the local K-12 and higher education systems. Such an intervention can further inspire and challenge Dan Thân fellows and others who have come to the Gulf Coast to "be the change they wish to see" while enhancing the contributions of local Vietnamese American youth who wish to engage directly with their own communities. Indeed, our analysis suggests the Gulf Coast community rebuilding process can serve as a powerful opportunity for introducing and integrating Vietnamese American Studies into the curriculum of public and higher education while, at the same time, critically grounding the field in the context of transforming schools and empowering communities. We recognize that such commitments were central to the founding of Asian American Studies, but have been largely sacrificed as the field has become more institutionalized over time (Chang & Kiang, 2002; Wong, 1995).

The development of Vietnamese American Studies (or Vietnamese Diaspora Studies) as a distinct field of study — intersecting both with Asian American Studies in the tradition of ethnic studies and Vietnamese Studies in the tradition of area studies — has accelerated during the past decade as more Vietnamese Americans have established a presence in U.S. universities (Bowen et al., 1999; Bowen et al., 2003; Lê Espiritu, 2006). The recent publication of two new professional journals, the *Journal of Southeast Asian American Education & Advancement* (http://jsaaea.coehd.utsa.edu/index.php/JSAAEA) and the *Journal of Vietnamese Studies* (http://ucpressjournals.com/journal.asp?j=vs), for example, suggest that the call articulated a generation ago by pioneering scholar Chung Hoang Chuong for Vietnamese American Studies to stand on its own is receiving greater attention (Chung, 1988; Kiang, 2004).

Nevertheless, the number of Vietnamese American Studies courses offered nationally at U.S. colleges is still small, perhaps fewer than ten. At the University of Massachusetts Boston, for example, while the Asian American Studies course, "Southeast Asians in the US" has been offered regularly since 1989, an additional course, "Resources for Vietnamese American Studies," was developed by one of the authors in 2003, and has been taught annually since then in order to connect curricular content more directly with Boston's local Vietnamese American community, which is the fifth largest in the United States (Bùi, Tang, & Kiang, 2004). This newer course introduces students to the field of Vietnamese American Studies — what theories, methods, resources, and voices are helpful to examine the migrations and reconstructions of identity, culture, and community for Vietnamese in the United States and their diasporic relationship to Viet Nam and around the world. The course includes presentations by local Vietnamese American researchers, writers, and community leaders.

In spring 2007, "Resources for Vietnamese American Studies" was taught by one of the authors while he served as NAVASA's Gulf Coast regional director. Through online instructional capacities, the course connected students with Gulf Coast-based MQVN CDC staff and Dan Thân fellows who were actively working on a range of community development projects. During their spring break week, the faculty member and all 21 students in the course traveled to the Gulf Coast, where they comprised five work groups with specific assignments linked to Vietnamese community rebuilding efforts in New Orleans East and East Biloxi. The five project-based groups were structured as follows:

- **Language Access Organizing.** Students gathered bilingual baseline survey data in the Federal Emergency Management Agency (FEMA) trailer lot where 199 resident trailers were parked. They went door to door to gather information in Vietnamese or English from residents about living in the trailers and plans for housing after their FEMA contracts expire.

- **Environmental Justice.** Members of this group addressed the issue of illegal dumping and plans for a community-based recycling campaign. They assessed the effects of dumping on the Vietnamese community and the larger environment. They also created a short video documentary to share findings with community members as well as policy makers.

- **Business Development.** Students crafted a strategic business planning template to support local business owners who had recently received loans from the ASI Federal Credit Union. They conducted bilingual mini-surveys on-site at local Vietnamese American businesses in both New Orleans East and East Biloxi to match the plans and needs of business owners with access to loans and other resource assistance from lenders and government agencies.

- **Urban Farm.** Members of this group evaluated the economic potential and community value of a 20-acre parcel of land in New Orleans East to support local production of culturally familiar vegetables, herbs, and other produce, and to assess the viability of establishing and sustaining a farmers market within the community.

- **Real Estate.** Members of this group surveyed land in both New Orleans East and East Biloxi and produced maps of the areas with locations that would be ideal for future community development projects in conjunction with a land-banking strategy to support permanent land acquisition.

Students engaged in community work in these five areas, and their efforts contributed directly to MQVN CDC's ongoing community rebuilding strategies, while also fulfilling the curricular intentions of the course to produce "Resources for Vietnamese American Studies."

Moreover, the work completed in this course deepened a curricular commitment initiated in a previous course on "Boston's Asian American Communities" through which four bilingual/bicultural undergraduate students and two graduate students traveled to the Gulf Coast to document the impact of Katrina and Rita specifically on Vietnamese American communities, given that those voices and experiences had been ignored or neglected by the mainstream media (Smith, 2005). In November 2005, prior to the more visible coalescence of community members to "return, recover, reclaim, and rebuild" (NAVASA, 2006), UMass Boston students spent four days in New Orleans, Biloxi, and Bayou La Bâtre (Alabama) interviewing Vietnamese community members in Vietnamese and English. From these images and footage, a Cambodian American student (the only non-Vietnamese American on this trip) created a short video documentary, both to show the effects of the storm on the land and communities, as well as to capture moments of peoples' resilience (Leong et al., 2007).

This initial documentation of post-Katrina Vietnamese American community realities enabled subsequent groups of students to contribute to the communities' actual rebuilding efforts and reflect seriously on their learning (Magni, 2007; Vo, 2007a).

CULTURALLY RESPONSIVE SERVICE LEARNING AND COMMUNITY EMPOWERMENT

The "Resources for Vietnamese American Studies" course was designed to contribute directly to Gulf Coast Vietnamese American community development and empowerment efforts. Reciprocally, the activism of those Vietnamese American communities enabled students to reflect not only on their own team projects, but also on the meaning of their education and connections to their own communities. Of 21 students in the class, 17 were bicultural, bilingual Vietnamese Americans. A sampling of their voices and reflections, along with those of their non-Vietnamese classmates, illustrate some aspects of their learning (Vo, 2007a).

For example, one student — a Trinidadian immigrant of mixed Indian descent — was able to connect with the Vietnamese community as well as with classmates through the team projects despite having limited prior knowledge of Vietnamese contexts. She noted, "Before, I never thought about the Vietnamese community outside of Boston; I have a lot more Vietnamese friends now" (Magni, 2007). Moreover, she was then able to apply her learning directly to her own role as a substitute teacher in a local elementary school in Boston that serves a substantial population of Vietnamese American students and families. Similarly, a Cape Verdean American student reflected on the significance of interacting with communities different from his own. As part of the Language Access Organizing group that went door to door to conduct surveys with FEMA trailer residents from various racial backgrounds, he observed, "I was just amazed by how the people let us into their lives. The survey is somewhat intrusive. But no one was reluctant, nor did they hold back. Just getting people's experience is important" (Vo, 2007a).

A Vietnamese American student involved with the Environmental Justice project team commented, "I learned a lot from just one week compared to one month of classroom instruction. The learning in class is so out of context. This experience was actually in context" (Magni, 2007). Her involvement in mapping the geographic extent of 26 waste sites and landfills located within a two-mile radius of the New Orleans East Vietnamese community enabled her to find deeper meaning in her own Environmental Science major. Prior to the trip, she had been unsure of what to do with her degree once she graduated, but after one day of mapping landfills, she realized how her academic work could be readily integrated with her commitments to community (re)building.

Beyond working on specific projects, students also drew deeper lessons from their direct experience with the rebuilding process. One Vietnamese American student explained,

"This class is one of the class at UMB that I learned more from and would keep, instead of forget. This was a life experience" (Magni, 2007). A Vietnamese immigrant student added, "I told my parents that I'm proud of myself, I could contribute to the community" (Magni, 2007). A Filipino American student who worked in the Language Access Organizing group further reflected:

> *The voices of the community need to be heard...I'm just seeing what effort and time it takes to be a community developer: a lot of time and commitment. And I hope it should be pushed by the love of the people. I'd like to take it back and bring it wherever I go (Vo, 2007a).*

Reinforcing this insight, a Dan Thân fellow who provided technical assistance for the Real Estate project team in East Biloxi encouraged the students to put into practice what they learned: "Go back to your own community, and see how you can invest in it" (Vo, 2007a). Although students initially may not have known how to compare the Vietnamese community of Boston with those in the Gulf Coast, many concluded that there are serious needs in their own communities that are also still unaddressed. The deep learning from this course, therefore, is not simply about post-Katrina New Orleans East or East Biloxi, but the ways in which students reevaluate the needs and resources within communities, including their own current and future roles and responsibilities. This example of reflective and engaged, community-centered learning demonstrates the potential power of Vietnamese American Studies as a field of study in both higher education and K-12 schools (Beevi, Lam & Matsuda, 2001).

CONCLUSION: THE DEEP WATER OF VIETNAMESE AMERICAN STUDIES IN POST-KATRINA EDUCATION

to have a good memory: có trí nho tot

ao sâu tot cá: in the deepest water is the best fishing

By considering the intersecting challenges of K-12 and higher education in relation to Gulf Coast Vietnamese American community rebuilding, this case study suggests that models of culturally responsive service learning and community-centered instruction can enable students to apply and extend what they learn from the classroom to critical issues and activities within local community settings. Specifically, the example provided here illustrates how Vietnamese American Studies can serve as a powerful educational intervention that connects students' identities and multilingual/multicultural capacities with Vietnamese American community development.

This learning experience has provided relevant educational contexts from which to support community rebuilding efforts in New Orleans East and East Biloxi and capacity-building dynamics such as the "reverse brain drain" phenomenon of younger generation Vietnamese Americans. Short-term student participation has contributed not only to longer-term community-based initiatives related to environmental justice, business and land development, and civic advocacy, but students have also independently produced numerous other "Resources for Vietnamese American Studies," including multiple conference workshops and papers (Vo, 2007b), a master's thesis (Nguyen, 2007), three documentary videos, and a wealth of interview transcripts, photographs, and documentary audio/video footage. In addition, photographs taken by one student during the November 2005 Gulf Coast visit were selected to be shown in the national traveling exhibition, "Exit Saigon, Enter Little Saigon," curated by the Smithsonian Institution's Asian Pacific American Studies Program in 2007. Video footage from that same November 2005 visit has also been included in a new documentary by transnational independent filmmaker, Leo Chiang about the Versailles Vietnamese American community.

We are clear, however, that these accomplishments are far less significant than the actual social/cultural/spiritual/economic/political transformation of Vietnamese Americans in the Gulf Coast and the resulting generation of new resources and sustainable capacities for continued community development. Given the day-to-day distance of our own institutional location geographically from the Gulf Coast, we look forward to learning more deeply from documentary narratives and critical analyses by those who have directly facilitated these history-making processes and outcomes, which range from stopping an illegal landfill to establishing new models of neighborhood organization and multilingual, city-wide civic engagement to developing affordable senior housing and a revitalized commercial business district to leveraging millions of dollars in new funding and nurturing home-grown, indigenous leadership independent of the "reverse brain drain's" social capital.

Recognizing, for example, that educational reform in Gulf Coast communities is linked with the development and implementation of Vietnamese American Studies curricula in both public K-12 and higher education, the Mary Queen of Viet Nam–Community Development Corporation gained approval in December 2007 to establish, in partnership with the Edison Schools Corporation, a new "Intercultural Charter School (ICS)" to serve the New Orleans East community (Simon, 2007). Scheduled to open in August 2008 with up to 400 students in grades K-5, the mission of the ICS is to "create an excellent school for our community, one of academic rigor, great pride in the diverse cultures that make up home populations, and a passion for learning throughout life...to build on the community's many strengths without shying away from tackling problems that threaten to distract or impede our children's academic and social progress." Numerous challenges, from fiscal and managerial to instructional and philosophical, will confront MQVN CDC in establishing and then sustaining ICS — one of only a handful of charter schools in the United States to emerge directly from the visions and demands of Asian American communities. Nevertheless, creating the opportunity to establish a neighborhood-based school in New Orleans East with a strong Vietnamese American Studies curriculum (perhaps to be developed comparatively with Latino Studies perspectives in light of the growing number of Latino workers, businesses, and residents who are also settling in New Orleans East since Katrina) is a significant accomplishment that integrates community capacity-building with educational reform in both process and outcome.

In East Biloxi, too, modest efforts are under way to establish a culturally responsive, community-based, after-school youth program targeting Vietnamese American children and families through the Community Science Workshops model (www.scienceworkshops. org/site/csw/). This intervention reflects, in part, a vision articulated in the East Biloxi Community Plan to create community facilities for multi-aged educational activities while also organizing a civic coalition of stakeholders to rebuild the city's public educational system (Warnke Community Consulting, 2006). Interestingly, two undergraduate students with strong science and Asian American Studies backgrounds — each of whom participated in the Gulf Coast community-centered "Resources for Vietnamese American Studies" course worked in Biloxi during summer 2008 to support the development of this fresh educational model, which is designed to connect youth with local Vietnamese American family and community cultural contexts, involving aquaculture, environmental justice, recycling, gardening, and other areas of science, technology, ecology, and health.

The decision to deepen one university's Vietnamese American Studies involvement in Biloxi reflects an analysis of that city's relatively underresourced post-Katrina profile, especially in comparison with New Orleans. Vietnamese community leadership and organizational capacities differ dramatically between East Biloxi and New Orleans, just as Katrina's storm surge engulfed Biloxi in ways that were radically different from the effects of levees failing in New Orleans. Over time, however, as local youth and K-12 interventions continue to take root in these settings, the importance of establishing Vietnamese American Studies at local colleges and universities in the Gulf Coast region should also be clarified and prioritized. Though there are no signs of this currently, perhaps the post-Katrina evolution of local institutions will also include developing Vietnamese American Studies courses, if not programs, to address such issues, just as we continue to center our primary curricular and programmatic involvements within our own local contexts.

By grounding our collective commitments and contributions to Vietnamese American Studies — both conceptually and concretely — in relation to post-Katrina (Cá Trí Nho) community rebuilding, we suggest that the development of Vietnamese American Studies as a field can meaningfully articulate with the foundational intentions of Asian American Studies to empower students and communities and to transform schools and society. While maintaining a good memory (Trí Nho) of those original visions in Asian American Studies, we also wish to explore further what fish (Cá) move in the deep water of Vietnamese American Studies, particularly as charted by Gulf Coast Vietnamese American communities.

REFERENCES

Adamo, R. (2007, Summer). Squeezing public education: History and ideology gang up in New Orleans. Dissent. [Online]. Available: http://www.dissentmagazine.org/ article/?article=862.

Beevi, M., Lâm, J., & Matsuda, M. (Eds.). (2001). Vietnamese Americans: An interdisciplinary curriculum and resource guide. Garden Grove, CA: Orange County Asian and Pacific Islander Community Alliance. [Online]. Available: http://www.tolerance.org/ teach/web/vietnamese/index.jsp.

Bowen, K., Kiang, P. N., LaFargue, M., Nguyen, C., Nguyen, T. T. T., & Srikanth, R. (1999). (Re) Constructing identity and place in the Vietnamese diaspora. [Unpublished essay]. Prepared under the auspices of the William Joiner Center for the Study of War and Social Consequences. University of Massachusetts Boston.

Bowen, K., Kiang, P. N., LaFargue, M., Nguyen, C., Srikanth, R., & Tang, S. S-L. (2003). Culture, art, trauma, survival, development: Vietnamese contexts. [Unpublished essay]. Prepared under the auspices of the William Joiner Center for the Study of War and Social Consequences. University of Massachusetts Boston.

Bùi, J. D., Tang, S. S-L., & Kiang, P. N. (2004). The local/global politics of Boston's Viet-vote. AAPI Nexus: Policy, Practice & Community, 2(2), 10-18.

Butler, R. O. (1992). A good scent from a strange mountain. New York: Grove Press.

Campanella, T. J. (2006). Urban resilience and the recovery of New Orleans. Journal of the American Planning Association, 72(2), 141-146.

Catania, S. (2006, October 16). From fish sauce to salsa: New Orleans Vietnamese adapt to influx of Latinos. [News feature]. New America Media. Pacific News Service. [Online]. Available: http://news.newamericamedia.org/news/view_article.html?article_id=3e0ffe22e e7a7bcbd9a2e1d4fb79f676

Chang, M. J., & Kiang, P. N. (2002) New challenges of representing Asian American students in U.S. higher education. In P. Altbach, K. Lomotey, & W. A. Smith (Eds.), The racial crisis in American higher education Vol. 2, (pp. 137-158). Albany: SUNY Press.

Chen, A. C. C., Keith, V. M., Leong, K. J., Airriess, C., Li, W., Chung, K.Y., et al. (2007). Hurricane Katrina: Prior trauma, poverty and health among Vietnamese-American survivors. International Nursing Review, 54(4), 324-331.

Chung C. H. (1998). Vietnamese American studies: Notes toward a new paradigm. In L. R. Hirabayashi (Ed.), _Teaching Asian America_ (pp. 175-185). Lanham, MD: Rowman & Littlefield.

Donato, K., & Hakimzadeh, S. (2006). _The changing face of the Gulf Coast: Immigration to Louisiana, Mississippi, and Alabama_, Washington, DC: Migration Policy Institute.

Dyson, M. (2006). _Come hell or high water: Hurricane Katrina and the color of disaster._ New York: Basic Books.

Greater New Orleans Community Data Center. (2008a). Open public schools in New Orleans for Spring 2008 (as of April 30, 2008). [Online]. Available: http://www.gnocdc.org/maps/orleans_schools.pdf

Greater New Orleans Community Data Center. (2008b). Public school enrollment 2000-2007. [Online]. Available: http:// http://www.gnocdc.org/school_enrollment.html

Green, J., Kleiner, A. M., & Montgomery, J. P. (2007). The texture of local disaster response: Service providers' views following Hurricane Katrina. _Southern Rural Sociology, 22(2)_, 28-44.

Hill, P., & Hannaway, J. (2006). The future of public education in New Orleans. In M. A. Turner & S. R. Zedlewski (Eds.), _After Katrina_ (pp. 27-35). Washington, DC: Urban Institute.

Kao, G. (2006). Where are the Asian and Hispanic victims of Katrina? A metaphor for invisible minorities in contemporary racial discourse. _Du Bois Review_, 3, 223-231.

Kiang, P. N. (2003). Pedagogies of PTSD: Circles of healing with refugees and veterans in Asian American studies. In L. Zhan (Ed.), _Asian Americans: Vulnerable populations, model interventions, clarifying agendas_ (pp. 197-222). Sudbury, MA: Jones & Bartlett.

Kiang, P. N. (2004). Checking Southeast Asian American realities in pan-Asian American agendas. _AAPI Nexus: Policy, Practice & Community_, 2(1), 48-76.

Kiang, P. N., Suyemoto, K. L., & Tang, S.S-L. (2008). Developing and sustaining community research methods and meanings in Asian American studies coursework at an urban public university. In T. P. Fong (Ed.), _Handbook of ethnic studies research: Approaches and perspectives_ (pp. 367-398). Lanham, MD: Rowman & Littlefield.

Kiang, P. N., & Tang, S.S-L. (2006). Electoral politics and the contexts of empowerment, displacement, and diaspora for Boston's Vietnamese and Cambodian American communities. Asian American Policy Review, 15, 13-29.

Kromm, C., & Sturgis, S. (2007). Blueprint for Gulf renewal: The Katrina crisis and a community agenda for action. Durham, NC: Institute for Southern Studies.

Le, U. (2006). The invisible tide: Vietnamese Americans in Biloxi, MS. Silver Spring, MD: National Alliance of Vietnamese American Service Agencies.

Lê Espiritu, Y. (2006). Toward a critical refugee study: The Vietnamese refugee subject in US scholarship. Journal of Vietnamese Studies, 1(1-2), 410-433.

Leong, K., Airriess, C. A., Li, W., Chen, A. C. C., & Keith, V. M. (2007). Resilient history and the rebuilding of a community: The Vietnamese American community in New Orleans East. Journal of American History, 94(3), 770-779.

Louisiana Department of Education. (2005, April). District composite report 2003-2004, Orleans Parish. [Online]. Available: http://www.louisianaschools.net/lde/pair/DCR0304/ DCR036.pdf

Magni, P. (Producer). (2007). AsAmSt 294 class reflections. [Video]. Available: University of Massachusetts Boston Asian American Studies Program.

Mississippi Department of Education (2008). Mississippi assessment and accountability reporting system: Biloxi High School, 2004-2005. [Online]. Available: http://orsap.mde. k12.ms.us:8080/MAARS/maarsMS_TestResultsProcessor.jsp?userSessionId=18&SchoolId =1315&TestPanel=1

NAVASA. (2006). Return, recover, reclaim and rebuild: A grassroots response from the Vietnamese American community. Silver Spring, MD: National Alliance of Vietnamese American Service Agencies.

Nguyen, J. (2007). Stand for something or fall for anything: The building/rebuilding of the Vietnamese American community of New Orleans. Unpublished master's program final project. American Studies Program, University of Massachusetts Boston.

Ratliff, B. (2006). Good crop, many obstacles for Gulf Coast shrimpers. Mississippi State University Office of Agricultural Communications. [Online]. Available: http://msucares. com/news/print/fwnews/fw06/060803.html.

Schmidt, A. (1995). Down around Biloxi: Culture and identity in the Biloxi seafood industry. *Mississippi Folklife*,28(2), 6-19. [Online]. Available: http://www.olemiss.edu/depts/south/publish/missfolk/mfcurris/biloxi2.html.

Simon, D. (2007, December 4). Eight new charters endorsed for N.O.: State Board expects to vote Thursday. *Times Picayune* (New Orleans), 1.

Skelton, Z. (2000). *The Biloxi public schools, 1924-2001.* Biloxi, MS: Biloxi Public School District.

Smith, A. (2005, December 16). Students document forgotten Katrina victims: Vietnamese Americans. *Sampan*, 1, 3.

Tang, E. (2006, Spring). Boat people.[Letters]. *Colorlines*, 22-25.

Tang, E. (2007, January/February). Rebel survivors. *Colorlines*, 35-38.

Tang, S. S-L. (2008a). Community-centered research as capacity/knowledge building in immigrant/refugee communities. In C. R. Hale (Ed.), *Engaging contradictions: Theory, politics, and methods of activist scholarship* (pp. 237-263). Berkeley: University of California Press.

Tang, S. S-L. (2008b). Challenges of policy and practice in under-resourced Asian American communities: Analyzing public health education, health, and development issues with Cambodian American women. *Asian American Law Journal*, 153-175.

Vo, J. (Producer). (2007a). *AsAmSt 294 class documentation.* [Video]. Available: University of Massachusetts Boston Asian American Studies Program.

Vo, J. (2007b, May 12). *Post-Katrina Gulf Coast Vietnamese community rebuilding: Education and the role of Vietnamese American Studies.* Paper presented at the Conference on Southeast Asian Americans, Carleton College, Minnesota.

Warnke Community Consulting. (2006). *East Biloxi community plan.* [Unpublished report]. Biloxi, MS: Biloxi Relief, Recovery and Revitalization Center.

Wong, S. L. C. (1995). Denationalization reconsidered: Asian American cultural criticism at a theoretical crossroads *Amerasia Journal,* 21(1&2), 1-27.

Zhou, M., & Bankston, C. L. III. (1998). *Growing up American: How Vietnamese children adapt to life in the United States.* New York: Russell Sage Foundation.

CHAPTER 10
ASIAN AMERICAN MODELS OF LEADERSHIP AND LEADERSHIP DEVELOPMENT IN U.S. HIGHER EDUCATION

Patricia Akemi Neilson, EdD, MPH

A projected wave of university and college presidential retirements combined with a national push to diversify leadership within higher education affords an unprecedented opportunity for Asian Americans to fill these leadership roles. Another factor contributing to this window of opportunity is the "graying" of senior administrators of higher education institutions in this country. It is time for a new generation of leaders who reflect the changing demographics of the United States to assume these leadership positions.

According to a recent report from the American Council on Education, Asian American undergraduate enrollments at leading higher educational institutions run from 25 percent to over 50 percent.[1] Nationally, of 15,928,000 total enrolled college students, 1,019,000 were Asian Americans, or 6.4% of total enrolled students (An Overview, 2004). Yet, Asian Americans represent less than one percent (0.9%) of presidents and chancellors (Bridges et al, 2008) and a little over one point five percent (1.6%) are full-time administrators (King & Gomez, 2008). The paucity of Asian American senior administrators in higher education is glaring and often leads to a misperception regarding the leadership ability of Asian Americans.

This chapter identifies models of leadership development and multiple pathways to senior leadership positions in higher education for Asian Americans. It explores the career pathways of ten Asian American senior college/university administrators and shows the importance (or absence) of planning, mentoring, and opportunities to practice leadership within professional associations. More importantly, this chapter reveals the critical and powerful influence cultural values had for each senior administrator, both internally and in their development and decision-making as highly visible senior administrators. In addition, this chapter highlights the Leadership Development Program in Higher Education (LDPHE), the only national training program that provides culturally relevant leadership development for Asian Americans. One of the primary goals of this formalized training program is to strengthen the leadership pipeline so Asian Americans will be poised to assume senior leadership positions as they become available. With the documentation of the importance of cultural values and the efforts of the LDPHE in the stories of the ten senior administrators who broke through the "glass ceiling," Asian Americans will be able to claim positions in presidencies and senior level positions in higher education. As faculty work with Asian American undergraduate students, they need to help those students see career possibilities they may not have envisioned for themselves, and help them think about how to achieve such goals and move into such leadership positions.

Career Pathways of Asian American Senior Administrators

A qualitative study (Neilson, 2002) about the underrepresentation of Asian American (AA) senior level administrators at two- and four-year institutions in higher education explored the career paths and mobility of ten AA senior administrators who have broken through the glass ceiling. With a commitment to do purposeful sampling and the recognition of the importance of differences in perspectives, the sample used in this study included five men and five women. Seven of the ten administrators were U.S. born (including Hawai'i); one was born in China, one was born in Taiwan, and one was born in India. The ethnic profiles were predominantly East Asian (four Japanese Americans, four Chinese Americans, one Okinawan American, and one Asian Indian). There were no Southeast Asian Americans (Vietnamese, Cambodian, Lao, or Hmong) that were identifiable at the time of the study in senior administrative positions, despite purposeful, snowball sampling efforts. The sample represented both two-year community colleges and four-year universities. The senior administrative positions held by the ten administrators included one associate president of a university system, a chancellor of a community college system, the president of a four-year institution, two community college presidents, a vice chancellor of a community college district, a vice president of academic affairs of a four-year university, a vice president of academic affairs of a community college, a vice president of student services at a four-year university, and a vice president of student affairs of a community college.

Upon conducting interviews, and analyzing the narratives of the ten administrators, four primary thematic categories emerged:

1. *Career Paths as Plans/No Plans.* Only one of the interviewees planned to become an administrator; the other nine described ascents to senior levels of administration that were "unplanned." Once three of the administrators had achieved a considerable amount of success in administration, they assessed their situations and did make plans for the positions they currently hold.

2. *Organizational/Occupational Career Paths.* For the purpose of this chapter, the definition of an "occupational career path" is a series of progressively more responsible experiences within an occupation as opposed to an "organizational career path," which is a sequence of increasingly responsible jobs within the same institution (Slocum, 1974). Of the ten participants, seven had occupational career paths and three followed organizational career paths. Some moved laterally to fill career gaps, while others shifted between and among systems. This contrasts with existing literature, which suggests that minorities and women are more likely to advance organizationally from within rather than from outside the organization. Participants reported having held an average of nearly six full-time professional positions in higher education prior to their current senior administrative position.

3. *Professional Opportunities Outside the Institutions.* All ten participants belonged to multiple professional organizations or social networks. Participation for most was meaningful, providing access to information and relevant professional networks as well as connections, in some cases, to Asian American colleagues

and perspectives. For a few, involvement with these associations represented pivotal reference points and leadership opportunities in their careers that were not possible within their own institutions.

4. *Role of Mentors.* Mentoring was a visible factor to administrative advancement for all but one participant in the study. The 90 percent finding is significantly higher than the 56 percent reported for the presidents and provosts in Moore's 1983 study. Participants reported having an average of three mentors, though the numbers ranged from 0 to 7. While their mentors were individuals of diverse backgrounds, participants reported having very few Asian American role models in their professional lives.

The findings outlined above and their implications are noteworthy. Stereotypic assumptions framed by the model minority myth and structural barriers characterized as a glass ceiling continue to limit the entry of Asian Americans into senior level administrative positions as reflected in their occupation of less than one percent of CEO positions in higher education. Even without sustained and intentional planning, this study revealed that mentoring, involvement in professional organizations, and other combinations of organizational/occupational experiences have made it possible for the ten individuals in this study to shatter the glass ceiling and rise to senior leadership positions.

More importantly, the analysis of the data yielded a thematic category centered on the influence of culture and values. Identifiable cultural behaviors played a pivotal role in the professional development of the participants in this study. Based on the frequency of similar cultural influences surfacing when analyzing the data in the study, three internal values were identified that directly point to the success of these administrators. These values are informed by the traditional principles of okage sama de[2] and kodomo no tame ni,[3] which traditionally lead to:

1. hard work as honor, legacy, and moral obligation;

2. collaboration as interconnection in the present; and

3. risk-taking for the sake of the children.

HARD WORK AS HONOR, LEGACY, AND MORAL OBLIGATION

Over and over again, the narratives referred to hard work in order to achieve excellence. The associate president of a university system's story, for example, was filled with instances where he took the time to read grant proposals to get a better idea of research projects in the institution, re-wrote memos until his supervisor didn't have any more corrections, and produced a major admissions compendium in one week. He observes:

I would suggest to Asian Americans who are considering a career in higher education administration to write, learn to speak and work really, really hard. I know this about myself. I tended to work harder than anyone else, in terms of actual output and actual time spent. Also, I do a lot of reading and am broadly curious. But frankly, the thing I see that holds back most people, of any race, is that they don't work as hard as the people who preceded them. I've worked with a lot of people who worked 8-5 and worked on balancing their lives and I think that's wonderful and I wish I'd done it, but you're not going to be competitive with the person who puts in 10-hour days and works 25 percent more than you. I don't know if that's good or fair, but I know that it's a fact. What doesn't work in the world is insisting that you get the same opportunities as someone else who works harder. I'm not saying that that's a good deal but I am saying that that might be what it takes.

Because of the strong influence culture played in his childhood, the president of a community college credits his father for instilling the work ethic in him:

Working hard is not a big deal. I learned this value from working in the family grocery store in Tucson. All the kids, the whole family, worked and, as I think back, it's amazing how many hours my dad put into the family business; I mean that he was the business. My dad's philosophy was: if there's work to do, you do it. You don't ask whose work it is. And I believe that until this day, that is how I approach projects and things that I do. I wash windows if I need to...it doesn't matter what my title is.

For these two administrators, hard work was second nature. It was part of getting their job done — an internalized expectation rather than a professional orientation. They felt and acted on senses of commitment, responsibility and obligation to the institution that employed them based on values instilled in them from childhood. The expectation of hard work, then, is not simply to achieve career advancement. It is meant to honor the legacy of hard-working family members.

Collaboration as Interconnection in the Present

The sense of interconnectedness and the internalizing of the concept of okage sama de — that we are extensions of one another and everything is connected — go a long way to explain and illuminate the intensely collaborative nature of many of the administrators in the study. The chancellor of a community college system, for example, characterized himself as "a leader of teamwork, collaboration and consensus building. I also always take risks." Three other administrators were also able to link collaboration with their style of leadership. The vice president of student affairs at a four-year institution credits her Asian values with the way she conducts business on a daily basis:

I didn't realize it at the time, but now as I look back, I really believe that the work I did in administration was congruent with whom I am as an Asian American. My style, which I believe is collaborative, includes nurturing people and caring for people. I also believe that those behaviors are very, very Asian. Consulting and being consultative is also related to collaboration. I believe in touching base with people, bringing them on board and giving them a sense of ownership. Sharing ownership, teamwork. Coincidentally, that is how leadership practices have evolved over the past three decades...is it a coincidence or recognition that this process works?

Her rhetorical question infers that in her thirty years in higher education she has seen "her way" of doing things validated. U.S. business management training during the 1980s, for example, adopted many elements of Japanese business practices and some of their underlying cultural principles. For the administrators in this study, this approach was, in all likelihood, an outgrowth of their own cultural values.

A community college president's way of tracing his collaborative nature, for example, dates back to his childhood:

I was raised in a Chinese family, so a lot of things that are part of me are of the Chinese culture. I think, for instance, I am more group-oriented than individual-oriented in the way I see life in the administrative structure. It wasn't hard for me to develop a very strong and real shared governance process with faculty and classified staff at the college. Part of the openness that I use in administration is looking at using groups to make decisions, to use the wisdom of the group and not the individual. These are things that are part of the Asian culture. I think the sense of wanting to accomplish not for myself but for the greater good is part of that.

By using this style of leadership to facilitate greater openness on campus, he changed the culture of his institution. Two years after he became president, there was a fiscal crisis and he had to preside over the first lay-offs in the institution. He recalls, "People were not happy about the situation, but they understood that it had to be done." He continues by saying, "There have been a lot of other things that have happened there, but the fingerprint that I have left is that it is a place that is much more open. I feel that the morale is very high."

Another community college president also practices collaboration in her position. As soon as she accepted the challenge of the presidency, she set out to implement the set of core values that she had outlined during her interview for the presidency, which were: trust, openness, integrity, honesty and forgiveness. Where did these values come from? This was her reply:

I have to say I do a lot of reading in organizational development. Most of the literature is based in business. Somewhere in the literature it points out that a leader of an organization needs to convey his or her own personal values to the organization. The way you are going to lead is based on what you personally believe in. We can have institutional values but if I don't believe in them or follow them, then there's a disconnect. So, I said, these are my values: trust, openness, integrity, honesty and forgiveness.

She did not declare that these core values were Asian values, but they sound very similar to the norms that were presented earlier in this chapter. In her first year as president, she was able to operationalize these core values into the culture of the campus. She established a mission-based governance, her own version of shared governance. This plan was based on consensus building, another form of collaboration. She created round table groups that met on issues or projects that affected the institution as a whole. The outcomes of the round tables were then reviewed by the governance group. In light of the institution's strategic plan, these outcomes were prioritized, resources were allocated and the results presented to the president, who generally viewed these decisions as final. This "collective governing body" had the authority to make final decisions, but usually deferred to the president, who has never used her veto option and trusts that the personnel of the institution will make the right decisions collectively.

In contrast, the vice chancellor of a system shared an incident from his graduate school experience — a setting in which he had no power — when his collaborative values were directly criticized for being inappropriate. After trying to work together with classmates in a graduate ecology class, his professor told him explicitly, "You cannot share data." He responded, "I'm not talking about copying results, I'm talking about sharing data so each of us can have enough data to make an analysis to come up with whatever we come up with to conclude something." The professor then responded, "If you do, I'll penalize you. That's graduate study." This example clarifies that even the micro-level articulation of Asian cultural values and commitments within U.S. higher education institutions is not necessarily accepted or acceptable. Cultural conflicts are a shared dynamic, and not simply experienced by one side. It is the exercise or threat of power by one side in a cultural conflict that forces the other side to adapt, submit, depart or resist. In this case, with his professor threatening to penalize him, he chose to drop out of his master's program at that university. Rather than sacrifice his integrity and lose face, *haji* [4] (shame), this vice chancellor's example points to a third cultural concept that integrates several aspects of the norms with needs or commitments to make sacrifices in order to have longer-term impact in the future.

Risk Taking — For the Sake of the Children

In addition to hard work as a moral obligation that honors the legacy of those in the past and collaboration as an active, present recognition of reciprocity and interconnectedness (okage sama de), a third quality echoed over and over in the career stories of participants in the study is risk-taking at important moments to have impact on the future. It may seem contradictory that risk taking is being considered as an Asian cultural value when the norms and concepts of the Asian values introduced thus far seem to imply otherwise. To stick out or to call attention to oneself is seen as undesirable and counter to a norm such as *enryo.*[5] However, the experiences shared by the administrators in this study exemplify risk taking of a different nature. The risks taken were about making a point, doing the right thing, fulfilling a moral obligation, or righting a wrong. In this way, risk-taking reflects an additional cultural principle, *kodomo no tame ni,* that, in conjunction with *okage sama de,* is fundamental to the framework of cultural values suggested from this study.

The linking of experiences of poverty and racial discrimination with commitment to a struggle for a better life for future generations was a powerful theme in the interviews with the ten Asian American senior administrators in this study. Three of the ten had parents who were sent to Japanese American internment camps during World War II, and six of the ten were the first in their families to gain a college degree, thereby making the relationship of the study's subjects to issues of access and educational opportunity direct and personal. Some individuals, for example the vice president of student services of a four-year institution, specifically recall "not having role models, coming from a poor family, not having opportunities, my family couldn't afford opportunities, so I didn't have the kind of opportunities that some of my colleagues and friends experienced."

Coming from these backgrounds, individuals repeatedly describe examples in which they chose particular directions or took personal risks because of internalized commitments to struggle for equity and justice on behalf of vulnerable populations, especially within higher education. For example, the vice chancellor of a community college system recalled being a biology graduate student at San Francisco State University during the tumultuous period of the Third World student strike in 1968 that forced the university to establish the first College of Ethnic Studies in the United States:

I felt strongly about the strikes, so I walked with the picketers and didn't go to class when the strike was going on....Very few faculty in the Biology Department supported the sympathies of the strikers....I told the faculty member that I couldn't come to class, but I would make up all the work, and more if necessary.

His later decision to prioritize working with "minority students and those students who historically have not participated in higher education" in his role as a community college senior administrator revealed his continuing commitment to support the underserved many years later.

Similarly, when asked about her most important professional contribution, the vice president of student affairs at a community college answers:

It has to do with what I've created in terms of access and equity. I've...[made]...efforts that bring in students to the institution that nobody else wanted to serve. These students are admitted and I am committed to making them successful....They are the students who are most at risk, the students who fail. But among the failures there are incredible success stories....Someone at the institution has actually called me the "conscience" of the institution, reminding them about what we are there for.

A vice president of academic affairs at community college also insists on prioritizing a commitment to students of color at her institution. Though she is a vice president of academic affairs, she actively serves as a student adviser: "I specifically asked that they [her advisees each year] be students of color, not necessarily Asian students, but students of color, because I think it is important that they identify with someone on campus, and why not me?"

One example among several for the president of a community college was his involvement with establishing and sustaining the professional association, Asian Pacific Americans in Higher Education (APAHE). He recalled, "At its beginnings, it was an activist group that responded to issues, including the admission policy and the tenure case of a faculty member [Director of the Asian American Studies Center at UCLA whose initial denial of tenure galvanized a national advocacy campaign during the late 1980s]. We organized to make a difference." The associate president of a university system also recognizes the significance of his role as a founding organizer of APAHE.

In another example, the president of a four-year institution, who spent the first three years of his schooling in a Japanese American internment camp, gives an account of his role in helping Asian Americans gain protection under Federal affirmative action guidelines:

> When I was interviewing for a vice presidency, I was asked whether I myself was a minority protected under Affirmative Action. I said we are covered under the Executive Order for Affirmative Action. And the reason I know this [is] because when I was Chairman National Education Commission of the Japanese American Citizens League (JACL), I was also serving on the Advisory Committee for the desegregation of the Pasadena Public Schools. The program was called the Emergency Assistance Program, which was federally funded, to help districts undergoing desegregation. The Pasadena Public Schools had received a major grant to assist in this process and under this grant's guideline, 50 percent of the people who were hired in the program had to be minorities. The other half did not have to be. Asians were not defined as either a minority or majority, so they were not hired for the program because they were not considered a minority. But they were not considered white either, so they just were not hired. They just did not know how to classify us. So, as the chair of the National Education Commission of the Japanese American Citizens League, I wrote to a White House staff at the time. I told him about this situation, so he worked with the staff and submitted a labor bill. This legislation was able to get Asians included among the minority groups protected under the Executive Order for Affirmative Action. I knew that we were in fact considered a protected group, so I proceeded to tell him that and I actually sent them the Executive Order for Affirmative Action that specified that.

In each of these examples, participants in this study reveal various ways in which their professional careers as senior administrators intersect with issues and dynamics of access, equity, and social justice. The data from this study show that Asian American administrators' career paths reflect choices and priorities informed by a sensibility that recognizes the reality of discrimination and the value of contributing to a better collective future for the next generation. In essence, the above examples illustrate how these Asian American administrators practice the cultural principle of kodomo no tame ni, taking risks for the sake of the children. This is a sharp contrast to making choices and taking risks in one's career based on personal ambition and professional opportunities that arise.

In addition, given that between 80 and 90 percent of the Asian and Asian American doctoral degree recipients in the 1990s were foreign-born and not U.S. citizens (Harvey, 2002), the pool of candidates emerging in the next two decades for senior administrative positions is likely to include a substantial number of immigrants. Only two individuals with significant immigrant perspectives were included in this sample. Nevertheless, issues raised in their interviews, such as accent discrimination, deserve further study through purposeful sampling with greater numbers of immigrant senior administrators. This attention to more targeted sampling could also address the need for studies about non-Chinese and non-Japanese Americans, including Indian Americans, Korean Americans, Filipino Americans, Vietnamese Americans, and others.

Moreover, given the important linkage between risk taking for the sake of the children (kodomo no tame ni) and participants' personal experiences of poverty and discrimination, special attention should be invested in supporting and mentoring specific individuals and groups within the higher education pipeline, such as Southeast Asian Americans, whose experiences with war, refugee resettlement, and poverty might lead them to have similarly resilient, internalized commitments to *kodomo no tame ni* and related issues of access and equity.

IMPLICATIONS FOR PRACTICE

The findings of this research reveal that having mentors, belonging to professional organizations, and having an occupational career path with its possible combinations, even with no plan, can help shape a career path to senior administrative leadership. Although there is no prescribed pathway to success, the ten administrators' career stories in this study offer important insights about how it is possible to overcome the "glass ceiling."

Clearly, for Asian Americans with interests in or even curiosity about becoming senior administrators, this study highlights the value of career planning in conjunction with being open to both occupational and organizational career paths and strategies. Considering a range of institutional possibilities, particularly in geographic areas with large or historic concentrations of Asian Americans, the likelihood of professional advancement to senior levels increases. In addition, having a critical self-consciousness in relation to one's core cultural values and influences, together with developing a sociocultural awareness and using structural analysis regarding the overall status of Asian Americans will enhance the capacity of Asian Americans to prioritize and strategize more effectively in their process of professional advancement.

Findings from this study also have implications for decision-makers, affirmative action officers, hiring committees, and search firms who are responsible for assessing pools of qualified candidates for senior administrative positions fairly. It is important, for example, to recognize cultural assumptions and dynamics that may occur during interviews, particularly with Asian American candidates who are both individually modest and highly collaborative in their style of leadership. In addition, one subject in this study who recalled being "considered as a finalist because I was a person of color," refers to the practice of "tokenism" of search committees, in which qualified Asian American administrators contribute to the "diverse" pool of candidates required by affirmative action guidelines, but are not chosen because they were never intended to be selected, and it was assumed, based on the model minority myth, that they would not protest. All parties involved with searches should be able to recognize, challenge and work to eradicate any such biased practices.

If Asian Americans are hired, respected, and offered continuing professional development opportunities as administrators, however, these types of individual and institutional investments will likely yield high returns, particularly if those Asian Americans' values of reciprocity and moral obligation manifest in hard work and positive change, as they have been described in this study.

Mentors clearly have essential and multiple roles to play. Their influence and active interventions as both sounding boards and advocates are critical to counterbalance the inertia that is caused by and contributes to one's having no plans. Furthermore, participants in this study point to the need and desire to have more Asian American role models involved in the mentoring process. At campuses with a critical mass of Asian American senior and junior faculty, for example, an organized Asian American faculty caucus or comparable body with either formal or informal institutional status can provide a critical support and advocacy mechanism for professional advancement and problem-solving, especially from the perspective of one's organizational career path.

Many campuses do not have such proactive capacity among Asian American faculty and administrators at their own campuses, so outside professional associations such as Leadership Education for Asian Pacifics (LEAP) and Asian Pacific Americans in Higher Education (APAHE) become critical. In this study, the general literature clearly emphasized the value of affiliating with professional organizations outside one's institution in order to have generic access to information, networks, and opportunities for skill building and leadership development, but Moore (1983) and others did not mention the specific importance for minority administrators to belong to culturally responsive or ethnic/racial identity centered professional associations. The participants in this study saw a need for not only professional contexts that provided generic opportunities offered by other associations, but also connections to colleagues and training that shared their experiences dealing with race, cultural values, community aspirations and the model minority myth. A description of one such program, the Leadership Development Program in Higher Education (LDPHE) follows.

LEADERSHIP DEVELOPMENT PROGRAM IN HIGHER EDUCATION

The Leadership Development Program in Higher Education (LDPHE) was initiated when Bob Suzuki, the president of California State Polytechnic University, Pomona, became critically concerned about the lack of a pipeline of Asian and Pacific American leaders who could move into positions of influence and leadership within higher education. To address this problem, President Suzuki organized a "summit" meeting in 1995 with leading APA's in higher education, including the late chancellor of the University of California, Berkeley Chang-Lin Tien and President/CEO of Leadership Education for Asian Pacifics (LEAP), J. D. Hokoyama. (Yamagata-Noji, 2005)

After almost a year of planning with President Suzuki leading the effort, two organizations, LEAP and APAHE partnered to offer a leadership training program called Leadership Development Program in Higher Education. Currently, it is the only national vehicle for Asian American centered professional career and leadership development in the United States. The program provides a leadership pipeline for Asian Americans seeking executive level positions.

The LDPHE is an intensive, four-day experience with a format that focuses on in-depth interactions between participants and program faculty. It is a stand-alone residential program held at the Kellogg West Conference Center on the campus of California State Polytechnic University, Pomona, in a retreat-like setting that allows participants to focus on issues, skill building and relationship development in an atmosphere free from distractions. The curriculum for the program includes:

- "Path to leadership" stories from current and retired Asian American senior level administrators in higher education
- Assigned mentors
- Career-building leadership skills
- Insights on the "hidden" career ladder in higher education
- Tools to effectively position yourself as a leader
- Creation and implementation of a personalized Leadership and Career Action Plan
- Valuable relationships and networks among fellow AA professionals in higher education

The main session topics are:

- The 21st Century Leader: Surviving and Thriving in the Third Millennium
- Understanding Asian Pacific American Values and Leadership Skills
- Developing and Promoting Your Leadership Style
- Effective Communication Strategies
- Interviewing for Success (Mock Interviews)
- Mastering the Dynamics of Power: Making an Impact on Campus
- Successfully Surviving Leadership Challenges

The uniqueness of the LDPHE curriculum lies in the anchoring of the material in a context of Asian American cultural values. These values are ingrained at an early age and participants are encouraged to seek greater linkages between their thoughts and actions with how they were raised, their beliefs and their values (Yamagata-Noji, 2005).

Since the inaugural class of 1997, 331 college and university administrators, faculty, and staff have completed the LDPHE, many of whom have gone on to become college presidents, vice presidents, deans, and faculty chairs (Yamagata-Noji, 2005). This section examines the trends of the demographics of Asian Americans who have completed the LDPHE and occupy a place in the leadership pipeline.

The inaugural class enrolled 25 participants in June 1997. There was a decline in enrollment in years 1998, 1999 and 2000 with enrollments of 21, 14, and 17, respectively. The numbers increased and remained relatively constant in years 2001, 2002, 2003 and 2004 with enrollments of 27, 28, 31 and 27, respectively. In 2005, the enrollment figures jumped to 42 and in 2006 and 2007 enrollments climbed to 49 and 50. Eleven years after its inception, potential participants are encouraged to apply early. The program has gained momentum as it has become a known entity.

The gender breakdown in the program is 202 females, or 61 percent, and 129 males, or 39 percent. The program attracts Asian Americans from all over the country, but is predominantly attended by those from California (78 percent, or 262 of the 331 participants overall). Other regions overall include the East Coast and the South at five percent, or 17 participants each, and the Midwest, Pacific Northwest and Western Rockies/Plains states at four percent, or 14 participants each. The past four years has seen increased participation from the Pacific Northwest and the South.

The position categories reported in the LEAP Leadership Development Program for Higher Education Demographics are administration/management, faculty and staff. Of the 331 total participants who have completed the program, 37 percent, or 121, were administrators/managers, 28 percent, or 93, were faculty, and 35 percent, or 117, were staff. When compared to the earlier years of the program (1997-2002), there is more balanced representation from each of the categories since that time.

The ethnic representation in the program revealed 43 self-identified categories. Twenty-six of the categories had small numbers that fell into two general groupings: mixed Asian and biracial. The following is a list of the ethnic representation in descending order:

Table 10-1: Ethnic Representation in LDPHE 1997 - 2007[6]

Ethnic Group	Percentage	Number
Chinese	37%	118
Japanese	14%	46
Filipino	13%	43
Mixed Asian	7%	23
Korean	7%	22
Biracial	5%	18
Vietnamese	5%	17
South Asian	3%	11

The numbers show that there is room for improvement in attracting more Southeast Asians and South Asians. In the case of Southeast Asians, their total numbers in higher education are relatively low, making recruitment difficult.

But Bob Suzuki's vision of creating a pipeline of Asian American leaders who could move up into positions of influence and leadership within higher education has been realized. The LDPHE is training and growing leaders to be the new generation of senior administrators in higher education.

Conclusion

This chapter revealed some troubling statistics regarding the numbers of Asian Americans in presidential and senior level administrative positions in higher education. It has also documented the remarkable successes of ten individuals who were able to break through the glass ceiling — people whose persistence, risk taking, hard work, resilience, high standards, and collaborative approaches enabled them to achieve beyond the "norm" and make it into the 1.6% of Asian Americans who are in such leadership roles nationally. In the case of these ten Asian American administrators, however, understanding their career paths requires not only an analysis of factors such as mentoring and involvement in professional associations that might be important to the story of any administrator, but also an engagement with specific Asian cultural values that lie at the heart of both their philosophical commitments and day-to-day practice.

This chapter ends with this advice to Asian Americans from The Committee of 100's 2005 report:

> *Asian Pacific Americans need to do more to publicize the fact that a cohort of bright, talented APA academic leaders constitutes part of the United States' competitive advantage: If this trend toward underrepresentation is not reversed, the United States may risk experiencing reverse brain drain, whereby the APA academic leaders accept positions at fast-growing institutions in greater China or Asia that are actively recruiting administrators with managerial experience. This is already the case with distinguished APA faculty members and executives accepting teaching positions in India and China, at present, three of the top Hong Kong university presidencies are occupied by APAs.[7]*

References

An overview. (2004). [Almanac Issue]. Chronicle of Higher Education, 51(1), 3.

Ariyoshi, G. R. (1997). With obligation to all. Honolulu: University of Hawai'i.

Bridges, B. K, Eckel, P. D., Cordova, D. I., & White, B. P. (2008). Broadening the leadership spectrum: Advancing diversity in the American college presidency. Washington, DC: American Council on Education.

Harvey, W.B. (2002). Status report on minorities in higher education 2001-2002. Washington, DC: American Council on Education.

King, J. E., & Gomez, G. G. (2008). On the pathway to the presidency: Characteristics of higher education's senior leadership. Washington DC: American Council on Education.

Kitano, H. (1969). Japanese Americans, the evolution of a subculture. Englewood Cliffs, NJ: Prentice-Hall, Inc.

Moore, K. M. (1983). The top-line: A report on presidents', provosts', & deans' careers, leaders in transition: A national study of higher education administrators. Washington, DC: American Council on Education.

Neilson, P. A. (2002). Career paths of Asian American senior administrators in higher education: An inquiry into under-representation. Unpublished doctoral dissertation for the Graduate College of Education at the University of Massachusetts Boston.

Ogawa, D. M. (1978). Kodomo no tame ni: For the sake of the children. Honolulu: University of Hawai'i.

Slocum, W. L. (1974). Occupational careers. Chicago: Aldine.

The Committee of 100's Asian Pacific Americans (APAs) in higher education report card. (2005). New York: Committee of 100.

Yamagata-Noji, A. (2005). Leadership Development Program in Higher Education: Asian Pacific American leaders in higher education — An oxymoron? In D. Leon (Ed.), Lessons in leadership: Executive leadership programs for advancing diversity in higher education: Vol. V. Diversity in higher education (pp. 173-206). St. Louis: JAI Press. (ED492040)

FOOTNOTES

1   These figures are derived from the following list, which is taken from Leadership Development Program in Higher Education: Asian Pacific American Leaders in Higher Education — An Oxymoron? (Yamagata-Noji, 2005).

University of California, Irvine	52%
University of California, Berkeley	42%
Polytechnic University (NY)	41%
University of California, Los Angeles	39%
California Institute of Technology	34%
Massachusetts Institute of Technology	31%
Carnegie Mellon University	26%
University of Illinois, Chicago	26%
University of Washington	26%
SUNY, Stony Brook	25%

2   George Ariyoshi, the first Japanese American governor of Hawai'i used this phrase in his memoirs, With Obligation to All (1997). "Okage sama de, because of your shadow which falls on me, because of your help, because of you, I am what I am. I reminded myself of that idea often, and I tried to nurture that attitude in others. We are extensions of one another, and we are beholden to one another."

3   In his book about Hawaiian Japanese with the same title, Kodomo No Tame Ni, Ogawa (1978) speaks of this Japanese American phrase, which means "for the sake of the children":"The Issei [first generation] lived in a world of overt racial oppression, imposed poverty and social rejection. The Nisei [second generation] not only inherited a world of limited opportunity but had to confront the catastrophe of a war which seemed to spell doom for their way of life. But rather than succumbing to fatalism or racial bitterness, both generations were sustained by the belief that for the sake of the children, kodomo no tame ni, the quality of life in Hawaii could be improved. If one worked hard, saved, sacrificed, and gathered strength from one's cultural roots, then material, social, and spiritual well-being would be possible for the coming generations" (Ogawa, 1978, p. xxii).

4   Haji, the sense of shame, is said to form the core of the Japanese mentality. This is a concept that spread when anthropologist Ruth Benedict classified Japanese culture as a "shame culture," as opposed to the Western "guilt culture." According to this classification, in Western countries, the absolute moral standard of guilt forms the backbone, or inner principle, of people's behavior. In Japan, however, behavior is not ruled by an inner principle, but an external feeling of shame. There are various criticisms against this kind of simplification. For example, Western people, too, have a sense of shame like the Japanese, and the Japanese also have inner moral principles. Nevertheless, it is true that the Japanese place higher importance on the sense of shame. Particularly for samurai in the feudal period, being put to shame in public was as good as being dead (http://lfw.rog/shodouka, www.japanlink.com).

5   Enryo involves a complex of deference behaviors helping to establish the perimeters of the individual's freedom. Enryo helps explain much of Japanese-American behavior. As with other norms, it has both positive and negative effects on Japanese acculturation. For example, take observations of Japanese in situations as diverse as their hesitance to speak out at meetings; their refusal of any invitation, especially the first time; their refusal of a second helping; their acceptance of a less desired object when given a free choice; their lack of verbal participation, especially in asking for a raise in salary — these may be based on enryo. The inscrutable face, the noncommittal answer, the behavioral reserve can often be traced to this norm, so that the stereotype of the shy, reserved Japanese in ambiguous social situations is often an accurate one (Kitano, 1969; Ogawa, 1978)

6   LEAP Leadership Development Program for Higher Education, July 11-14, 2007. Demographics handout in participants' manual.

7   The Committee of 100's Asian Pacific Americans (APAs) in Higher Education Report Card (2005) cites Howard W. French's New York Times article, China luring foreign scholars to make its universities great (2005, October 25), International, p. 14.

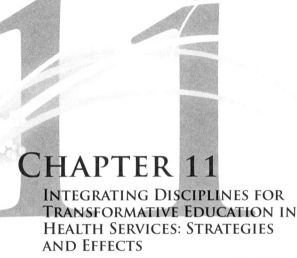

CHAPTER 11

INTEGRATING DISCIPLINES FOR TRANSFORMATIVE EDUCATION IN HEALTH SERVICES: STRATEGIES AND EFFECTS

Karen L. Suyemoto, PhD
John Tawa, MA
Grace S. Kim, PhD
Stephanie C. Day, MA
Susan A. Lambe, EdM
Phuong T. Nguyen, MA
Julie M. AhnAllen, PhD

The multicultural landscape of the United States challenges health service educators to develop ways to effectively teach increasingly diverse students and prepare them to provide services to increasingly diverse health care consumers. Traditional approaches to health services education (e.g., nursing or psychology) emphasize "objective" knowledge, such as standardized diagnostic and treatment modalities, taught through "objective" pedagogical approaches. However, these contents and approaches to education are rooted in Eurocentric values and primarily applicable to Eurocentric populations (Banks, 1996a; Freire, 1993). In contrast, transformative education (TE) emphasizes critical exploration of the content, production, and dissemination of knowledge. (Banks, 1996a; 1996b; Freire, 1993; Gay, 1995). Although systems-level disciplines such as ethnic studies are most frequently associated with TE, integrating TE approaches within individual-level, health science disciplines, such as nursing or psychology, can address health service provision disparities by making education more accessible and relevant to students traditionally underrepresented in health sciences as well as enabling all students to provide systemically sensitive services. Health services disciplines also offer approaches that could help meet the goals of TE. Nursing and psychology frequently provide practical applications of theory for working with individuals and groups that are less emphasized in systems-level disciplines. The integration of systems-level discipline and individual-level service-focused discipline approaches can contribute to meeting the goals of TE and service provision.

AN OVERVIEW OF TRANSFORMATIVE EDUCATION GOALS

The core principle of TE is that education should contribute to social justice rather than maintain social oppression (Banks, 1996b; Freire, 1993; Gay, 1995). The following strategies and approaches are therefore emphasized within TE:

1. *Examining Complex Social Variables and Power Relations.* TE explicitly examines and problematizes complex social variables, such as race, ethnicity, and social class. TE sees knowledge as creating power, and encourages explicit consideration of power and privilege in relation to these social variables. Thus, rather than discussing social variables primarily as equally valued differences, they are examined as distinctions with implications for resources, opportunities, and power relations between people. Including an individual perspective develops students' awareness of power and privilege in their own experiences and encourages students to examine intersections between individual, interpersonal, and systemic enactments of social variables.

2. *Including Marginalized Voices.* TE includes historical and current experiences and contributions of traditionally marginalized peoples. TE also addresses the legacies of misinformation about marginalized peoples that are based on stereotypes or myths (Banks, 1996a). Including an individual-level perspective attends to the ways that marginalization and associated legacies affect individuals and interpersonal relationships.

3. *Personalizing Knowledge.* TE facilitates connections between knowledge — in the form of didactic material — and lived experiences (Freire, 1993). These connections are made both in relation to what students know about others (connecting conceptual principles and research findings to lived experiences through narratives and case examples) and within students' lives (e.g., connecting material to the lived experience of students).

4. *Exploring Epistemological Validity.* TE critically examines what and who defines "valid knowledge" (i.e., epistemology; Banks, 1996a; Banks, 1996b). Therefore, TE challenges the traditional objectivistic approach that emphasizes a single "Truth." The traditional approach often obscures epistemological questions related to power and the construction and dissemination of knowledge, such as who conducts research studies, with which populations, and from whose perspective the findings are interpreted and passed on to the next generation through formal education. The inclusion of an individual-level perspective encourages students to examine how they themselves are knowledge consumers and producers, and how they may contribute to or challenge the maintenance of the dominance of some viewpoints over others.

TRANSFORMATIVE EDUCATION IN HEALTH SERVICES: THE EXAMPLE OF ASIAN AMERICAN STUDIES AND PSYCHOLOGY

Asian American Studies (AAS) is based in TE ideals. From its inception, AAS aimed to improve the experiences of Asian Americans through: (1) increased ethnic and racial consciousness; (2) community organizing and empowerment; (3) educational reform; and (4) providing students with accurate and contextualized information about Asian Americans (Endo & Wei, 1988; Hune, 1989). AAS focuses on communities and systems, rather than individuals, and offers insights about educational and community interventions that contribute to social justice for Asian Americans.

In contrast, Psychology reflects the medical traditions of emphasizing individual processes. Like nursing, clinical psychology traditionally focused on objective diagnostics and treatments, and quantitative investigations of controlled processes within a medical tradition (Doll, 1940). More recently, multicultural and feminist psychologists have criticized objective and individualistic stances as reductionistic and disconnected to peoples' lived experience and encouraged a more contextualized view of the person (Campbell & Wasco, 2000; Sue & Sue, 2003).

The benefits of integrating the individual health focus of clinical psychology (or nursing) with the sociopolitical systemic focus of AAS include: better understanding of the individual, social, and political experiences of Asian Americans; expanding methodologies of inquiry; translating psychological/nursing research and ethnic studies theory into a more positive impact on individuals and communities within and outside the university;

and working together to best serve and understand Asian Americans in the classroom and beyond.

In the following sections, we discuss specific strategies for integrating TE within the Health Services curriculum and pedagogy in order to contribute to student engagement, learning, and the betterment of the health of individuals and communities served by these students. Although we use examples from AAS and Psychology, the strategies and effects we discuss are applicable and relevant to nursing education and other health service areas. We then address ways in which multiple TE goals are incorporated into lived experiences of students through interpersonal relationships. We conclude by considering ways in which integration and TE can be institutionally supported.

CURRICULAR STRATEGIES FOR TE GOALS

A TE approach requires significant curriculum development planning. Nursing or Psychology educators may need to: (a) consider supplementing traditional textbooks with extra readings and case examples, (b) plan activities and assignments to aid students' appreciation for multiple lived experiences, and (c) create assignments that connect didactic materials to lived experiences.

Curricular Strategies for Examining Complex Social Variables and Power Relations

Social variables such as race, culture, and social class are now often included in traditional nursing and psychology curricula. However, TE seeks to move beyond basic discussion of these variables to actively explore their complex nature, interactions, and relationships to structural power and privilege. For example, there is considerable research comparing Asian Americans and White European Americans on a variety of psychological and health constructs. Including this research in classes is one step toward moving away from a Eurocentric approach. However, this research often grossly oversimplifies race and culture. For example, simple checkboxes with "race" categories (e.g., White/European, Asian) are often used to operationalize race and culture. This kind of operationalization tells us little about what it means to the participants to be Asian or White or whether participants are categorizing themselves racially or culturally (Suyemoto, 2002). We cannot know from a checkbox whether participants strongly endorse Asian cultural values such as collectivism, whether participants' self-categorization is related to racial or cultural experiences, or whether participants are simply endorsing a label imposed upon them. However, researchers frequently make complex cultural or racial interpretations; for example, attributing differences between Asian Americans and White Americans in conformity as being due to the Asian "collectivistic culture." Presenting only the results and traditional interpretations of such research when teaching contributes to oversimplification and misinformation about Asian Americans. Alternatively, a TE approach includes in the curriculum a complex analysis of the meanings of social variables, questioning, for example, what endorsing a checkbox might actually mean in relation to race *and* culture, and what interpretations can be realistically made when utilizing this methodology.

One way to examine the complexity of social variables is to explore the heterogeneity of meanings and power dynamics within a group. Utilizing examples of people who do not easily fit the narrower definitions of a group can expand students' understandings of social variables. For example, in my Introduction to AAS class, I (KLS) discuss experiences with students and research participants who have described themselves as: Korean and raised by an adoptive White European American family; White and raised by a Japanese foster family; and Black/Asian multiracial and raised by an African American family. We discuss how these individuals might see themselves or be seen by others in relation to race and ethnicity as two separate variables (Suyemoto, 2002). Through this discussion, we highlight ways in which race and ethnicity are extremely complex as students struggle to determine how each of these individuals would identify or be seen by others.

TE also aims to examine power on the individual, interpersonal, and systemic levels that differentially affect individuals' access to health resources. Thus, it is important for the curriculum to include content that reflects an analysis of structural power in relation to individual differences. For example, in considering health care disparities in racial and ethnic minorities, it is important to understand problems beyond an individual focus (e.g., the individual needs to improve English language skills or to acculturate and understand American norms or to prioritize health and take time from work for appointments in order to better utilize health services). Instead, TE encourages students to question how problems might lie within systems and reflect inequities in power and privilege. The view that individuals should acculturate in order to better access health care rests on the unquestioned assumption that health care is best when reflecting American values and norms. This assumption leaves unexamined the ways that the health care system privileges some, while excluding others, because of its values and structure. Various research studies point to the systemic issues and barriers associated with accessing health care that are particularly pertinent for racial and ethnic minorities (e.g., availability/ease of transportation; language options available in health care; issues related to citizenship and documentation; availability of financial, interpersonal, and other resources within a community (see review in USDHHS, 2001). A systems-focused conceptualization enables students to explore the complexities of privilege and lack of privilege posed by intersections of race, ethnicity, language, and socioeconomic class.

Discussion of the effects of structural oppression also includes exploring the ways in which *all* groups that lack sociopolitical power (e.g., women, working class/working poor; Weber, 1998) have converging experiences of oppression. These discussions help students consider their personal and community connections to others who experience oppression, their own relative privilege in relation to others, and the importance of resisting oppression in all areas, not just those where they personally experience oppression. For example, one African immigrant student shared that Asian American Psychology helped him understand his own experiences of oppression as an immigrant and as a person of color, as well as develop his racial connections to U.S.-born African Americans and his connections and empathy for Asian Americans.

Curricular Strategies for Including Marginalized Voices

TE recognizes the privileged position of what is usually considered the "norm" (i.e., the Eurocentric perspective), and therefore structures curricula to explicitly include experiences that are often ignored. Typically, educators in psychology, nursing, or other health sciences highlight seminal theories in each teaching module, and students learn these concepts for exams. For example, Introductory Psychology typically addresses content areas such as sensation and perception, emotion, cognition, intelligence, human development, health/mental health (e.g., stress and coping, mental disorders and treatment), and personality. However, the majority of the research and theory discussed in most introductory textbooks describes the average or modal experiences of White European Americans (WEAs). The experiences of WEAs are treated as normative both explicitly (e.g., through describing normative identity development as involving significant autonomy and differentiation that is characteristic of individualistic, rather than collectivistic, cultures) and implicitly (e.g., through the lack of inclusion or recognition of exclusion of the experiences of other racial and cultural groups). To move beyond this traditional Eurocentric dynamic, we (GSK and KLS) modified traditional approaches to Introductory Psychology to include the experiences of traditionally marginalized peoples by integrating cultural and racial minority psychology through additional readings (e.g., Matsumoto, 2000) and lecture content. For instance, in the perception section, my (GSK) class discussed whether optical illusions, seemingly "physical" phenomena, are viewed similarly across cultures. We compared findings from research studies covered in standard textbooks (conducted mostly with WEAs) to cross-cultural studies with British, Indian, and New Guineans (reviewed in Matsumoto) and discussed how the two latter groups perceived optical illusions differently from the British group. As students were exposed to the concept that perceptions are socially influenced and not simply biologically determined, they also questioned whether the "facts" in the textbook could be universally applied and whose experiences had been left out of the research literature.

Including marginalized experiences also means attending to differences within Asian Americans, and particularly to those marginalized within Asian American communities. Many health, nursing, and psychological studies focus on East Asians. Examples of addressing bias include ensuring that general topics such as acculturation include readings about Asian Americans less frequently researched, such as Hmong Americans or Pakistani Americans; exploring complexities within a topic, such as discussing the position of Arab Americans within the understanding of race and the meaning of Asian American; and including particular content on groups and individuals that are marginalized or discriminated against within the larger Asian American community, such as refugees, multiracial Asian Americans, or Asian adoptees.

Curricular Strategies for Personalizing Knowledge

Personalizing knowledge and including marginalized voices are frequently strongly connected and can be addressed by some of the same curricular strategies. Personalizing knowledge not only increases students' interest and reflection, but also aids in increasing empathy toward others. The use of films, stories, narratives, and case examples can bring experiences to life and demonstrate how abstract concepts are lived in more complex ways than group statistical analyses might suggest. For example, I (GSK) have used documentary films in my Introduction to Psychology class, such as *Misunderstood Minds* (learning disability and IQ; Kirk, 2002) and *Kelly Loves Tony* (transition to adulthood; Southeast Asian American experience; Nakasako, 1998). In our (KLS, GSK, PTN, JT) Asian American Psychology classes, we use fiction (e.g., Chang, 1997), as well as narrative essays (e.g., Park, 1997) and personal histories (e.g., Lee, 1992; Xiong, 1994) as additional readings for discussions of intergenerational family dynamics, cultural aspects in understanding depression and suicide, and issues of acculturation, racism, and immigration. We have also invited panel speakers to talk in our classes about their lived experiences (e.g., inviting immigrants to speak on a panel during a course section on acculturation in Asian American Psychology; this could be further focused, for example, on acculturation and accessing psychological or nursing services).

Personalizing knowledge also involves making connections between principles and facts, the experiences of other individuals, and the students' own experiences. In the Infancy and Child Development class, I (JMA) paid particular attention to exposing students in personal ways to various cultural norms and the complex role culture plays in child development. Topics such as physical discipline and theories of attachment were addressed from multiple cultural perspectives, in the context of how ethnic minority values are often understood to be in conflict with majority White cultural norms. I encouraged students to consider their own experiences and critically examine their judgment of different practices in light of understanding the diversity of cultural norms. For example, one assignment asked students to observe a child and interview the parent about his/her parenting styles. While this assignment was a customary project that many instructors had used in the past, I modified it by having students choose a family that represented a different cultural background from their own in order to expose students in personal ways to experiences different than the dominant norms. Students were required to consider their analysis within the specific cultural context of the family and to reflect on their personal learning from this assignment.

Curricular Strategies for Exploring Epistemological Validity

The final aim in developing curriculum to enact TE involves critically questioning epistemological assumptions. This means including readings that address the historical and sociopolitical backgrounds in which disciplinary knowledge has been created, and planning time to explore the hidden assumptions that disciplinary knowledge rests upon. For instance, in Introductory Psychology, discussion of individual differences such as intelligence focused not only on the meanings of IQ and examining widely used intelligence tests, but also on exploring the historical context of intelligence test development, the goals of such testing, and the resulting cultural biases embedded in these tests.

Similarly, for other content areas such as research methods, creative teaching methods can be utilized in psychology or nursing education to strengthen students' critical thinking and make the instruction more empowering. For example, when discussing methods in my (GSK) Introductory Psychology class, students are invited to consider the disciplinary bias toward quantitative methods, and how this bias may affect what knowledge is produced and disseminated. Students also learn how understanding and social equity can be undermined by utilizing only quantitative approaches, which frequently means data from minority groups are compared with the WEA norms; Asian Americans are overaggregated, resulting in limited understanding of diverse ethnic groups within the Asian American group because of the numerical dominance of East Asians; and/or race and racial groups are oversimplified in order to fit them into a quantitative paradigm (e.g., checking race boxes).

Questioning the dominant meanings within disciplines and the cultural and historical origins of these meanings is another way to explore epistemology. In Introductory Psychology and Asian American Psychology, for the module on health and mental health, we (GSK, PTN, KLS, JT) spend considerable time on various ways of defining "health" versus "disorder," and how disorders have differential meanings or symptomologies based on cultural and historical contexts (e.g., anorexia nervosa or gender dysphoria). Of particular importance to Asian Americans is depathologizing Asian American familial and cultural values. Asian American values (e.g., collectivism, emphasis on family cohesion and interdependence, emphasis on harmony as it manifests in conformity and expression, etc.) continue to be pathologized as they are compared with WEA values (Uba, 1994); students frequently feel that Asian Americans should adopt WEA values in order to be more well-adjusted in the United States, a view that is common, but criticized within multicultural psychology (e.g., Norasakkunkit & Kalick, 2002). We encourage students to discuss the sociohistorical and cultural aspects of Asian American values and their normative and health values in different contexts (e.g., within Asian communities and home countries). In doing so, students consider whether WEA experiences should be the universal norm for health, and examine how and why experiences of more privileged groups, instead of less privileged groups, have come to be considered "norms."

Epistemological questions can be linked to personalization of knowledge for greater impact. For instance, in my (PTN) Asian American Psychology class, students read "Homecoming" (Chang, 1997), a short story about intergenerational relationships in a Chinese American family. The American-born, second-generation daughter in this story has difficulty understanding the seemingly "harsh and academics-focused" parenting style of her father, and "silence" of her mother, who would not "stand up" for the daughter. Often, students struggle with understanding this family dynamic and tend to side with only the daughter's perspective. Dividing the students into small groups, I ask the students to separately consider the different lived experiences and values of the father, mother, and daughter; how these might impact their family relationships and world views; and I ask them how these family relationships may be perceived by others in the United States or in the Asian home country. This perspective-taking exercise helps students gain a broader understanding of Asian American experiences and contributes to depathologizing Asian American cultural values. It also frequently affects Asian American students' understandings of their own families and relationships.

PEDAGOGICAL STRATEGIES FOR TE GOALS

If the curricular aspects of TE refer to what we offer to students (i.e., course content and assignments), pedagogical aspects refer to how we approach, engage, and interact with students, as well as how we foster interactions between students in the classroom (i.e., relational process). More specifically, pedagogy refers to the teacher's method and style of engaging students and fostering a learning environment (Gay, 1995). In this section, we illustrate pedagogical approaches that can be effective in integrating TE in nursing, psychology and other health services.

Pedagogical Strategies for Examining Complex Social Variables and Power Relations

Social variables, such as race and culture, and their related power dynamics enter into the classroom with students and professors, regardless of the content covered. These variables and power dynamics affect student-professor and student-student relations. Attending to how these variables play out is important to meeting the goals of TE. Making these dynamics transparent by discussing the process of communication in the classroom is one way to simultaneously address these issues and engage students. For example, in our classes, we talk with students about research on communication styles, race, and culture and the effects of these variables on interpersonal relationships (e.g., as reviewed in Sue & Sue, 2003). We invite students to reflect on how these issues and variables might affect their own interactions in classes and in service provision, encouraging (inter)personal exploration of the complex interactions of power, race, and culture.

Professors can model awareness of power relations. Pedagogical strategies discussed below under Including Marginalized Voices and Exploring Epistemological Validity are also models of sharing power, as TE seeks to create cooperative learning environments. These strategies reflect a belief that students are not mere recipients of unidirectional knowledge from the teacher: both students and professors co-construct knowledge as students' voices and experiences of the students are privileged and validated. This does not mean that the professor surrenders all authority (e.g., the role as evaluator and discussion facilitator) to become another student in the classroom. However, it does mean that the professor explicitly attends to her or his educational privilege, power as an evaluator, and racial or ethnic privilege if relevant. Failure to attend to these aspects of ascribed "power" of the professor can serve to perpetuate social injustice and domination (Freire, 1993). For example, I (JT) am explicit in class that my Japanese heritage is more central to the dominant meaning of "Asian American" (i.e., East Asian) and that the achieved educational and economic attainment of Japanese Americans as a group affords me more privilege than, for example, many Southeast Asians. Drawing from group psychotherapy theory, we use the classroom as a "real life" context for enacting positive relationships between individuals in which there is an ascribed imbalance of power due to role (e.g., between the professor and students) or social status (e.g., me as a Japanese American and a student who is Vietnamese American).

Pedagogical Strategies for Including Marginalized Voices

Pedagogical strategies for TE aim to create classroom environments that encourage the participation of traditionally silenced students (e.g., racial, ethnic, and linguistic minorities) and students with particular cultural/learning styles that may discourage participation in traditional classrooms. Like most faculty, we would like all students to participate. We work to facilitate student-professor interactions through the implementation of strategies to address potential barriers, and shape a cooperative, culturally sensitive learning environment where students value each others' contributions.

In our classes, we frequently begin on the first day with a question or activity that encourages each student to participate in a personalized way. These questions vary among classes and can be more or less related to the course content. For example, in Asian American Psychology, we (KLS, GSK, PTN, JT) asked each student: "Are you Asian American? Why or why not?" In my (PTN) Vietnamese American Resources class, I asked each student to speak about themselves and their families. In Infancy and Child Development, I (JMA) showed *A Class Divided*, a documentary that follows a third grade classroom experiment on prejudice and discrimination and engage students in discussion of their personal responses and connections. After all students have spoken, we ask students if they have questions or comments for each other. While these discussions take considerable time, we believe that they are critical to the achievement of TE. By encouraging every individual student to speak, we communicate to students that (a) each one of them has a valued voice in the class; (b) we (the professors) are invested in making personal connections with them (the students) and are willing to take the time to do so; (c) connections among students is important; and (d) contextual issues of race, culture, and other social variables will be central to the ways in which we will approach the material. This approach also enables us to gain a sense of students' styles, in some ways performing "individual assessments" of variables that may affect the content and pedagogical approach. For example, level of English fluency, which may affect pedagogical approach (e.g., supplement class lectures with videos, supplement assigned readings with in-class exercises, or incorporate more small-group work). Thus, this initial approach establishes the structure of a cooperative learning environment for future class discussions, enables professors to consider pedagogical approaches that best meet the needs of all students, and contributes to students' increased feelings of engagement and empowerment.

Including the voices of marginalized students also involves facilitating connections between students and professors. When preparing to teach Adolescence, an intermediate level psychology course, I (SCD) was aware that many students are the first in their families to attend college. I also realized that cultural values (e.g., deference to authority, hierarchical relationships) might affect some students' comfort to connect with me. In my syllabus, I explicitly acknowledged how difficult it can be for students to come to office hours or contact me if they are having trouble. I made myself more accessible to students by briefly staying after class so students could connect with me "informally," by periodically sending email "check-ins" to all students, and by soliciting feedback about the class at the start of each session and responding to their feedback in subsequent classes.

We also include marginalized voices by using diverse interactive strategies. In standard lecture-format classes, there are usually only a few students who speak to the professor. The use of small group discussion formats or dyadic interactions provide students who are reluctant to speak in front of the entire class a place to engage. More than one "quiet" student in our classes was revealed as talkative or outgoing when interactive with two or three peers. Choosing reporters from these small group discussions through random means (e.g., who woke up earliest today?) rather than letting students choose the reporter also encourages student participation and challenges the dynamic of only having a few — usually more privileged — students who speak up in class.

Pedagogical Strategies for Personalizing Knowledge

We can encourage the application of lived experiences to theoretical perspectives by how we frame discussions. For example, in many of our classes, we discuss research on "personality" differences between Asian Americans and WEAs (e.g., emotional expressiveness). In order to increase understanding, I (KLS) give students a worksheet to write examples of each trait. In order to personalize the information, though, I ask students to offer examples from their own experiences or the experiences of people they know, rather than from the text. Small group discussions are also helpful in meeting this goal, as students are frequently less willing to share personal connections in front of large groups, particularly in earlier class sessions.

Encouraging students to attend to their emotional responses to the course content also creates a context in which course material actually becomes "alive" and has the potential to transform students. One example is through the evocation of empathy, frequently used in clinical interventions to personalize the experiences of others so that one might develop a greater understanding of one's own subjective experiences. In my (PTN) Vietnamese American Studies class, I aimed to develop empathy and personal connection through reading about a Vietnamese man who was brutally murdered by White supremacists. As a homework assignment, I asked the students, many of whom were Vietnamese, to write a reflection essay about how they felt knowing that the victim was Vietnamese and to imagine how it would feel to be the victim's friend or family. In our class discussion, I actively invited these emotions into the room. Some students reported feeling very angry, while others said that they were in shock and unsure of what to think. Many students reported feeling sad that someone could be killed for being Vietnamese and said they could not imagine how it would feel to lose someone in this way. This exercise had an impact on students because they could experience how racism affected them personally through the discussion of emotional reactions. It opened dialogue between students about the challenges of living in a racist society, and also allowed students to talk about the importance of recognizing and resisting racism.

Pedagogical Strategies for Exploring Epistemological Validity

How we teach can model critical examination of knowledge production and maintenance, or it can encourage students to passively accept what is taught as the only truth. A banking model of education (Banks, 1996a; Freire, 1993) suggests that the teacher holds the valuable knowledge, the student's job is to deposit that knowledge in their brains, and teachers withdraw this knowledge for exams. In this model, what the professor says is *right* and critical questioning is discouraged. In contrast, TE encourages students to critically evaluate knowledge offered in the class in light of their own experiences and from their knowledge in other areas. For example, we often say to Asian American Psychology classes: "My goal here is not to tell *you* about *your* experience, but rather describe what the literature states are common experiences in the Asian American group. You may have different experiences than what the literature says, but think critically about it, rather than accept that your experience is 'different' and therefore invalid or dismiss the literature because it doesn't match your own experience." Inviting students to challenge theories fosters critical analysis as engaged thinkers and promotes the validation of their voices. We model an approach where students learn to question the basis of knowledge, including the knowledge that we are offering.

We also encourage students to see themselves as consumers and producers of knowledge. In our experience, *all* students have much to learn from each other. For example, in my Adolescence course, I (SCD) viewed students as both learners and possessors of knowledge. With their permission, I provided a list of contact information for every student in the class and strongly encouraged them to use each other as resources. In my cross-listed Asian American Psychology class, I (JT) created interdisciplinary research groups, distributing students with experience in Psychology and students with experience in Asian American Studies. I encouraged them to think about the different types of knowledge, and ways of producing knowledge, in which they had expertise and to share their perspectives. For example, while Psychology students may have stronger understanding of psychological trauma (i.e., symptomology and diagnostic criteria) than AAS students, they may have less insight into the nuanced experiences of cultural trauma related to genocide and war that may be common to specific Asian American populations (e.g., South East Asian refugees).

The Importance of Interpersonal Relationships in Meeting TE Goals

Up to this point, we have emphasized the ways that we have incorporated TE goals and philosophies into our teaching. The goals of TE are also nurtured by interpersonal relationships that benefit from interdisciplinary connections. This section will highlight our (all authors except KLS) roles as students rather than professors as well as the complex, multileveled relationships that exist between students and professors/mentors outside the classroom (e.g., advising, consultation, social interactions). Through our interpersonal connections with individuals from Asian American Studies and Psychology who utilize TE approaches, we have been benefited by dynamic models of enacting and integrating the goals and values of TE.

As Asian American graduate students in Psychology we have all, at times, felt disempowered. We have had experiences where discussions within classes or with faculty about our research left us feeling marginalized and discouraged as students or as Asian Americans. These moments have been due to subject matter that silenced particular voices, lack of attention to the cultural context of students, or the acceptance of stereotypes (unintentional but still hurtful discrimination). At these moments, we frequently felt bad about ourselves, our potential, and our discipline. We needed safe spaces to discuss our concerns. And we needed greater understanding of the interpersonal and structural dynamics involved in these interactions. Faculty in AAS and in Psychology who utilized a TE approach provided this space through individual mentoring and student/social organizations and meetings. Because of their teaching philosophies, these mentors (who were frequently not our formal advisers or instructors) validated our feelings and helped us "recharge" and develop solutions. This process often provided a sense of empowerment that allowed us to return to our discipline and advocate for our own voice and the voices of others.

Our experiences with mentors who embrace TE approaches have also affected us by fostering deeper connections between academic goals, lived experiences, and the communities we aim to serve. When I (PTN) started in the Clinical Psychology program, I was the first Vietnamese American ever enrolled in a doctoral program at UMass Boston. Although the fact that Dorchester boasted the second largest concentration of Vietnamese Americans on the East Coast was significant in my decision to come to UMass, I had previously resisted identification as a refugee, which likely contributed to my uncertainty about how to connect with the community. But faculty in AAS conceptualized their role in ways that included reaching out to students like me, even though I was not in their programs or disciplines. They encouraged me to take opportunities that facilitated my learning about the history of Vietnamese Americans, my understanding of my own family's experience as Vietnamese refugees, and how this influenced my professional development. These experiences inspired me to embrace my identity and expand my vision of serving my community.

Similarly, I (SCD) came to the Clinical Psychology program with a long personal history of feeling excluded by the Asian American community and questioning my ability to connect with or serve Asian American people. As an international Korean American adoptee with White adoptive parents and a multiracial Black brother, my "authenticity" as a Korean American and/or Asian American has often been challenged and these experiences contributed to greater affinity for Black or African American communities than for the Asian American community. I was pleasantly surprised to be welcomed and included by Psychology and AAS faculty who conceptualize Asian Americans in nuanced ways that actively and explicitly include interracial, international adoptees. The abundance of emotional support that I received enabled me to develop my identity as an Asian American woman, see that I did have a connection with other Asian Americans, and ultimately make a commitment to work for positive change within the Asian American community.

Our understandings of epistemology as students have also been expanded by our relations with faculty in Psychology and AAS who embrace a TE approach. For instance, I (GSK) had an interdisciplinary dissertation committee from Psychology and AAS. As I approached my research project on racial identities, ethnic identities, and peer-group belonging and exclusion in Asian American high school youth, my committee members gave me the freedom to consider broad sociohistorical and political contexts about race, culture, and their intersections with psychological issues (i.e., identities). I was able to contextually expand my knowledge of psychological research and thoughtfully critique the existing psychological theories and methodologies without the fear of being silenced because I was questioning what "Truth" was in the discipline. The interdisciplinary committee members dialogued with each other in respectful ways about disciplinary connections and disconnections and links to the lived experiences of the Asian American youth I was studying.

One of the most important aspects of relationships with faculty in both Psychology and AAS who embrace a TE approach is our opportunity to have models who successfully balance multiple roles and academic identities through enacting the goals and philosophies of TE. By demonstrating interest in our personal experiences and being willing to share their own, faculty demonstrate the importance of self-awareness of our own cultural histories in the teaching process. Further, they have encouraged us to use these histories to connect with students, both within and outside the classroom. Faculty's interactions with us when we have felt marginalized served as models for us to listen to our own students' difficult stories without silencing them and expanded our understanding about the role of mentors who go beyond simply being good conveyors of accurate knowledge in the classroom.

Our interpersonal connections with individuals in AAS and Psychology who engage in TE approaches have provided us with examples of explicitly and implicitly acknowledging power dynamics, listening to our voices, making connections to our lived experience, and have helped us feel emotionally supported and empowered. We have, in turn, tried to pass these benefits along to others. Rather than engaging in direct reciprocation to those who have bolstered us, we have internalized the community emphasis of AAS and attempt to enact the goals and philosophies of TE in our personal and academic lives. We have transitioned from being students benefiting from TE to being educators and mentors utilizing TE as an alternative way of engaging and interacting with students, particularly those from marginalized populations. The cyclical, reciprocal nature of TE can best be summed up with a narrative that highlights the goals of TE and details one individual's progression from student to mentor and instructor.

In the Spirit of Reciprocity: A Personal Story of Transformative Education

In my junior year, on the first day of my Asian American Psychology class, the instructor (KLS) asked: "Are you Asian American? Why or why not?" Some of us looked around the room perplexed. I avoided looking at any of the students who didn't "look" Asian because I couldn't imagine what their responses might be. "At least I am 'half-Japanese,'" I thought. But was I "inside" the circle or "out"? Some of the "Asian looking" students had claimed they were not Asian American, for example, because they weren't born in America. If they were not Asian American, then certainly I was not. But I said: "Yes, I am Asian American." Although I didn't grasp the significance of it then, this was a political act of resistance, and a claim to an in-group that until that moment I didn't know could be my own. While I thought the "more" Asian students might be shaking her heads, I felt the instructor holding and validating my response. Throughout the course, the instructor continued to foster a classroom environment that supported my complex social experience as a multiracial Asian American, and as a parent of a multiracial African American/Japanese-European American child. Although course material included theories of Asian American Psychology, the instructor encouraged us to actively engage with these works, examining them in relation to other Asian American voices and our personal experiences.

I can recall one personal reflection essay in which I described feeling frustrated by the Asian American racial identity models that typified the Asian American experience exclusively in relation to White/European Americans: conforming to, emerging from, and integrating with White societal norms. Did this mean that my experience was somehow not the "true" Asian American experience? Instead, my instructor encouraged me to think about how my experience negotiating Asian American, European American, and African American social contexts might reflect limitations of these identity models, rather than limitations of my experiences. As a graduate student, I would develop a research focus on understanding Asian American experiences in relation to African Americans.

Karen eventually became my mentor as both an undergraduate honors student and graduate student in Clinical Psychology. As an undergraduate member of her research team, I established interpersonal connections that would become the foundation and sustenance of my own efforts to teach and mentor within a TE model of education. Using an intergenerational model of mentoring, Karen assigned me to a graduate mentor (GSK) who met with me weekly and guided me through my own independent research project, research assistant (RA) tasks, and graduate school application process. Two years later, I became a graduate member of the research team. In my first year, I was given the opportunity to mentor an undergraduate RA, a Vietnamese immigrant student who connected to our team through Karen's Introduction to AAS class. I enthusiastically accepted this opportunity as a chance to give back what I was given. It didn't take me long to realize that I wasn't just "giving back." I was still "being given." This time, as graduate student, I was learning to work closely with another student, a student with a vastly different "Asian American" experience, and guide him through his personal and academic challenges. I was learning to become a faculty mentor.

I am now in my fourth year of graduate school and teaching Asian American Psychology, the course in which I first claimed my identity as an Asian American. I have asked my students: "Are you Asian American? Why or why not?" I have tried to hold everyone's response in the way that Karen held mine. I often call on images of my AAS and Psychology instructors who embrace TE goals, sometimes modeling their subtle — both verbal and nonverbal — ways of acknowledging students' "truths." I could not ask for anything better than to know that I have held and validated someone in the way that I once was, empowering them to take identity stances, to become critical and engaged thinkers, and perhaps eventually become transformative educators themselves.

This narrative represents far more than my story alone. It is a story of collaboration between two disciplines that has become greater than the sum of its parts. This connection was deliberately created by faculty and administrators within the university with the explicit agenda of utilizing the strengths of the sometimes contrasting and sometimes complimentary pedagogies, curricula, and goals for social impact of both AAS and health services disciplines such as psychology or nursing.

INSTITUTIONAL SUPPORTS FOR TE

Interpersonal relationships and connections between students and faculty, students and students, faculty and administrators and within faculty are consequences of TE models of education as well as the foundations upon which they are built at an institutional level. Although curricular and pedagogical approaches and developing relationships with students are largely choices made by individual faculty, the support of departments and universities can strongly influence these choices. For example, the formal creation of split lines such as mine (KLS) in Psychology and AAS ensures interdisciplinary collaboration that encourages TE. Interdisciplinary collaboration means being exposed to different ways of thinking, teaching, researching, and valuing knowledge that encourages critical analysis of one's own practices. Cross-listed classes and interdisciplinary research committees are another structural support for integration of disciplines that supports TE through creating a formal structure for interdisciplinary collaboration. Although most graduate student research has one member of a committee that is not within their discipline, "external" members are frequently seen as observers or general "quality checks," rather than as contributing expertise and critical analysis that expands the impact of the research. Split lines for faculty, cross-listed classes, and interdisciplinary research committees of disciplines that emerged with TE goals at their core (such as Ethnic Studies, Women Studies, or Queer Studies) with disciplines that aim at service provision and intervention (such as Nursing, Psychology, Education) are particularly good matches. Students' engagement and the attention to social inequities that characterizes TE can be important contributors to meeting the goals of effective service provision in the latter disciplines.

Departments and institutions can support TE or can instead emphasize the narrower traditional educational goal of conveying knowledge in "objective" ways. Although perhaps not the explicit intention, the latter approach frequently serves to maintain the status quo of social inequities, partly because these inequities are embedded within the education system and institutions (Banks, 1996b; Gay, 1995). Therefore, one must be intentional in order to challenge them. TE approaches are frequently criticized as not "objective" enough and as too time consuming due to its focus on the learning process, leading to less time for content coverage in classes and less time for faculty scholarship. TE approaches are also criticized as not directly contributing to student achievement as measured by test performance, and as eroding traditional academic hierarchies. These criticisms, however, are also value laden. Decisions about curriculum and pedagogy are inherently biased (some things are not included, and some approaches reach some students better than others, etc.). Content coverage may come at the expense of student ability to retain or utilize information that is experienced as disconnected from lived experience. Emphasis on scholarship rather than student engagement, or testing as the best indicator of achievement rests on assumptions about what is valuable and how it is enacted. Our experience is that TE approaches are more effective in actively engaging students, addressing inequities in knowledge, and encouraging students to be active participants in their education and professions. We believe this is particularly important for students being trained in nursing, psychology, and other health service provision, where personal engagement and understanding of social inequities have direct relevance to their work.

REFERENCES

Banks, J.A. (1996a). The canon debate, knowledge construction, and multicultural education. In J.A. Banks (Ed.), _Multicultural education, transformative knowledge, & action: Historical and contemporary perspectives_ (pp. 3-29). New York: Teachers College.

Banks, J.A. (1996b). Transformative knowledge, curriculum reform, and action. In J.A. Banks (Ed.), _Multicultural education, transformative knowledge, & action: Historical and contemporary perspectives,_ (pp. 335-348). New York: Teachers College.

Campbell, R., & Wasco, S. M. (2000). Feminist approaches to social science: Epistemological and methodological tenets. _American Journal of Community Psychology,_ 28, 773-791.

Chang, C. F. (1997). Homecoming. In E. H. Kim, L. V. Villanueva, & Asian Women United of California (Eds.), _Making more waves: New writing by Asian American women_ (pp. 43-53). Boston: Beacon Press.

Doll, E. A. (1940). Some things we know in clinical psychology. _Journal of Applied Psychology,_ 24, 20-26.

Endo, R., & Wei, W. (1988). On the development of Asian American studies programs. In G. Y. Okihiro, S. Hune, A. A. Hansen, & J. M. Liu (Eds.), _Reflections on shattered windows: Promises and prospects for Asian American studies_ (pp. 5-7). Pullman, WA: Washington State University.

Freire, P. (1993). _Pedagogy of the oppressed._ New York: Continuum.

Gay, G. (1995). Mirror images on common issues: Parallels between multicultural education and critical pedagogy. In C. E. Sleeter & P. L. McLaren (Eds.), _Multicultural education, critical pedagogy, and the politics of difference._ Albany, NY: State University of New York Press.

Hune, S. (1989). Opening the American mind and body: The role of Asian American studies. _Change,_ 21(6), 56-63.

Kirk, M. (Producer/Director). (2002). _Misunderstood minds: Searching for success in school._ [Film]. Available: http://www.pbs.org/wgbh/misunderstoodminds/about.html.

Lee, J. F. J. (1992). *Asian Americans: Oral histories of first to fourth generation Americans from China, the Phillipines, Japan, India, the Pacific Islands, Vietnam and Cambodia.* New York: New Press.

Matsumoto, D. (2000). *Culture and psychology: People around the world* (2nd ed.). Florence, KY: Wadsworth.

Nakasako, S. (Producer/Director). (1998). *Kelly loves Tony.* [Film]. United States: Independent Television Service and the Center for Asian American Media. Available: http://distribution.asianamericanmedia.org/browse/film/?i=116.

Norasakkunkit, V., & Kalick, S. M. (2002). Culture, ethnicity, and emotional distress measures: The role of self-construal and self-enhancement. *Journal of Cross-Cultural Psychology, 33,* 56-70.

Park, L. (1997). A letter to my sister. In E. H. Kim, L. V. Villanueva, & Asian Women United of California (Eds.), *Making more waves: New writing by Asian American women* (pp. 65-71). Boston: Beacon Press.

Sue, D. W., & Sue, D. (2003). *Counseling the culturally diverse: Theory and practice* (4th ed.). New York: Wiley.

Suyemoto, K. L. (2002). Redefining "Asian American" identity: Reflections on differentiating ethnic and racial identities for Asian American individuals and communities. In L. Zhan (Ed.), *Asian Americans: Vulnerable populations, model interventions, and clarifying agendas* (pp. 195-231). Sudbury, MA: Jones and Bartlett.

Uba, L. (1994). *Asian Americans: Personality patterns, identity, and mental health.* New York: Guilford Press.

USDHHS (U.S. Department of Health and Human Services). (2001). *Mental health: Culture, race, and ethnicity — A supplement to Mental health: Report of the Surgeon General.* Rockville, MD: Author.

Weber, L. (1998). A conceptual framework for understanding race, class, gender, and sexuality. *Psychology of Women Quarterly, 22*(1), 13-32.

Xiong, M. (1994). An unforgettable journey. In S. Chan (Ed.), *Hmong means free: Life in Laos and America* (pp. 118-128). Philadelphia: Temple University.

APPENDIX A

AUTHOR PROFILES

LIN ZHAN, PHD, RN, FAAN

Dr. Zhan is Dean and Professor, School of Nursing at Massachusetts College of Pharmacy and Health Sciences, Boston, and a Fellow in the American Academy of Nursing. Dr. Zhan's research and teaching interests include immigrants' health and quality of life; race, gender, and class in health and health promotion; theoretical foundations in health promotion; philosophy of science; intervention research in health promotion, women's health, and diversity in higher education. Dr. Zhan serves on the American Academy of Nursing Expert Panel on Aging and on the Board of Governors of the National League for Nursing. In addition, she serves as a consultant for the HRSA funded project that provides a tailored intervention to promote retention and graduation of underrepresented students in nursing. Dr. Zhan is a visiting /honorary professor in seven Chinese universities.

JULIE M. AHNALLEN, PHD

Dr. AhnAllen is a psychologist and co-facilitates a seminar on culturally competent practice at Boston College University Counseling Services. She is passionate about issues of cultural diversity in practice and research. Current clinical interests include complexity of immigration and acculturation, identity development in college students, development of positive self image in marginalized groups, bereavement issues, trauma, and eating disorders. Research interests include identity development of marginalized populations, Asian American psychology, and racial and ethnic identity development in interracial relationships.

JAMES ĐIEN BÙI, MSW

Mr. Bùi is the Regional Director of the National Alliance of Vietnamese American Service Agencies (NAVASA) and oversees that group's Gulf Coast operations in communities devastated by hurricanes Katrina and Rita. Recently, he helped to establish a local community development corporation in New Orleans East that shut down a controversial landfill and secured over $18m to fund neighborhood projects including 84 units of affordable senior housing, a 20-acre urban farm and open market, a community health clinic and $500k in capital to stabilize and expand local businesses. He has worked with community development agencies in Boston and Los Angeles and also in South Viet Nam and Northern India on micro-credit economic development projects. Mr. Bùi is President of Hong Bàng, a US-based NGO that focuses on rural development in Viet Nam. He is also an adjunct lecturer/faculty at the University of Massachusetts Boston in the Asian American Studies program.

STEPHANIE C. DAY, MA

Ms. Day is a doctoral candidate in the Clinical Psychology program at the University of Massachusetts Boston. She is currently working on her dissertation, Adopted Korean Women: The Interactive Processes of Negotiating Identities and Becoming First-Time Mothers. Her past research has examined the racial and ethnic identities of Korean transracial adoptees and the identity and social justice development of Asian American adolescents. Ms. Day has clinical experience with adults, adolescents and families from diverse urban populations. As a teacher, researcher and clinician, Ms. Day is committed to using psychology for social justice and collaborating across disciplines.

KHANH THI DINH, PHD

Dr. Dinh is an Associate Professor of Psychology at University of Massachusetts Lowell. Dr. Dinh's primary research interests are in the area of immigrant psychology and communities, particularly pertaining to the acculturation and psychosocial adjustment of Asian and Latina/o immigrant families and youth. She served as a Research Fellow for the Institute for Asian American Studies at the University of Massachusetts Boston and as a Scholar-in-the-City for the Patrick J. Mogan Cultural Center in Lowell. Dr. Dinh is a recipient of an NIH National Health Disparities Research Service Award and a co-recipient of a grant award from the American Psychological Association for Ethnic Minority Recruitment, Retention and Training in Psychology.

IVY KA-MIN HO, PHD

Dr. Ho is an Assistant Professor of Psychology at University of Massachusetts Lowell. Dr. Ho's research interests are in health psychology, psychophysiology, and the associations between victimization and physical health among women. Dr. Ho is a co-recipient of a grant from the American Psychological Association: Commission on Ethnic Minority Recruitment, Retention and Training in Psychology.

PETER NIEN-CHU KIANG, EDD

Dr. Kiang is a Professor of Education and Director of Asian American Studies Program at University of Massachusetts Boston. Dr. Kiang's research, teaching, and advocacy in both K-12 and higher education with Asian American immigrant/refugee students and communities has been supported by the National Academy of Education, the National Endowment for the Humanities, the Massachusetts Teachers Association, and the Massachusetts Association for Bilingual Education. He is co-president of the Chinese Historical Society of New England. He holds a BA, EdM, and EdD from Harvard University and is a former Community Fellow in MIT's Department of Urban Studies & Planning.

GRACE S. KIM, PHD

Dr. Kim is an Assistant Professor of psychology in the department of Human Development at Wheelock College. Her interests in teaching and research center on the intersections of race, culture, identities, and psychological well-being in immigrants, particularly Asian Americans. She has conducted mixed-method and qualitative studies on racial and ethnic identities and sense of belonging/sense of exclusion in Korean transracial adoptees and in Asian American high school youth. Her current research interests include adjustment and racial and ethnic identity negotiations in transnational families and identities in Southeast Asian youth and young adults.

SUSAN A. LAMBE, EDM

Ms. Lambe is a student in the Clinical Psychology Doctoral Program at University of Massachusetts Boston. She is interested in racial identity development, post colonialism, inter-minority relations, radical pedagogy, and the psychological effects of racism on people of color. She is the founder of Swirl Boston, a community organization for multiracial people in the Boston area.

WINSTON LANGLEY, PhD, JD

Dr. Langley is Provost and Vice Chancellor for Academic Affairs at University of Massachusetts Boston. He has been within the academy for over 35 years and has written widely in the area of political science and international relations. His scholarly works include Human Rights: Major Global Instruments (1992); The Encyclopedia of Human Rights Since 1945 (1999); and Kazi Nazrul Islam: The Voice of Poetry and the Struggle for Human Wholeness (2007).

NANCY J LIN, MA

Ms. Lin is a doctoral candidate in the Psychology Department at University of Massachusetts Boston. Ms. Lin's area of interest is in refugee-related issues, including identity and trauma in people who have fled conflict in Southeast Asia and East Africa. She has a background in medical anthropology from the School of Oriental and African Studies, University of London. Ms. Lin plans to develop psychotherapeutic treatments that are culturally salient for war-related trauma and that can be implemented in refugee camps and throughout the journey towards healing. In her spare time, she enjoys volunteering with newly resettled refugee families in the Boston area.

LUSA LO, EdD

Dr. Lo is an assistant professor of Special Education at the University of Massachusetts Boston. Her research interests include family-school-community partnerships and educational planning and practice for language minority students with disabilities. In addition to teaching at the graduate level, she provides information, support, and workshops to Chinese families of children with disabilities and the professionals who work with them.

SAMUEL D. MUSEUS, PHD

Dr. Museus is an Assistant Professor in the Higher Education Doctoral Program and an affiliate faculty member of the Asian American Studies Program at the University of Massachusetts Boston, where he teaches courses on qualitative and quantitative research methodology, the impact of college on students in general, and students of color in particular. His research is aimed at understanding the various factors that affect the experiences and outcomes of college students of color, specifically, the role of institutional environments in racial/ethnic minority college student adjustment, engagement, and persistence.

PATRICIA AKEMI NAKAMOTO NEILSON, MPH, EDD

Dr. Neilson is the Director of the Center for Collaborative Leadership in the College of Management at the University of Massachusetts Boston. Dr. Neilson also served as academic Dean of Human Services at North Shore Community College and is on the board of Asian Pacific Americans in Higher Education (APAHE), a national organization.

PHUONG T. NGUYEN, MA

Mr. Nguyen is a doctoral candidate in the Clinical Psychology program at the University of Massachusetts, Boston. Mr. Nguyen's general research interests include Asian American psychology, intersections between identity, culture, and social environments, and Asian American mental health (particularly within Vietnamese communities). Mr. Nguyen's clinical experience has included work with individuals and families from marginalized and undeserved populations (many of whom are Asian/Asian American) in the greater Boston area.

KAREN L. SUYEMOTO, PHD

Dr. Suyemoto is an Associate Professor in Psychology and Asian American Studies at the University of Massachusetts Boston. Her interests in teaching, research, and consultation focus on cultural diversity and anti-racist practice, with particular attention to Asian Americans. She has published and presented on topics related to racial and cultural identities, feminist connections with multicultural understandings in psychology, and diversity issues in education. Dr. Suyemoto is co-editor (with Marsha Mirkin and Barbara Okun) of Women in Psychotherapy: Exploring Diverse Contexts and Identities (2005). Her current research interests are in ethnic and racial identities in multiracial and Asian American individuals, and in the intersections of psychological and educational experiences for Asian American urban college students. She is currently (2008-2009) President of the Asian American Psychological Association.

SHIRLEY SUET-LING TANG, PHD

Dr. Tang is an Assistant Professor of Asian American Studies and American Studies at the University of Massachusetts Boston. Dr. Tang's research and teaching interests include: Southeast Asian American community studies; multiracial/ethnic community history; Asian American Studies; and American Studies. She is working on a book manuscript that examines the development and displacement of the Khmer (Cambodian) American community in Revere, Massachusetts.

JOHN TAWA, MA

Mr. Tawa is a doctoral candidate in the Clinical Psychology program at the University of Massachusetts, Boston. He is currently developing his dissertation on processes of decreasing social distance between Black and Asian individuals and communities. This research falls under a broader social justice aim of fostering positive relations between minority communities. Mr. Tawa's other research foci include: understanding how people conceptualize race and ethnicity, the effects of perceiving racism on racial minorities' psychological well-being, and multiracial experiences. He also works in a community health center with young men who have had exposure to community violence.

JANET HONG VÕ, BA

Through her Asian American Studies training and interests in social justice and community work. Ms. Võ aims to continually connect, support and learn from various Asian American communities (particularly the Vietnamese American). She intends to pursue a Juris Doctor degree. She is currently a co-coordinator of the Asian American Student/Studies Outreach, aiming to connect students and the community with the positive impacts and resources of UMass Boston's Asian American Studies Program. In Spring 2007, she supported Instructor James Bùi's class, Resources for Vietnamese American Studies, by documenting students' service learning projects in the Gulf Coast Vietnamese communities.